CHOOSE COSTA RICA
FOR RETIREMENT

HELP US KEEP
THIS GUIDE UP TO DATE

Every effort has been made by the author and editors to make this guide as accurate and useful as possible. However, many things can change after a guide is published—establishments close, phone numbers change, facilities come under new management, etc.

We would love to hear from you concerning your experiences with this guide and how you feel it could be improved and be kept up to date. While we may not be able to respond to all comments and suggestions, we'll take them to heart and we'll also make certain to share them with the author. Please send your comments and suggestions to the following address:

The Globe Pequot Press
Reader Response/Editorial Department
P.O. Box 480
Guilford, CT 06437

Or you may e-mail us at:
editorial@GlobePequot.com

Thanks for your input, and happy travels!

INSIDERS' GUIDE®

CHOOSE RETIREMENT SERIES

EIGHTH EDITION

CHOOSE COSTA RICA
FOR RETIREMENT

Information for Travel, Retirement, Investment, and Affordable Living

JOHN HOWELLS

INSIDERS' GUIDE®

GUILFORD, CONNECTICUT
AN IMPRINT OF THE GLOBE PEQUOT PRESS

The prices and rates listed in this book were confirmed at press time. We recommend, however, that you call before traveling to obtain current information.

To buy books in quantity for corporate use or incentives, call **(800) 962–0973, ext. 4551,** or e-mail **premiums@GlobePequot.com.**

INSIDERS' GUIDE®

Copyright © 1992, 1994, 1996, 1998, 2001, 2003, 2005, 2007 by John M. Howells

Text design: Linda R. Loiewski
Map design: Lisa Reneson
Overview map: Stephen Stringall

Spot photography throughout © Photodisc

ISSN: 1543-6411
ISBN-13: 978-0-7627-4164-9
ISBN-10: 0-7627-4164-3

Manufactured in the United States of America
Eighth Edition/First Printing

CONTENTS

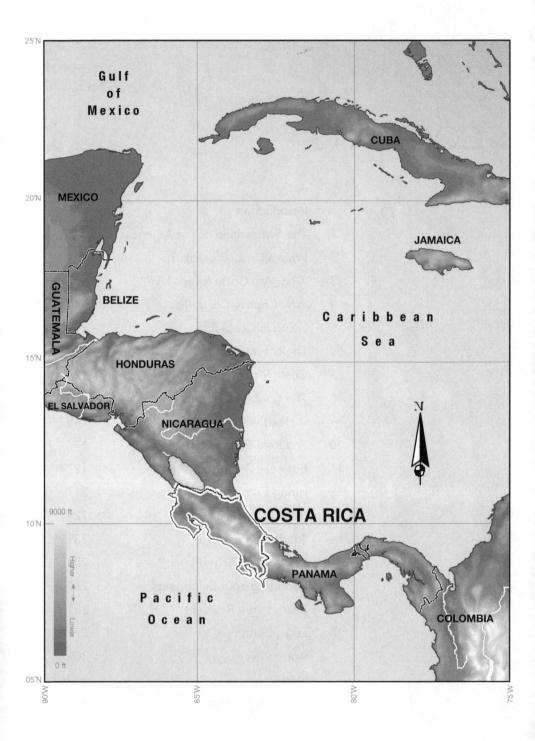

INTRODUCTION

This eighth edition of *Choose Costa Rica* is the outcome of more than three decades of traveling in, living in, and writing about Latin America, Central America, and my favorite country, Costa Rica. My bias for Costa Rica comes through quite clearly, but I try to balance the picture by reminding readers that living in a foreign country is definitely not everyone's cup of *café con leche*. (Costa Ricans don't drink tea.) It takes a special type of person to create and enjoy an interesting and challenging life in a foreign setting. Hopefully, this book will help you determine if you are that type of person.

Costa Rica has always been a magnet for those seeking unspoiled and pristine tropical destinations for vacations and retirement. As the country's rain forests, tropical beaches, and marvelous wildlife gain ever more fame, foreign tourism increases exponentially. Today tourism has displaced coffee and bananas as Costa Rica's major industry. The estimated 30,000 to 40,000 foreigners who have taken up residence here exert a powerful and beneficial influence on the economy and social betterment of Costa Rica. This book is partially an attempt to explain these phenomena.

Enthusiastic and eager North Americans and Europeans are attracted to Costa Rica's charming environment in constantly growing numbers. They first visit as tourists, later returning as residents seeking a new beginning in a tropical paradise. Traditionally the country has been a mecca for retirees, but an increasing number of newcomers are too young to retire. This influx of younger North American families with children creates a demand for schools catering to English-speaking students. Too young to sit around and play bridge or golf like their parents, today's newcomers want to try their hands at business, land development, teaching, or volunteer work.

This book is also designed as a guide for those individuals who manage to have part or all of the year free for doing exactly what they feel like doing. It's for the professor on sabbatical, the schoolteacher on a summer vacation, the construction worker with chronic winter unemployment, the executive who can take a leave of absence. This book is also for self-employed individuals who can trust their businesses to others while they enjoy life now instead of waiting for the "someday" that may never come. *Choose Costa Rica* is especially oriented toward those who seek a "new start," who might wish to invest time and resources into launching a new business career as well as enjoying a fascinating lifestyle in an exotic foreign country. Costa Rica is also a magnet for the newly divorced or widowed who are casting about for a new social niche, new friends, and a new start in life.

Although this is partly a travel book, the emphasis is on "how to do it" rather than "where to stay." A hotel, bed-and-breakfast, or restaurant may be mentioned from time to time but only as an adjunct to the narrative and should not be taken as a personal recommendation.

After reading through this book, maybe you'll understand why Costa Rica has such a good reputation among North Americans and Europeans. You might even find a haven for you and your family. A word of caution: *Costa Rica is not for everyone.* There are those who cannot keep from comparing conditions in Costa Rica with those in the United States or Canada. Remember, Costa Rica is still a developing third-world country. This means a world of difference. For those of us who love Costa Rica, we thank our lucky stars for the difference!

By the way, throughout this book you will see Costa Ricans referred to as *Ticos* and North Americans as *gringos*. These are not terms of disrespect and are commonly used in Costa Rica, which will be explained later in the book. These nicknames actually carry an affectionate context, since both groups like and respect each other.

If you have access to the Internet, you might want to check my Costa Rica Bulletin Board, an Internet forum that connects those interested in knowing more about living in and traveling in Costa Rica. The Web site can be found at: http://discoverypress.com/CostaRica.

About prices quoted throughout this book: They are accurate as of the time of writing, based on the current dollar exchange rates in Costa Rica. In fall 2006 the approximate exchange rate was 520 colones to the dollar.

NOTE: Unless otherwise stated, all phone and fax numbers in this book are in Costa Rica, and to connect, you must dial the proper access and country code. See "Dialing Costa Rica," in chapter 5 (pages 89–90).

CHAPTER ONE

THE SWITZERLAND
OF THE AMERICAS

My love affair with Costa Rica began more than thirty years ago. While researching Guatemala for a freelance travel article, my wife and I decided to travel a little farther south to see what Costa Rica was all about. Three more days of travel was nothing after the long trip thus far, and we'd always been curious about that little Central American country so often referred to as "The Switzerland of the Americas." (Have you ever found a guidebook that *doesn't* claim a similarity between Costa Rica and Switzerland?)

We expected Costa Rica to be okay, but we were stunned by the country's breathtaking beauty and abundant wildlife. We were captivated by the friendliness of the Costa Rican people. Yet, try as we might, we found little resemblance to Switzerland. Not the Switzerland *we* knew. Costa Rica is as much like Switzerland as a watermelon is like a pumpkin. The only obvious similarity between the two countries is that they are about the same size. Switzerland is actually a bit smaller than Costa Rica—one of the world's few countries with that distinction.

Costa Rica is lushly tropical and continuously swathed in luxurious green vegetation—a place where coffee, sugarcane, and mangoes

thrive, where snow never falls, and many inhabitants are laid-back coffee growers. It's the exact opposite of Switzerland, with its snowcapped peaks and rocky terrain, wildlife limited to dairy cows, and a population of seriously intense watchmakers.

Yet the more one travels in Costa Rica, the more apparent the parallels with Switzerland become. Both are peaceful, progressive countries where democracy and stability are hallmarks. Although Costa Rica's tropical beaches are incongruent with Swiss landscapes, Costa Rica's higher mountains rival the beauty of the Alps. Well, some of the Alps' lower elevations perhaps.

Even closer similarities between the two countries appear in their political philosophy and economic structure. Both are places of small farms and small businesses, with an air of prosperity and a feeling of equality among citizens. Both countries have renounced aggressive militarism, diverting resources instead toward education, medical care, and other services that benefit society in general. In short, both places are affluent, happy, and tranquil. Both are locations where North Americans can feel at home, safe, and welcome.

There are differences, of course. Costa Rica is closer to the United States and Canada, making it somewhat more accessible than Europe. Costa Rica also enjoys a dramatically lower cost of living than Switzerland. And best of all, Costa Rica has a climate that can be enjoyed year-round by those of us who hate wearing snow boots and earmuffs. Costa Rica's higher elevations (commonly known as the Valle Central, Meseta Central, or the Central Valley) enjoy springlike temperatures year-round; brightly colored flowers seem to glow in the crystal-clear atmosphere. The countryside is so fertile that fence posts sprout and become trees despite all the farmers' best efforts. Crossing over the mountains, you drop down to tropical lowlands where North Americans own plantations of coffee, macadamia nuts, black pepper, and other exotic crops for export. (Macadamia-nut plantations are exceedingly rare in Switzerland.) Beaches flank either side of the country, dotted with small communities where North Americans and Europeans live in communion with surf and jungle.

A UNIQUE **HISTORY**

Costa Rica stands out in this hemisphere in many ways, but its biggest contrast is with its Central American neighbors. When you drive across

the border into Costa Rica or when you step off an airplane arriving from another Central American country, you know immediately that you are in a special place. Relative affluence stands out in contrast to the grinding poverty of most other Central American locations. People living in neighboring republics point to Costa Rica as an example of the kind of world they would hope to imitate. "If Costa Rica can be prosperous, democratic, and free," the envious neighbors ask, "why can't we?"

Clearly, there's a world of difference between Costa Rica and other Central American countries. How did it get that way? Why does Costa Rica have so much less poverty and so large a middle class in comparison with neighboring countries? Answers to these questions can be found in a series of historical events—some accidental, some planned.

In 1502, when Columbus happened upon Costa Rica during his last voyage to this hemisphere, he anchored somewhere near the present-day city of Limón and dispatched an expedition ashore. Thinking he had found an island, Columbus waited on the ship for a report from his landing party. His explorers returned with news of an inhospitable jungle and impossible swamps, plus ferocious natives who owned but a few paltry ornaments of thinly pounded gold, probably trade goods from Panama. In short, the Limón Coast offered little to excite the imagination of these avaricious explorers.

According to legend, Columbus gave his new discovery the name *Costa Rica* (rich coast) to impress the King of Spain. The explorers sailed away as soon as the ships were repaired, without any thought of colonization. The Caribbean Coast was left virtually ignored by Europeans for several centuries. In contrast with the rapid colonization and development of other parts of the Americas, Costa Rica grew very slowly.

It was the custom for the Spanish Crown to grant huge tracts of land to the conquistadores as a reward for their services. Indians were considered a part of the land, and although not exactly slaves, they essentially belonged to the enormous haciendas: They were forced to work as peons for the aristocratic conquerors. In places like Peru, Mexico, and Guatemala, the Indians meekly accepted their new rulers and continued working the same lands as before, paying tribute to new overlords. However, the Indians of Costa Rica (like their cousins in North America) proved to be determined, fierce fighters who resisted the idea of accepting this subjugation. Experts in defending their heavily forested lands, the natives simply withdrew farther into the jungle when defeated. They clearly weren't interested in tilling fields for the pink-faced intruders. Archaeological evidence suggests that at least some tribes were headhunters, similar to the Jívaro tribes in Ecuador, whose warriors dangled their enemies' shrunken heads around their necks as ornaments. In short, these people were unlikely candidates for being docile field laborers for the pink-skinned intruders.

This left the newcomers in a position they hadn't counted on. Instead of being lords over huge estates and overseeing gangs of laboring peons, the Spanish conquistadores were forced to work the land for themselves. This required hard manual labor and a marginal existence on small, family-run farms. From the beginning, all were equal in their struggle for existence. Even the royal viceroy had to raise chickens and tend his own garden to avoid starvation. Small wonder that many early settlers moved on to easier pickings; others ignored the country completely.

Costa Rica remained a backwater of Spanish colonization, all but forgotten over the ensuing centuries. It grew in its own way, ignoring the ineffective Spanish governors sent by the royal court of Madrid. Costa Ricans lived quiet lives, isolated and unaffected by events in other colonies. In fact, when Spain granted independence to the Spanish colonies in 1821, Costa Rica was the last to know (and probably cared the least). For all practical purposes, it had always been on its own. Independence was no novelty.

COFFEE ECONOMY Fortunately, Costa Rica's first president turned out to be a progressive thinker, a visionary who wanted to see the country develop socially and economically. He was convinced that growing coffee for export could be a major economic breakthrough, a key to modernization. Coffee profits could build roads, schools, and cities.

But the country was scantily populated. More people were needed to grow coffee in order to fulfill the president's dream. Consequently, free land was offered to anyone willing to grow coffee plants. Since coffee production in Costa Rica is ideally suited to small farms, European families began immigrating to take advantage of Costa Rica's opportunities. They came from Italy and France as well as Spain. Instead of huge plantations owned by a few wealthy families as in other Central American republics, hundreds of small farms sprang up, selling coffee beans to merchants who processed and exported the product. This resulted in a tradition of independence and equality, with a preponderance of middle-class farmers and a few moderately wealthy, coffee-exporting families. The spread between rich, middle class, and poor was much narrower than anywhere else in the hemisphere and remains so to this day.

Troubled times in Europe during the last half of the nineteenth century brought new waves of economic and political refugees to the Americas. This was their chance for a new beginning. The standing offer of free land to grow coffee was irresistible. These refugees, instilled with contemporary Europe's liberal intellectual and political philosophy, contributed substantially to the notions of freedom, equality, and individual rights that were already in place.

This is not to say that Costa Rica didn't develop a wealthy oligarchy of elite families whose positions rested upon their control of coffee exports. But because of their tradition of being "self-made" families and their respect for hard work, their mentality was different from that of the arrogant Spanish conquistadores who worshipped royalty and privilege.

Free and compulsory education was an early development, starting in 1869 and setting a tradition of literacy that ranks Costa Rica higher than most other countries of the world. A university was founded in 1844, staffed in part by intellectuals who fled Europe's political and economic maelstrom of that era. These and other modern European traditions developed in Costa Rica in stark contrast with the medieval, feudal heritage of Mexico and other Central American countries.

DISMANTLING THE MILITARY A truly significant event that totally separated Costa Rica from the ranks of other Latin American nations occurred in 1948. The ruling party decided not to recognize the results of an election and refused to give up power, ordering new elections because of the closeness of the vote and accusations of fraud. A crisis of democracy threatened. Pepe Figueres, a charismatic member of one of the wealthy families, stepped forward to lead an uprising against the government and its illegal attempt to use the army to hold on to power. The result of this successful revolution (the first and only in Costa Rican history) was a decision to abolish the army and replace it with the Guardia Civil, a civilian-controlled police force that augments the local police. In some smaller towns the Guardia Civil is the only police force.

This was a brilliant and bold step. Barracks were turned into schools. Ex-soldiers were given jobs building roads. Money that would normally be absorbed by military corruption and graft was devoted to highways, education, and medical care. Today a huge percentage of the national budget goes to education and culture. Public money pays for four universities, three symphony orchestras, and five autonomous state publishing houses. Of the gross national product, about 10 percent is spent on medical care; Costa Rica has an average of one physician for every 700 inhabitants.

Some North Americans shake their heads in dismay at the lack of a standing army. They ask, "Without a military, how can you defend your country from aggression?" The answer is simple: The function of a Central American military has *never* been to deter aggression. The military's duty is to protect the rulers of the country from its citizens, to keep the people in line, to maintain privileges for the military and the country's financial elite. Democracy doesn't stand a chance when army officers nominate candidates, and armed soldiers threaten voters, conduct elections, and then count the ballots. Are we surprised when a general is elected president?

A WELCOMING **DEMOCRACY**

Many North Americans expatriates will tell you they decided on Costa Rica for a new beginning in life because they feel at home here. Costa Ricans like and respect us. We find it easy to make friends among the sizable community of fellow countrymen who have planted roots in Costa

Rica. It's a place where North Americans feel comfortable living in just about any neighborhood, not forced to huddle together in enclaves of other expatriates for mutual support. That's not to say Costa Rica is crime-free (is there such a place?) but compared with other foreign retirement destinations in this world, Costa Rica gives you an unusually safe feeling.

Costa Rica is a country where your conscience isn't continually assaulted by grinding poverty, malnourished children begging in the streets, or social injustice. Juvenile gangs and graffiti are the exception, not the rule. It's a country of full employment; anyone who wants a job can find one, and wages are the highest of any country between the Panama Canal and the United States' Rio Grande.

The Costa Rican personality resembles that of North Americans in many ways: how they view the world, their social behavior, and their value systems. They are open, friendly, and egalitarian. Most North Americans feel right at home in Costa Rica. (The only other Latin country where I feel this way is Argentina.)

Because of these ingrained attitudes, Costa Rica has avoided the problems that have mired its sister Central American republics in a quicksand of turmoil and tragedy. Costa Rica's devotion to democracy and peaceful cooperation with its neighbors has enabled the country to retain its enviable position as a showcase of prosperity, respect for law, and personal freedoms.

HONEST ELECTIONS More than a century-and-a-half tradition of free and honest elections forms the basis for today's political life. Instead of the frequent military takeovers so common in neighboring countries, Costa Ricans change their government via the ballot box. Although members of the affluent families often win elections, they are civilians and intellectuals and for the most part are working for the good of the country as a whole, not just for one particular class. Election Day is Costa Rica's most important holiday, a riotous celebration with a joyous spirit that goes far beyond mere politics. Voting is mandatory—nonvoters pay a token fine—but few citizens would think of passing up the fun and excitement of an election. Weeks prior to Election Day, all parties campaign vigorously, with folks everywhere waving their party's flags, cheering enthusiastically when a car displaying a favored flag drives past, or booing good-naturedly when an opposition flag passes by. On the day of an election, all stores, bars, and businesses are closed, and liquor cannot be sold the day before and the day after the election. Traditionally, public transportation is supposed to be free on election day. Buses, taxis, and even private cars are expected to stop when someone indicates he or she wants a ride to a polling booth. In practice, most autos will stop for anyone who waves and asks for a ride in whatever direction the auto is headed. After all, this is a fiesta!

It's interesting to note that many Costa Ricans, when they move from their hometowns to another part of the country, do not change their voting registration to their new address. Elections are considered an opportunity to return to their hometowns to vote, to visit friends and family, and to party at the same time. Reunions and celebrations are a vital part of Election Day.

Voters must dunk their thumbs into indelible ink to prove they've voted (and cannot vote again), and this purple digit is worn as a proud badge of civic duty. Automobile drivers honk their horns and wave their discolored thumbs in the air as they drive along the streets, to show everyone that they have voted, while shouting, "Have you voted yet?" There are so many horns blowing on Election Day that it sounds like New Year's Eve at midnight.

The result is a country intensely dedicated to notions of democracy. All segments of the political spectrum, from extreme right to far-out left, are represented; all are totally legal. The crucial point is this: The electorate has a free choice. Voters can vote right, left, or center, choosing whichever party presents the best ideas. Because citizens can change their government at will, Costa Rica is virtually revolution-proof.

The end result is a free, prosperous, and peaceful country.

Please don't misunderstand: I'm not implying that Costa Rica has no poverty or that Costa Rican workers are highly paid compared with industrialized countries. But compared with Mexico and Central America, workers here enjoy excellent working conditions, living wages, and government guarantees of fair treatment from employers. Even those at the poverty level live far better than in most other third-world countries and better, in my opinion, than millions of people living at the poverty level in the United States. You'll see few if any "street people," panhandlers, or beggars on Costa Rican streets. Children never beg. As a friend observed, "Among the world's poor, Costa Rica's poor are probably the most affluent."

Welfare is an unknown concept in Costa Rica. Family and friends are always there to help in case of disaster. Jobs are plentiful and unemployment a fraction of that in most highly developed countries. Food is abundant; medical care and education are free. Much agriculture here depends on illegal aliens from Nicaragua to harvest crops and tend banana plantations; Costa Rican workers prefer not to do this kind of backbreaking work. (Does this sound familiar to Californians and Texans who depend on illegal Mexican immigrants for their crops?) Open-air markets have a tradition of giving food to the poor, with vendors handing out their surplus to those asking. If a family wants land to grow food, the government does its best to set them up with a farm.

Although wages are higher here than in neighboring countries, they appear to be extraordinarily low to us *Norteamericanos*. How can workers be expected to survive on as little as $60 a week, much less be considered well-off? The answer is that even though the cash salary is small, fringe benefits connected with the job make a big difference. In addition to their cash salaries, workers are guaranteed benefits such as sick leave—at the rate of 50 percent of their salary—from the first day of illness up to a lifetime of disability. Workers receive a month's pay as *aguinaldo*, or Christmas bonus, every year and a minimum of two weeks' paid vacation every year. Medical care is free. Women receive six weeks' maternity leave (at full salary), and all receive a Social Security pension upon retirement. It isn't necessary to put aside money for the children's college tuition, because education is virtually free, a basic right provided by the government. Since medical care is free, a worker can spend his or her entire salary on living expenses without having to put a portion aside for medical emergencies or illnesses.

All these benefits are guaranteed by law, and all Costa Ricans know exactly what their rights are. Since there's usually a shortage of help in many regions of Costa Rica, anyone who really wants to work can find a job. The result is that employers have to pay more than minimum wages in order to attract competent workers. This is in contrast with other Latin American countries, where the minimum wage and the maximum wage are considered the same.

When you measure these benefits and put a cash value on them, you'll find that Costa Rican workers are ahead of many North Americans. In the United States a woefully inadequate medical-insurance monthly premium can cost a worker more money than many Costa Ricans' total monthly earnings! Since few low-paid U.S. workers can afford medical insurance, one short visit to a hospital can push them over the financial edge. Sick leave? In the United States only large, affluent companies can afford such extravagance. Paid vacations are not mandatory in the United States; they're granted at the discretion of an employer. In Costa Rica, paid vacations are the law.

I'm always amused when I hear ultraconservatives point to Costa Rica's health-care system as evidence that the government is socialist. They overlook the point that if universal health care makes a country socialist, the United States would be one of the few nonsocialist countries in the world! So where does the money come from for health care, pensions, sick leave, and such? It comes out of workers' wages in the form of Social Security contributions and matching funds paid by employers as part of the wage package. Costa Rica's system should be a model for other third-world countries.

LARGE NUMBER **OF EXPATRIATES**

Most reliable sources estimate between 30,000 and 40,000 North American citizens reside in Costa Rica—some full-time, others making their homes here seasonally. Exact figures are impossible to come by. Some make the mistake of counting the number of Social Security checks sent to Costa Rica and counting them as U.S. citizens, thus arriving at a much higher figure. Almost all of these checks go to Costa Ricans who worked in the United States and returned here to retire. Since the U.S. government refuses to direct-deposit Social Security payments into overseas banks, and few U.S. citizens would trust the Costa Rica postal system to deliver the goods, the number of Social Security checks sent here say nothing about the number of U.S. retirees living in Costa Rica.

The percentage of Canadian versus U.S. citizens is difficult to state with precision, but you can be confident that plenty of Canadians are represented. A few North Americans live in other Central American countries—Guatemala, Honduras, Belize, and even El Salvador and Nicaragua—but their ranks are scanty compared with those in Costa Rica.

Because of its small size and economically homogeneous native population, Costa Rica has a high percentage of North Americans (and foreigners in general) who are "starting over" or living part-time in this exotic semi-paradise. Furthermore, you'll find these newcomers scattered all around the country—almost every nook and cranny has a few of us living there—instead of everyone concentrated in enclaves or colonies, as is the case in many other foreign countries.

Costa Rica graciously welcomes seasonal residents, retirees, and business investors, placing fewer restrictions on newcomers than most foreign governments. The government makes it easy to own property or start a business. In fact, you can do both, even as a tourist or part-time resident. To live in Costa Rica permanently as a *pensionado* (retiree), you need only have proof of a $600-a-month retirement income. Actually, living on $600 a month is possible, on a basic level, but it isn't recommended. Because of Costa Rica's affordable cost of living as compared to that of the United States, a retired couple can easily cover their living expenses on an average U.S. Social Security check of $1,129. On that amount you should be able to afford a part-time housekeeper and gardener, and travel when you feel like it. Just consider the lifestyle you would lead in the U.S. on that amount! You might be looking for part-time work yourselves. I personally know people who live well in Costa Rica on less than $800 a month—and others who spend $2,500 and feel they are economizing.

Those who do not receive a company pension or Social Security can still qualify for permanent residency in Costa Rica by showing they have enough income to prove they aren't indigent. The amount required is $1,000 a month. Details are discussed in chapter 17. You should be aware that the national legislature has been considering raising this amount to $2,000 a month, but at the time of this writing, that hasn't happened. You can check on the status of the proposed legislation at my Web site: www.discoverypress.com/update.

Two other conditions make Costa Rica special as a destination for part-time or full-time living. Most important is the almost perfect weather. The central plateau is wonderfully temperate, with thermometer readings virtually the same year-round, with highs in the 70s. Beaches are exquisitely tropical yet, like Hawaii, seldom extremely hot or humid.

The second favorable condition is Costa Rica's exciting investment climate. Instead of placing barriers to prevent foreigners from going into business, as do most other countries in the world, Costa Rica encourages foreign investment. To lure investors, the government offers tax incentives and duty-free imports. Again, you don't have to be a citizen or even a legal resident to own property or conduct a business. You can do it on a tourist visa! Not many desirable countries permit you to do this.

PLANNING YOUR **VISIT TO COSTA RICA**

One publication I strongly recommend for anyone considering Costa Rica for anything more than a short vacation is San José's English-language newspaper, the *Tico Times*. If you read every issue from front to back, including the advertisements, by the time you actually get to Costa Rica, you will know so much about the place that you will feel as though you are returning home. The classified ads keep you up to date on rental costs, housing prices, and what secondhand furniture and appliances sell for. Display ads tell you what you should pay for a hotel room or a bed-and-breakfast. You'll find the best places to dine as well as where to go for a beach excursion. The news columns are well written, with complete and unbiased news of what's happening in Costa Rica as well as in neighboring countries—news not available in U.S. or Canadian newspapers. Featured are articles relating to foreign residents, governmental actions, or changes in law that may affect them, as well as news of social activities and club events. An extensive letters-to-the-editor section prints opinions of tourists and residents alike, telling of exceptionally nice places to go and which places are rip-offs, giving opinions about the country, kudos and complaints, political views, and just about anything else you can imagine. By all means, start your subscription several months before you leave. An interesting innovation is that you can subscribe online. That's what I do; not only do I read the paper every week, I store a copy on my computer for future reference (in Adobe Acrobat format). Go to www.ticotimes.net to subscribe.

A second essential for your first visit is a good travel guide: *Choose Costa Rica* is not intended to be a travel book. This is a guide to retirement, long-term living, and investment in the country. United States and Canadian bookstores are loaded with excellent travel guidebooks packed with information about obligatory places to visit, detailed descriptions of the locations, and what to do when you get there. Here again, the *Tico Times* comes to our rescue. Every year the newspaper publishes a new edition of *Exploring Costa Rica,* a most detailed and comprehensive listing of accommodations and restaurants in almost every community you'd care to visit. The book is free with a subscription or can be ordered by mail.

A final essential for your trip is a sense of adventure and an ability to go with the flow. Things are going to be very different in Costa Rica, as you will learn by reading this book. Folks who love Costa Rica are those who savor the differences. Those who can't stand Costa Rica are those who are disappointed because it isn't at all like it is back home.

EASY ACCESS To enter Costa Rica, you simply show your passport and you are automatically granted a ninety-day visa. Technically, you are supposed to carry your passport with you at all times, but it's okay to carry a photocopy of the page with your photo and another copy of the page with your entry stamp, so it can be determined when you entered the country. Be aware that although a copy is acceptable, the police have the right to accompany you to your hotel to see the original. (This only happens when someone is suspected of wrong-doing or is using a touched-up photocopy.) Be careful not to lose your passport—it's a bummer to have to go to the embassy and apply for a replacement before you can return home.

It's possible to apply for a ninety-day visa extension through the Department of Immigration (some travel agencies claim to be able to do this for you). However, most people take the option of leaving the country for seventy-two hours, visiting the beaches of Nicaragua or the islands of Panama for a three-day vacation. When they reenter the country, they are granted another ninety-day visa. This makes a stay of six months possible, allowing plenty of time to investigate and tour all the nooks and corners of Costa Rica to see whether it would be an appropriate place to retire or go into business.

Theoretically, this "seventy-two hour turnaround" is allowed once in a six-month period; that is, after the second visa you should remain out of the country for three months before reentering the country. Although still on the books, this rule hasn't been enforced broadly for years. Many foreigners have lived in Costa Rica for years, leaving the country every three months. They should be aware that there could come a time when the law is enforced. They know that at that point they'll have to consider applying for residency. The government refers to these people as "perpetual tourists." Occasionally, the ministry of tourism threatens to crack down on perpetual tourists but rarely takes action, except in the case of a few undesirables. Of course, being in the country with an expired visa, over ninety days, could get you into trouble. You should take this rule seriously.

Don't misunderstand, I am not encouraging anyone to violate any rules; I am merely reporting how the laws have been enforced over many years, probably many decades. My personal opinion is that the government recognizes this group of North Americans as law-abiding and peaceful residents who benefit the economy by spending millions of dollars here, thus creating employment. The government's attitude is always subject to change, just as the government is subject to change every four years. Therefore, I encourage anyone who wants to live for long periods of time in Costa Rica to apply for permanent residence.

Finally, I emphatically urge that you make no decisions about permanent moves or business investments without spending several months "on location," getting to know the country, meeting the people, and learning what it's all about. Before making any financial moves, find a good lawyer, one recommended by someone in the North American community. Above all, don't hand your money to someone simply because he or she comes from Akron or Atlanta and has an honest face. Honest faces and firm handshakes are the marks of successful swindlers! Costa Rica has suffered its fair share of sweet-talking gringos with designs on your pocketbooks. There's something about a foreign country that tends to bring out latent larceny in some people. Later on in this book, we'll discuss ways to protect yourself from theft.

RETIREMENT TOURS Although travel in Costa Rica is easy and plans can be very casual, some folks prefer to take a guided tour to the more popular areas for relocation. An organized tour is more efficient and saves time because the tour guide knows exactly where the expatriates prefer to live, and the guide will be able to introduce you to North Americans who have made the move to Costa Rica. One tour that comes highly recommended is conducted by Christopher Howard, a longtime resident of Costa Rica and author of several guidebooks on living and retiring here. His tours are in-depth and take you all over the country. Visit his Web site at www.liveincostarica.com.

Another Costa Rica tour operator, George Lundquist, features a retirement tour called "Expose Me to Life for the Non-Rich in Costa Rica." His four-day tours take guests to some nontraditional retirement locations as well as some of the standard places. He places an emphasis on retiring on Social Security checks. George's website is www.costarica retireonss.com.

INTERNET RESEARCH Another valuable preplanning tool is the Internet. Allow me to strongly recommend that if you don't already have a computer with a Web connection, get one right away. The amount of Costa Rica information available on the Internet is almost unbelievable, and it grows even more comprehensive by the day. With today's simplified Web browsers, anyone can learn to tap in to this information with an hour's instruction. Do your research, then take the computer to Costa Rica with you so that you can stay in constant contact with friends and family. Fortunately, the Costa Rican government places low or no import duties on computers. They are priced similar to what you would pay in the States.

In addition to in-depth descriptions of various sections of Costa Rica as places to live, the Internet brings you Web pages with regional descriptions of Costa Rica, as well as real estate, homes for rent, and online expatriate clubs. If you want to correspond directly with folks living in Costa Rica or others who are considering moving there, you'll find forums and bulletin boards where they post their e-mail addresses. You might make some Costa Rica friends before you ever leave for the airport!

One Internet source of information is my own Costa Rica Bulletin Board. This has been on the Internet for ten years now and has attracted over 600,000 visitors. Discussions range from items such as how to find a shipping company, buying furniture in Costa Rica, where to rent a house, which is the best bed-and-breakfast in Jacó Beach, and how to cook *gallo pinto*. The Web address is http://discoverypress.com/CostaRica.

Costa Rica Living is a very popular and essential expatriate Web site. It's a great way for expatriates to keep in touch by e-mail and socially, with frequent gatherings, dinners, and luncheons, both scheduled and impromptu. Newcomers are welcome: www.groups.yahoo.com/group/ CostaRicaLiving.

Reflecting the trend for younger people moving to Costa Rica, a new social club called Young Expats of Costa Rica has established their own Internet news group for expatriates under the age of 40. It's found at www.youngexpatsofcostarica.org.

To keep you informed about important changes in laws or conditions since the publication of this edition of *Choose Costa Rica*, I maintain an "update" page at www.discoverypress.com/update.

CHAPTER TWO

WHAT'S
COSTA RICA LIKE?

Costa Rica is a small country, even though it doesn't appear so from the standpoint of the traveler who is driving a rental car from one end of the country to the other over winding roads, uphill and down. Every turn in the road brings a new vista, something else to contemplate. Actually, the country contains a little less than 20,000 square miles, much of it almost unpopulated.

Travel articles and guidebooks traditionally describe Costa Rica as being "the size of West Virginia," but that's not really accurate. The truth is, Costa Rica is smaller than West Virginia by 20 percent. Would it help to say that Costa Rica is about half the size of Kentucky? If that makes the country sound small and insignificant, we can balance the equation by pointing out that Costa Rica is larger than Albania, Denmark, Belgium, Holland, Israel, or Switzerland (plus several countries you and I have never heard of).

Few countries of any size offer such a diversity of scenery and climate or such a wide variety of flora and fauna. Probably no other country in the world devotes as large a percentage of its territory to national parks and wildlife refuges. About 27 percent of Costa Rica's land is thus protected. These preserves range from cloud forests to tropical beaches, from vol-

canic craters to jungle swamps and inland waterways. The national park system is a major attraction for tourism.

Costa Rica's bewildering assortment of wildlife includes 850 species of birds—more than in all of the continent north of Mexico. Representative mammals are monkeys, coatis, jaguars, and ocelots, as well as sloths, tapirs, and agoutis. One evening down on the Pacific Coast, a large anteater ambled in front of our car, its long snout almost touching the ground in front and an equally heavy tail drooping behind, looking very prehistoric. Turtles, colorful frogs, and toads of all descriptions are found, as are crocodiles and iguanas. Snakes? Of course. They range from huge boa constrictors to tiny coral snakes. Experts say there are more varieties of butterflies in Costa Rica than in all the African continent; more than 2,000 species have been collected so far and more are being discovered. The number of orchids and bromeliads boggles the mind. This is truly a naturalist's paradise.

Many tropical countries offer beaches and vacation accommodations, but nowhere else in the world can a tourist find such a combination of beaches, mountains, friendliness, and tropical wonder that's accessible year-round.

The Costa Rican government recognizes these unique assets and actively involves its citizens in both the preservation and the exploitation of nature at the same time. How do you protect as well as exploit the environment? Just one example: By hiring local people to guard and preserve endangered-turtle-nesting beaches, jobs are created. Beach villages then become tourist attractions, complete with motels, restaurants, and shops, thus creating even more jobs. Visitors from all over the world can now visit cloud forests, turtle-nesting beaches, and nature preserves—in comfort. In the process, they leave much-needed foreign currency with Costa Rican businesses and banks.

North Americans and Europeans are scrambling to join this bandwagon and, with government encouragement, are investing heavily in tourist businesses, particularly in motels, restaurants, and endeavors of a like nature. Some enterprises become instant successes, with full bookings and plenty of business. Despite occasional slow spells, Costa Rica's commerce and tourism have forged ahead through the past decade and continue healthy and growing into the new century. (Details about starting and operating a business in Costa Rica are presented in chapter 11.)

A COUNTRY **OF CONTRADICTIONS**

Before readers are left with the impression that everything is perfect in paradise, that Costa Rica is the best of all worlds, let's examine some contradictions.

The first contradiction: Even though the Costa Rican government is totally committed to preserving the environment and tries to control illegal deforestation, it also permits foreign companies to bulldoze forests in order to make more banana plantations and tourist resorts. The government puts large tracts of land into biological and wildlife reserves, forest reserves, national parks, and Indian reservations, yet at the same time, farmers and agribusinesses cut down forests on private tracts almost at will. The economy destroys in the name of progress, while the government tries to preserve in the name of conservation. But at least the government does try, and its efforts are improving.

Another contradiction: The growth of ecotourism in Costa Rica brings hundreds of thousands of visitors to enjoy the ecological wonderlands, but large numbers of visitors tramping through delicately balanced wilderness systems threaten to destroy the very ecological treasures that lure them to Costa Rica in the first place. The government raised admission fees to national parks in an effort to cut traffic to some extent. Some say the increase was merely to bring in more revenue, which may well be true, but it did indeed lower the number of visitors and traffic in national parks. The fee increase had a beneficial side effect in directing more business toward private ecological parks and developments.

Yet another contradiction in Costa Rica is the high incidence of petty crime among such a peaceful population, particularly in larger cities. In fact, a major criticism this book has received in the past was that it did not place proper emphasis on the crime rates. I have to admit that I've had a tendency to overlook this issue, in part because I feel that the problem is lightweight compared with the crime situation in other Latin countries. And crime here is almost insignificant when matched with the crime rate in many U.S. communities of similar size. We'll discuss crime in more detail in chapter 5.

Some will disagree, but I feel that Costa Rica's substandard roads, heavy traffic in some areas, and serious potholes are a bigger annoyance than petty crime. I must admit, the government is trying its best to

upgrade the roads and fill in potholes. But chronic shortage of funds, ever-increasing traffic, heavy trucks, and sometimes intense rainfall, all make road maintenance difficult.

Combine treacherous pavement with too many automobiles in and around the heavily populated San José and suburban areas, and you have a situation that encourages taxi rides into congested parts of San José. Fortunately, cab rides are cheap, and more than 7,000 taxis roam the streets. You won't have a long wait between rides. The problems of potholes and heavy traffic in the city will always be another of those fly-in-the-ointment nuisances you'll have to accept if you want to live in paradise. Nothing's perfect. The farther you get from downtown San José, the less the annoyance. When you are really deep into rural areas, the biggest obstacle to driving might be a herd of cattle being driven down the road or a sow and litter of piglets ambling across the way.

Another situation that could become a problem as the foreign population increases is foreign ownership of most of the coastal lands. Although the Costa Rican people are friendly, gentle, and welcoming, you would assume they feel some level of resentment as they see foreigners bid up the price of property until it is out of their price range. The big-money players are heavily represented by North American, German, Swiss, and Italian buyers (more or less in that order). However, this resentment, when evidenced, is low and balanced by an appreciation of how foreign investment creates jobs and bolsters the economy. Where my wife and I own property, local people tell us they'd much rather see foreigners own the land, because Ticos tend to clear-cut the forest to make room for cattle. From their viewpoint, trees don't make money until they are chopped down, but cattle are renewable resources. Ticos know well that cattle ranches create few jobs other than mending fences, while businesses, construction, and working for foreign residents mean full employment and prosperity to all.

Visitors and foreign residents can do little to resolve these contradictions, but they need to be aware that problems do exist and may crop up in the future. The best we can do is try to minimize our impact upon the natural resources of the country. None of these problems have gotten out of hand, and solutions are constantly being sought by the Costa Rican government. But in any democracy, the going is slow and cumbersome. Just be aware that not everything is perfect in paradise—but for my money, it's still paradise!

MENU OF **CLIMATES**

For such a small country, Costa Rica has an astonishing variety of climates. From the misty mountaintops of Talamanca and Monteverde to the dry northern Guanacaste province, from the permanent spring weather of the Arenal area to the jungle lushness of the Caribbean Coast, Costa Rica has every kind of climate one might desire. Well, except frozen snow and bitter cold; but you don't want that anyway. Yes, there are seasons, but the differences between them are minimal, mostly measured in differences in rainfall rather than in temperature variation. Unlike many other choice world vacation spots, Costa Rica isn't a one-season destination; almost any time of the year can be a perfect time to visit. For those who live here full-time, the seasonal changes add spice to retirement. September and October are probably the least popular months, though, for these are the rainiest ones. (Some expats prefer these months because there are fewer tourists.)

In Costa Rica people transpose the meanings of winter and summer. They call the months of December, January, and February summer, or the dry season. These are the months that children take their "summer vacation" from school. To a Costa Rican, winter is June, July, and August! Conversations can become very confusing when Costa Ricans and North

Americans discuss the seasons, with summer and winter having opposite meanings for each. To avoid misunderstandings, I generally say, "June, July, and August" instead of "winter," or better yet I'll say "dry season" or "rainy season"—then everybody knows what I mean.

The dry season, which actually begins around the end of November and lasts until May in many parts of the country, isn't parched and arid as the name might imply. Occasional showers keep plants and lawns pleasantly green and flowers blooming in the higher elevations, where most folks live. Some Pacific coastal areas are truly dry January through April, very much like California summers, when it almost never rains between June and October. On the Caribbean Coast and the northern areas around Lake Arenal, "dry season" is just a figure of speech; rain knows no seasons here.

A common misconception is that "rainy season" means continuous downpours. Typically, even in the most rainy parts of the country, the day begins with glorious sunshine, with blossoms glowing in the sparkling-clean air and birds singing happily. Then clouds roll in after lunch. Rain, sometimes heavy, falls between 2:00 and 4:00 P.M. (In some places you can almost set your clock by it.) The downpour sends people indoors for a couple of hours (an ideal time for a nap). Then sunshine returns, and the world is once again refreshed, ready for another glorious sunset. Other sections of the country enjoy sunshine all day, with rain falling mostly at night. This is the "best" rain; falling asleep to the drumming sound of raindrops on a metal roof is soothing. Seldom does it rain every day; several days in a row can be perfectly dry.

Because most North Americans customarily think of the tropics as a place to visit during their winter season—to escape the snow and ice of their homelands—they are often surprised to find that the months of June, July, and August are the favorite time of year for many who live in Costa Rica. "You can't really appreciate this country until you've experienced our winter months," says my friend Graham Henshaw, an expatriate from England. "When the rains start in May, the grass and trees change to an bright, emerald color. Flowers that bloom only in July and August are absolutely stunning. That is my favorite time of year."

To further complicate matters, what is true of the mountain valley environment around San José isn't necessarily true on the Caribbean side, which can be flooded with sunshine while the capital is awash in *aguaceros* (rainstorms) and vice versa. The truth is, no matter what time of year you choose to visit, you're guaranteed a serving of nice sunny weather—and possibly some rain as well.

Seasons in the tropics are largely determined by altitude. At ocean level the climate is a year-round summer; at moderate elevations year-round spring is a better description. The higher you go, the cooler it gets. A sweater or jacket can be worn almost every evening of the year in higher elevations. Your travel wardrobe should include shirts, sweaters, and jackets you can peel off or pile on, depending on whether you're dining at a beach restaurant, visiting a volcano, or traveling somewhere in between. Be sure to bring rain gear and sturdy shoes if you plan any jungle exploring, plus sunscreen for visits to mountains or beaches; the tropical sun is persistent at all altitudes.

On the northwestern Pacific side, the dry season is exactly that, with very little rain falling from early December until the beginning of May. The grass turns brown, and many trees lose their leaves, just as they do in North America in the winter. But the reason for leaf loss is to conserve water, not because of frost and freezing weather. Most trees are evergreen, but even some of these lose a portion of their leaves. It isn't as bleak as it sounds, for many of these trees replace leaves with brilliantly colored blossoms, as this is the time of year to attract bees, butterflies, and other pollinating insects.

Even on the dry Guanacaste Coast, you'll find microcosms of green environments tucked away in the interior valleys, where sporadic rains are coaxed from the westerly Pacific winds. Farther south along the Pacific Coast, the dry-season rainfall is even more frequent, keeping things pleasantly green during the driest months. The weather chart at the end of this chapter provides statistics on the microclimates of Costa Rica. You will find an interesting interactive weather map on the Internet at www.costa-rica-guide.com/weather/weathermap.html.

INSECTS AND **THE TROPICS**

An odd thing about the weather checkerboard of Costa Rica is that, contrary to what one might think, the more humid areas are not necessarily the most insect-plagued. Of course, bring your insect repellent, but I'm convinced that you need it less in most places in Costa Rica than you do in the American Midwest, Florida, or most certainly in many Canadian locations. Along the forested Pacific Coast and the Nicoya Peninsula—where the insect varieties are amazingly abundant—mosquitoes and flies pester you far less than in the dry regions of Guanacaste. On the humid Caribbean Coast, where rain can fall almost any time of the year and where bugs can get so large you'd think they'd been taking steroids, household cockroaches and flies are not nearly as plentiful as I've seen in Houston or New Orleans. (We've seen many interesting beetles but surprisingly few ordinary cockroaches in our Costa Rica travel and homemaking.)

In parts of Costa Rica, even in the most tropical locations, insects are so benign that many natives don't bother with screens on their windows. Of course, the rainy season in some areas will make a liar of me, so it would be best to carry repellent. This is particularly advisable when staying in one of the areas where dengue fever has been reported (mostly around the outskirts of Puntarenas and near Liberia). There's a vigorous campaign continually under way to eliminate the mosquito that spreads the flulike ailment. Although it is potentially dangerous for those who contract the ailment more than once, very few deaths have been recorded in Costa Rica from dengue fever.

Why flies and mosquitoes are relatively scarce might seem puzzling. I believe the answer is that the natural environment in Costa Rica is largely intact. Natural enemies of pests such as flies and mosquitoes haven't been eliminated by pesticides, chemicals, and other methods, as they have back home. By day, birds of all descriptions flit back and forth, snacking on insects, keeping them in balance with nature. Many birds consider houseflies to be special treats. By night, squadrons of bats keep up the good work, finishing off mosquitoes before they get a chance to do much damage. According to one naturalist, a small bat can catch about 600 mosquito-size insects per hour, and a large colony of bats will consume thousands of pounds of insects every night. (Costa Rica has more than thirty species of bats, thank you very much.)

Meanwhile, lizards, geckos, and chameleons patrol the walls and corners of houses, cleaning up cockroaches and water bugs before they have a chance to infest the kitchen or make a condominium out of your bathroom. The fearsome-looking praying mantis sometimes prowls about the edges of rooms, snapping up bugs that the lizards miss. Ugly as the mantis is, we love 'em!

ATTACK OF THE ARMY ANTS Folks living in the tropical lowlands have additional help in keeping their homes bug-free. From time to time our Costa Rica house is invaded by army ants. Black and about a quarter of an inch long, they march in broad formation up the concrete columns to our veranda and spill over the floors in a busy wave of housecleaning. They remove moths and other night-flying insects that committed suicide against the porch lights the previous night, and they scour the base-boards, corners, and ceilings in search of bugs, beetles, and insect eggs. Scorpions flee in terror; they have no defense against army ants—if they tarry, they are dismantled and served as snacks. Even snakes fear the ants. We simply stay out of their way or prop our feet out of range on a foot-stool while we read a novel, until their twenty-minute cleaning expedition is finished. We say good-bye and thank them as they continue on their way to their next housecleaning duties.

To our dismay, when our housekeeper sees army ants coming, she runs for the insecticide can and sprays profusely. This stops the wave of ants immediately, and they retreat. She is totally deaf to our protests and won't stop spraying until the ants completely disappear.

Actually, I'm exaggerating somewhat. (My wife has asked me a million times to stop exaggerating. No, two million times!) The truth is, these army ant invasions don't happen all that frequently, maybe once a month or so, depending where you live. If they happen to come while you are out shopping, you'll miss them. But they are spectacular.

Not that insects can't make one suffer. Some very small creatures made a recent trip to the Pacific beaches memorable for several weeks. These were the dreaded "no-see-ums," a generic name given to any tiny bug that bites without your knowing you are being attacked but makes you suffer afterward. In this case, they were probably some kind of minia-ture sand flea because they got me on the ankles and lower legs. (Mos-quitoes and gnats bite wherever they please.) However, it was my own fault; I should know better than to stroll along the beach at dusk without repellent on my bare legs. Not all beaches are plagued with no-see-ums; local residents can warn you as to which ones are troublesome.

During a visit to Cahuita, on the Caribbean Coast, I was about to enter my cabin when I encountered an enormous beetle. It was about the size of a teacup, shaped like a giant ladybug, and the color of an olive drab army helmet. Feeling brave, I gingerly picked it up by its back, correctly

figuring that its wicked-looking legs couldn't reach around the shell. I carried it to a nearby restaurant and proudly displayed my beetle to the people sitting at the bar, figuring that I'd raise a few eyebrows. The bartender looked at my discovery with a bored expression as he remarked, "Yes, those little ones are females."

It turned out that I was holding a rhinoceros beetle, possibly the largest bug of the entire insect world. They tell me the male, which I never happened to confront, grows to a length of 10 inches (25 centimeters), sports enormous horns, and is colored in brilliant metallic hues. Harmless, though.

CENTRAL AMERICAN **EARTHQUAKES**

All along the mountain chains that stretch from the tip of South America to Alaska, you will feel earthquakes. As a Californian, I've become accustomed to them and seldom experience more than a slight feeling of excitement when windows start rattling and my desk sways a bit. We Californians expect to have several minor quakes a year and a big one every twenty-five years or so.

So it should come as no surprise that Costa Rica has its share of shakes and tremors. Actually, more than its share. The really big ones here are spaced by decades instead of generations. Yet Costa Ricans are just as calm about earthquakes as most Californians are. After all, compared with the 700 or so tornadoes that slam the midwestern and eastern parts of North America, claiming eighty to a hundred victims each season, an occasional shaker seems relatively mild.

The last big tremor—a whopping 7.4 on the Richter scale—hit the Caribbean Coast near the city of Limón in April 1991. Older structures suffered the most damage, particularly those not constructed to modern-day standards. However, by the beginning of the next tourist season, most of the damage had been repaired, hotels were operating, roads were open to traffic, and tourism was going full blast.

A few months after the quake, I visited Cahuita, not too far from the epicenter. Expecting to see a lot of damage and hear horror stories, I was delighted to learn that there were no fatalities in the village and that, except for one major building (which had been made of nonreinforced cement) and a few other smaller structures, the town came through relatively unscathed. Cahuita construction is of wood, which may shake, rattle, and twist but doesn't usually tumble down.

Costa Rica's 7.4 shaker claimed about forty lives, one of the worst ever. But compare this earthquake with the one in Iran the year before: It was 7.5 on the Richter scale and claimed more than 50,000 victims. A horrible 6.9 quake in Armenia in 1989 killed 25,000 people; one in Costa Rica the following year was just as strong yet nobody was killed. Why the difference?

One answer to this question, besides lower population density, is sensible construction methods. Costa Rican homes and businesses are designed with earthquakes in mind. Costa Rica has prohibited the use of adobe in constructing homes for more than eighty years. This is the only nation in the hemisphere with a ban on adobe, a material that has a tendency to collapse and bury earthquake victims. Wood, reinforced concrete block, or stressed cement is infinitely safer. Instead of picturesque tile roofs, which can crush inhabitants under tons of heavy beams and broken tile, most Costa Rican roofs are of ordinary-looking corrugated aluminum, plastic, or sheet metal. These lightweight roofs may slide about during a quake, but they won't collapse and kill people by burying them.

An interesting feature of the 1991 quake was an uplifting of the coastline. The force raised the land as much as 5 feet near the town of Puerto Limón and 1½ feet at Puerto Viejo. What once were coral reefs are now dry land at the edge of surf where fishermen once hauled in crab, shrimp, and red snapper. This lifting of the land from the sea is a wonderful example of how the Central American land bridge was formed some two or three million years ago when quake activity began pushing the land ever higher. Geologists find coral fossils on mountaintops now 9,000 feet above sea level.

TEMPERATURES AND RAINFALL
FOR SELECTED COSTA RICAN LOCATIONS

Alajuela

AVG.	JAN.	FEB.	MAR.	APR.	MAY	JUN.	JUL.	AUG.	SEPT.	OCT.	NOV.	DEC.	ANNUAL
				(In degrees Fahrenheit and inches)									
HIGHS	81	83	85	85	82	81	81	81	80	80	80	81	81
LOWS	62	62	63	63	64	64	64	63	63	63	63	63	63
RAIN	0.3	0.5	0.6	3	11	11	7	10	1	14	20	1	92

Golfito

	JAN.	FEB.	MAR.	APR.	MAY	JUN.	JUL.	AUG.	SEPT.	OCT.	NOV.	DEC.	ANNUAL
HIGHS	91	92	92	91	90	89	89	90	89	89	89	90	90
LOWS	71	72	73	73	73	72	71	71	71	71	71	71	72
RAIN	6	6	8	11	19	18	18	22	28	28	23	12	199

Cahuita

	JAN.	FEB.	MAR.	APR.	MAY	JUN.	JUL.	AUG.	SEPT.	OCT.	NOV.	DEC.	ANNUAL
HIGHS	86	86	87	87	87	87	86	86	87	87	86	86	86
LOWS	68	68	69	71	71	71	71	71	71	71	69	69	69
RAIN	13	8	8	11	11	12	17	13	6	8	16	18	141

Nicoya

	JAN.	FEB.	MAR.	APR.	MAY	JUN.	JUL.	AUG.	SEPT.	OCT.	NOV.	DEC.	ANNUAL
HIGHS	91	93	95	96	91	89	89	89	87	87	87	89	87
LOWS	69	71	71	73	73	71	71	71	71	71	69	69	71
RAIN	0.2	0.4	1	3	11	13	10	12	16	16	5	1	89

Manuel Antonio

	JAN.	FEB.	MAR.	APR.	MAY	JUN.	JUL.	AUG.	SEPT.	OCT.	NOV.	DEC.	ANNUAL
HIGHS	87	87	89	89	89	87	87	87	86	86	86	86	87
LOWS	69	69	71	71	71	71	69	69	71	71	71	69	71
RAIN	3	1	2	7	16	17	18	19	21	26	16	7	153

San José

	JAN.	FEB.	MAR.	APR.	MAY	JUN.	JUL.	AUG.	SEPT.	OCT.	NOV.	DEC.	ANNUAL
HIGHS	73	75	77	78	78	78	77	77	78	77	75	77	77
LOWS	59	59	60	60	62	62	67	62	60	60	60	59	62
RAIN	0.4	0.2	0.5	2	9	12	9	10	13	13	6	2	77

CHAPTER THREE

WHAT ARE
COSTA RICANS LIKE?

Most travelers will agree that every country has its own distinct person-ality. Native citizens of each country have unique ways of behaving and viewing the world. My favorite story to illustrate differences in national personalities is *Traveler's Heaven* and *Traveler's Hell:*

"Travelers' Heaven is when you are greeted by the British, the French do the cooking, Italians plan the fun and games, and Germans keep order. But Traveler's Hell is when you are greeted by the French, the British do the cooking, Italians keep order, and Germans plan the fun and games!"

Americans and New Zealanders, for example, are stereotypically outgoing, friendly, and loud talkers. Russians are pictured as dour and morose, with no sense of humor. British are said to be terrible cooks. Of course these are stereotypes, and we all agree that it's unfair to apply stereotypes. (Except in the case of the Brits, who tend to boil every-thing they can't fry.) Yet there is more than a kernel of truth here. The reasons for a nation's personality differences often can be explained by the historical development of each country.

In South America, for example, Argentina has a personality that reflects the heritage of its large Italian immigration, while next-door Chile

was influenced by English and German newcomers who joined the original Spanish settlers. The result is an outgoing, vivacious, and self-confident Argentine personality compared with Chile's more reserved, polite, and introverted temperament.

Costa Rica's distinct personality also is a product of history. In chapter 1 we discussed Costa Rica's isolation during the early Spanish years and how, during the early days of the republic, Costa Rica invited Europeans from all nations to immigrate and start coffee farms. Italian and French refugees from a severe European economic recession joined Spaniards in the land rush, each nationality bringing its customs and personalities to blend together into Costa Rica's unique way of European–Central American life and creating the Tico personality of today.

One way Ticos differ from residents of some other Latin American countries is tolerance toward other religions and other points of view. Costa Ricans are predominantly Catholic but without the zeal and rigidity sometimes found in other countries. This, too, has a historical explanation. In the early days, small villages were so isolated that the Church either couldn't or didn't bother to install chapels or send priests. The result was an informal observance of religion as something remote and almost irrelevant (except for the celebration of village saints' days). Even today the Catholic churches in many villages are often attended by visiting priests. This situation creates fertile ground for evangelical denominations to establish churches. Numerous small villages have evangelical Protestant churches only.

Yet curiously, one of the country's most important celebrations is on August 2, when thousands of Costa Ricans end a pilgrimage walk of several days to pay homage to the *Virgen de los Angeles* in Cartago. And Catholics and Protestants alike enthusiastically celebrate their villages' religious fiestas with dances, bullfights, parades, and fund-raising events. It's more like a carnival than a religious observance. Don't miss attending these celebrations. The local people appreciate gringos joining in and will welcome you with enthusiasm. You'll have a great time.

WHY **"TICOS"?**

Throughout this book you'll see the term *Tico* used when speaking of Costa Ricans. This is the appropriate nickname for a Costa Rican citizen, just as *Nica* is a Nicaraguan, and *gringo* describes North Americans in general or any foreigner who speaks English. The term *gringo* is an accepted nickname for both Canadian and U.S. citizens—no one takes umbrage by it. Costa Ricans call themselves Ticos when distinguishing themselves from foreigners, instead of the more cumbersome *Costarricenses*.

The name Tico comes from an archaic practice of using the sound *-tico* on the end of a word as a diminutive instead of the normal *-tito*. For example, whereas a Mexican would say *momen**tito*** for "just a tiny moment," some Costa Ricans (not all) might say *momen**tico.*** Thus, a kitten would be a *ga**tico*** in Costa Rica but a *ga**tito*** in Mexico. Not all Costa Ricans use this ending, but enough do to keep the tradition alive.

THE TICO **PSYCHE**

An outstanding difference between the psyche of Costa Ricans and other Latinos is the way they view the world and their place in it. Because of a long tradition of democracy and equality, the country has developed an egalitarian society similar to the United States and Canada in terms of social equality. Unlike many other Latin American countries, the spread between Costa Rica's rich, poor, and middle classes is narrow. The middle class is large and relatively prosperous; the upper class is small and only moderately wealthy. People here do not bow to anyone, regardless of who they are. This is a country where you can see the president and his wife pushing a grocery cart in a supermarket. People look you in the eye and shake your hand, fully convinced that everyone is equal.

Because Tico attitudes are similar to North Americans', we feel perfectly comfortable when socializing with them. However, there are some subtle differences in the Tico psyche that need to be understood. First of all, it is considered ill-mannered to be loud, brash, argumentative, and overly competitive, as Americans tend to be. (The exception of course, is when playing soccer or driving a car.) In fact, they hate confrontation so much that they'll do anything to avoid giving you bad news. When your contractor tells you that the transformer for your new home didn't arrive today but is coming *mañana,* he may be avoiding the bad news that it might be a week or a month before you have electricity. Costa Ricans want to tell you what you would like to hear if at all possible. If it's not possible, they avoid talking about it so you won't feel bad.

In line with the hesitation to give bad news is a tendency to avoid saying no to a request or business proposal. If saying no might make a Tico appear rude or might hurt your feelings, they become vague. So when doing business, remember that you can only count on an outright "yes" or "no" as being definitive. A hesitant "yes" or "maybe" could mean anything.

Another interesting trait is the reluctance to accept blame. When our maid drops a plate on the floor, she says, *"Se quebró el plato,"* or "The plate broke itself." I once tried to convince an electrician that he had installed my telephone incorrectly. (The problem was obvious: He had shorted the wires by pounding a staple across the cable shroud.) He insisted that the problem was a temporary glitch at the telephone exchange. "Pretty soon they'll find their mistake and fix it." He installed a new cable at my insistence and according to my directions, after which the phone worked. "You see?" he crowed in triumph. "While I was putting in the new cable, the telephone company found their mistake and fixed it!" I agreed with him so he could save face.

Something I do *not* believe is the often heard claim that Ticos deliberately mislead you about directions rather than admit that they don't know the answer. For example, some claim that when asked directions, Ticos might give any response, pointing whichever direction they think you might like. I've often wondered where that notion came from. I have never, in all my years of traveling in Central America, had anyone do that. (I ought to know, because without street signs, I have to ask for directions frequently.) When Ticos don't know the answer to a question, they simply say so, like anyone else. On two occasions the people I asked didn't know, so they flagged down a passing car to ask. Giving misleading directions would be the height of rudeness and a violation of Tico etiquette.

The well-known *mañana* attitude of Latin America is present in Costa Rica but not nearly to the extent as in some other Latino countries—at least in my experience. Our workers are usually always at the job on time and work hard while they are there. (They also quit exactly on time.) The exception to this rule is after a local weekend fiesta, when workers might be late to work on on those Monday mornings. Nobody expects all of their workers to show up on time Monday morning or to be really capable of work. Guests to your dinner party will be late anywhere from fifteen minutes to half an hour. Your auto mechanic will be an hour late changing your oil, but seldom a day late.

In several ways, Ticos are very much like us, except that they speak more softly and seem more stoic about the world's problems than some of their Latin American counterparts. They laugh just as much as we do and share the same sense of humor. The best part of all: They really like North Americans, probably because our personalities mesh. Most of us who live in Costa Rica reciprocate this instant friendship; we like Ticos, too.

TICO **SPANISH**

Because of Costa Rica's early isolation, the country developed some unique linguistic differences from other Spanish-speaking countries. Furthermore, within Costa Rica itself, local accents developed in isolated parts of the country back when communication was extremely difficult. For example: An oxcart journey from San José to Limón used to take nearly two weeks. That's how they used to transport coffee to the coast, and that's why they built the railroad.

These accents vary from being so slight that it takes an expert to distinguish them, to being all but unintelligible to those not fluent in Spanish. The differences are similar to the way words are pronounced in Minneapolis, Minnesota, as compared to the way they're pronounced in Montgomery, Alabama. This is most noticeable in Guanacaste (northwestern Costa Rica). Like the Alabama accent, the Guanacaste accent is the result of dropping consonants and slurring vowels together. This lingo is similar to that spoken in Nicaragua (not surprising since Guanacaste originally was part of Nicaragua). Once you get used to this blending of sounds, it becomes clear.

Don't worry too much if you are just learning Spanish. Almost all people can and will speak "proper Spanish" when they realize you don't understand them. They simply repeat their words with a more careful pronunciation and avoid using local slang—just as they learned to do when they were in school. English is mandatory in all grammar schools, by the way.

There is one outstanding difference between Tico Spanish and standard Spanish grammar that might puzzle those who have studied the language in high school or college back home. Instead of using the polite *usted* and informal *tu* forms of Spanish normally taught in our high schools and universities, Costa Ricans use the archaic Spanish *vos* instead of the more common *tu* for the familiar first person singular. Originally, *vos* was the polite form of Spanish first person singular, and *tu* was familiar. Then somewhere in the late sixteenth century, the use of *vuestra merced* (your grace) became the polite form, later shortened to *usted*. This downgraded the formal pronoun *vos* to informal use, and the pronoun *tu* was used only when speaking to inferiors or animals. Later, the use of *vos* was totally dropped and *tu* once again became standard for informal speech in Spain. However, the first Costa Rican immigrants from Spain came *before* that switch in grammar occurred and therefore retained the old custom. To make things more confusing, the *tu* form is sometimes used as a form of intimacy between lovers.

Verbs have a different declension or word ending when using *vos*. Unfortunately these grammatical verb forms aren't taught in U.S. schools, even though the *voseo* mode is used by several million people in the western hemisphere. (Yes, they teach the *vosotros* form, but that is plural and is used mostly by Catholic priests when addressing a congregation.) It takes some time to become comfortable with the *vos* form; in the meantime play it safe by using *usted*. Look at the chart below and note the differences.

	Usted **Form**	*Tu* **Form**	*Vos* **Form**
Do you want?	*¿Quiere Ud?*	*¿Quieres tu?*	*¿Queréis vos?*
You speak . . .	*Usted habla*	*Tu hablas*	*Vos hablás*
You are . . .	*Usted es*	*Tu eres*	*Vos sos*

You'll also encounter some interesting differences between Tico expressions and Spanish usage in other countries. Some are quite charming. For example, in most Spanish-speaking countries, the term for "you're welcome" is *por nada* ("it's nothing"), or *no hay de que* ("don't mention it"). Costa Ricans feel those expressions somewhat impolite. To

say "you're welcome," they say *con mucho gusto,* which translates as "with much pleasure." (Now, is that polite or what?) Of course, they're used to hearing gringos use the other expressions, so they won't be surprised when you say *"de nada."*

Instead of greeting close acquaintances with ¿*Como está usted?* ("How are you?") they'll often ask, ¿*Como amaneció?* ("How did you wake up this morning?").

Another curious custom: For some reason Ticos feel that asking for something using the verb *dar* (to give) is impolite. Instead of *"Dame una coca, por favor,"* meaning "Give me a Coca-Cola, please," they consider it more polite to use the verb *regalame,* which means, "give me," but also could mean "make me a gift of. . . ." So to be polite in a Tico sense, you might say *"Regálame una coca, por favor."* A Tica friend told of her first visit to Mexico and of ordering a cup of coffee in a restaurant by saying *"Regálame un café con leche, por favor."* The waitress was obviously embarrassed when she said, "I'd love to give you some coffee, but the owner would be angry with me if I did!" My friend laughed about this, saying she hadn't realized that she could be misunderstood.

One uniquely Costa Rican term, solidly ingrained into the language, is *pura vida.* I suppose this would translate as "it's a great life," but in effect it means "okay," "cool," "all right," or sometimes an emphatic *"aw-right!"* Instead of asking "Would you like anything else?" a clerk in a store might say, *"Pura vida?"* A gas-station attendant might ask, "Is your oil *pura vida,* or should I check it for you?" When you greet someone with *"Como está usted?"* the answer is often, *"Pura vida!"*

A couple of strictly Costa Rican expressions initially puzzled me and could be puzzling to those learning the language. This is a tendency to begin sentences with the words *vieras que,* or simply *vieras.* Literally it means something like "You see" or "You know." Also used in the same way is *digamos que* or *digamos* ("let's say. . ."), but since the sound *d* is often softened or dropped entirely, it comes out *"igamos."*

COSTA RICA **SLANG**

You should be careful not to use sayings with obscene implications and also realize that slang changes over time. Many years ago I ran across a series of tapes with Tico slang expressions, bought them, and put them away, vowing some day to master Tico slang. Twenty years later I actually began to study those tapes. Armed with this knowledge of Tico slang, I ventured forth to display my proficiency and was shocked to see smiles and laughter. Then I realized that over the years, this slang had fallen from favor. I was saying things like "Twenty-three skidoo!" or "Groovy!" and "Oh, you kid!"

For those who would like to study Costa Rican slang, an excellent Web site can be found at www.isls.com/costarica/destination/pachuco spanish.html. A word of warning: Those who have learned and used Spanish slang in another country should be careful when using it in polite company in Costa Rica. Some expressions that might be clever and inoffensive in Mexico, for example, could mean something obscene or insulting here, and vice versa.

CHAPTER FOUR

WHY CHOOSE
COSTA RICA?

North Americans choose Costa Rica for a new beginning for many of the same reasons that tourists choose to spend their vacations here. They've heard all about this small Central American democracy, the rain forests, lofty mountains, marvelous wildlife, and gorgeous beaches. They love having the choice between year-round spring in the mountains or year-round summer at the ocean. Costa Rica's cleanliness and welcoming citizens make tourists feel at home and inspire many of them with an idea of moving here to start a business, work, or retire. Those who relocate here are, in a sense, going on a permanent vacation. They get to enjoy all the attractions that bring foreign tourists to Costa Rica's shore without leaving home.

Some point out that Costa Rica's relative affluence and absence of obvious poverty make them feel more comfortable while experiencing the stimulation of foreign retirement. The fact that Americans genuinely feel welcome makes it easy for retirees to settle anywhere we choose and not feel confined to expatriate enclaves.

Costa Rica's unique selection of climates is a definite drawing card, with fugitives from bitter-cold winters or suffocating summer heat finding welcome relief from weather extremes. "I grew up in Kansas," one

retiree explained, "and we had blizzards and frozen ground in the winter, then 110-degree days trapping us indoors in the summer. Where we live now (on the hillside above Escazú) we only need one set of clothing—springtime."

Many who fall in love with Costa Rica and resolve to live here are much too young to retire. So they come here with the goal of combining a business enterprise with enjoyment of all Costa Rica has to offer. Starting a business or buying a business is easily done, but as anyone with business experience knows, success is never guaranteed. Later in this book we have a chapter on doing business in Costa Rica and why some make a success of it and others do not.

Some relocate to Costa Rica for the sheer exhilaration of living in a foreign country. When asked how she and her husband made the decision to move to Costa Rica, Hilary Aeschliman said, "We probably did things differently than most sane people do. We decided to move here without even visiting. We had traveled in Mexico, and everyone we spoke with compared it favorably. In fact, many people liked Costa Rica better than Mexico. So we decided we could handle Costa Rica without testing the waters first. Our initial plan was to spend a year in Costa Rica, rent furnished homes, learn the language, and take our experiences back home when it was over. However, our children are enjoying school here, so after one year into it, neither of us feel an inclination to hurry back to the States. I suspect that we'll be part-time Ticos for a long time to come."

LOW COST **OF LIVING?**

Sometimes I hesitate to say this, but one of the side benefits of living in Central America is a significantly lower cost of living than can be found in most parts of the United States or Canada. The reason I'm reluctant to say this is that most of those who come to Costa Rica solely because they want a cheap place to live usually suffer frustration and disappointment. They end up not seeing the beauty of the country because they are continually comparing prices of everything. They don't understand that there is a difference between "affordable" and "cheap."

It's always amusing to hear tourists—and even an occasional resident—complain about high prices in Costa Rica. For some reason people assume that property, goods, and services ought to be dirt cheap in a developing Central American country like Costa Rica. They feel cheated to discover some things cost as much here as they do back home—some imported goods even more.

They tend to forget what prices were where they came from. When they pay 550 colones for a bottle of beer, it sounds like a lot of money. Yet 550 colones is more or less one dollar. (Probably less than half the price back home.) Over time the price of a beer will no doubt increase from 550 colones to 1,100 colones—then they'll complain that the cost has doubled. But when that happens, the exchange doubles as well. Yet the price of a bottle of beer could rise to 1,100 colones, but the exchange rate will *still* make the cost of a bottle of beer one dollar!

A few months ago my wife and I happened to be having dinner with a couple from New England who were visiting Costa Rica for the first time. They reluctantly admitted they were somewhat disappointed with Costa Rica as a place to retire. When asked why, they replied that they felt that Costa Rica was not the beautiful and interesting place described in magazines and guidebooks. (They didn't know that we were authors of a guidebook.)

Dumfounded by their answer, I politely inquired how long they had been in Costa Rica and where they had visited. They admitted that they had just arrived three days earlier and that their travels were limited to taxi rides around the San José area.

"Okay, we realize there must be more to Costa Rica than San Jose," the husband admitted. "But we were under the impression that everything is cheap here. We see houses advertised in the *Tico Times*, and they cost almost as much as they would back home in South Dakota." They admitted that they hadn't actually *looked* at any of the houses. They had expected to find a nice home for around $30,000.

Their concern over high prices amused us. They were enjoying a delicious sea bass dinner priced at $5.00 including dessert. They were drinking Costa Rican beer priced at $1.00 a bottle. They were staying at a nice bed-and-breakfast for about $40 a night. To be polite, we agreed with the couple; Costa Rica probably wouldn't be the ideal place for them to retire.

Although I have a hard time imagining a quality place in the United States or Canada that makes Costa Rica look expensive, my routine reply to bargain hunters is: "If rock-bottom prices are your priority, look at Mexico, Guatemala, or Nicaragua." Many third-world countries offer cheaper living than Costa Rica. But is the quality of life the same? Is the weather as nice? Are the people as friendly?

The bottom line is: You're in for disappointment if you expect to pay $5.00-a-day wages for your gardener or maid, or purchase ocean-view property at Texas Panhandle prices. If you anticipate luxurious $10.00-a-day hotel rooms and lobster dinners for $3.00, this might be the time to stop reading this book.

AFFORDABLE, NOT CHEAP In general, I estimate most Costa Rican prices at about two-thirds the cost in most North American communities. Of course, imported goods can be much more. The hotels Costa Rica expatriates patronize usually range from $35 to $65 a night, including breakfast. These aren't luxury establishments by any definition, but they clearly offer far more than budget hotels do in the United States or Canada for the same price. Backpackers are delighted to find rooms for $5.00 to $10.00, since they don't mind sharing the bathroom.

Go to just about any nice restaurant in Costa Rica and check the menu. Few entrees are priced over $9.00. A juicy steak goes for about $8.00, pasta Alfredo for $4.00. If the entree exceeds $13.00, you're probably ordering lobster or jumbo shrimp. (For some reason, jumbo shrimp is expensive in Costa Rica.) If you're into *tipico* Costa Rican food, you can order a *casado* for about $3.00—a delicious plate of beans, rice, fried banana and yucca, and salad, with your choice of chicken, fish, or pork chop. My favorite Tico restaurant serves a butterflied pork chop half the size of a dinner plate!

Let's forget about hotel prices and restaurant costs; they don't figure heavily in most long-term residents' budgets. More important is comparing the cost of everyday living here with the lifestyle the same amount of money provides elsewhere. You would be hard-pressed to find another place with so much to offer for such a reasonable outlay.

CAN YOU LIVE ON SOCIAL SECURITY? The answer is maybe yes, maybe no. Numerous surveys here show that most expatriate couples report spending between $1,200 to $1,600 in Costa Rica to maintain a comfortable lifestyle. This would involve comfortable living accommodations (not deluxe), an inexpensive auto, a part-time housekeeper, and a certain amount of travel around the country. Clearly, their standard of liv-

ing on budgets like these will be much higher than they could ever hope for in the United States or in Canada for the same outgo. Some people spend a lot more, but their living standards are much higher as well.

Since average Social Security benefits for a couple amount to $1,648 (February 2006), those drawing that amount should be able to make basic expenses just with their monthly benefits. Additional income could be banked or saved for emergencies. These average Social Security checks amount to about to $400 a week, which is more than most Tico families earn in a month. Yes, they probably could do okay living back in the United States—depending on where they lived—but clearly not without some budget trimming. This $1,648 figure is average, of course, which means half of the Social Security beneficiaries make less than that. Some much less.

One way of economizing is by living in ordinary rather than deluxe housing. In many foreign countries North American residents feel they must live in certain "safe" areas, for which they pay premium prices. Because Costa Rica is not a highly stratified society, North Americans feel comfortable living in almost any neighborhood or village. This translates into a wide selection of rents and housing prices. While you can pay $1,500 a month to rent in a luxury section of Escazú, you can often find a nice place for $400 a month in the same neighborhood. For $300 you can find accommodations in very livable areas such as Alajuela or San Pedro. Just a few minutes away from shopping and conveniences, it's quality living with a superb climate. If you're content with less sumptuous digs, your rental costs can be even less. I have a friend who lives in a small house near San José that he rents for $170 a month. (Understand, we are not talking about premium beachfront properties with ocean views!)

Utilities, a significant part of most budgets, seem almost free in Costa Rica when compared with the United States or Canada. Our telephone bill is usually around $7.00 a month. Homes in the higher altitudes seldom have furnaces or air conditioners to drain money from budgets. Electric bills for our condominium in Rohrmoser averaged $13 a month, a tiny fraction of what we pay back in California. At our Pacific Coast home, electric bills are more, about $30 a month (exactly why it is more, I can't say). In this particular community, our nongovernmental-water-company bills are very high (only because our water bills include road maintenance and other services). No matter, we have friends in Missouri and Ohio who spend more just to heat or cool their homes every month than most Costa Ricans earn in a month. Compare the cost of living here with your own hometown and then tell us Costa Rica is expensive!

Property taxes are almost nothing, at least for North Americans accustomed to forking over big money for taxes. According to people I interviewed for this book, an average middle-class home—with three bedrooms and two baths—is taxed at the rate of $40 to $200 a year. Most U.S. communities collect more taxes than that every month. Tax reform laws passed in 1996 boosted some property taxes but were basically aimed at collecting from those who previously had evaded taxes altogether. However, new tax reform laws passed the following year cut property taxes back to the original amount.

Besides affordable housing, utilities, taxes, and food costs, what other bargains does Costa Rica offer? Oh yes: servants. A full-time housekeeper will clean your house and wash and iron clothes for about $250 a month. That includes all benefits such as Social Security, paid vacation, and a Christmas bonus. (See chapter 12 for further details.) We pay our gardener-handyman $2.00 an hour for part-time work, and that's well above minimum wage. We have a friendly cleaning lady who comes in one half-day each week. She washes clothes, changes bed linens, mops and disinfects floors, and waxes the veranda deck—also for $2.00 an hour. (By the way, what do you pay servants in *your* hometown?)

Is everything inexpensive in Costa Rica? (Don't we wish!) Gasoline is more expensive, depending on the current world price of crude oil and whether the government needs more tax revenue. Automobiles are heavily taxed, and repair parts can be costly. Since the bulk of Costa Rica's governmental income comes from customs duties, obviously anything imported can be pricey.

High import taxes are a way of life in almost all Latin countries. This makes automobiles very expensive. You'll need to brace yourself before asking the price. Until a couple of years ago, customs and sales taxes cost as much as 100 percent of appraised value! It's a little better today, running from 40 to 77 percent of the vehicle's value. These tax rates change frequently, but you can be sure that autos in Costa Rica will always be expensive. Calculations for automobile duties are made from something called the *Black Book,* listing new- and used-car wholesale auction prices—the bible for U.S. car dealers, loan officers, and Costa Rican customs agents.

Fortunately, public transportation is excellent and inexpensive. Depending on where you live, a family car may not be the absolute necessity that it is back home. Buses travel all over the Valle Central, at frequent intervals, for as little as 20 cents, 70 cents for longer distances. Taxis are plentiful and inexpensive. Even in the country, far from city conveniences, buses and taxis are abundant. Where public transportation is all but nonexistent, the custom is for automobiles and trucks to pick up pedestrians. We've made several Tico and gringo acquaintances that way. Would you consider picking up hitchhikers back home? I wouldn't!

LOW-BUDGET EXAMPLE Before I go any further, I want to emphasize: In no way do I encourage anyone with a limited budget and no backup funds to move to Costa Rica simply because of the low cost of living. That would be an invitation for disaster. At home, low-income people can qualify for Medicaid, welfare, food stamps, and other programs. This safety net doesn't exist in Costa Rica. However, if you have sufficient funds to cover emergencies and money to splurge for luxuries on a regular basis, you are welcome to investigate further.

For two-thirds of all U.S. retirees, Social Security is the major source of income. About one-third of U.S. elderly survive on Social Security as their only income. That's an average of $1,129 a month for a man, $870 for a woman, and $1,648 for a married couple (figures as of February 2006). Depending on your lifetime accumulation of benefits, your checks could be more or less. The thought of millions of retirees having to survive on Social Security checks is not a happy one, but people have to do the best they can.

Of course, not everyone has the luxury of drawing average Social Security checks. Fifty percent of the beneficiaries draw below the national averages, and if that's their only income, they have to make do.

Following is the experience of Californian Tom Stafford, who, like several million other U.S. retirees, draws Social Security benefits of $700 a month or less. Although Tom had accumulated a modest nest egg as a backup, he knew he had to live conservatively and live within his Social Security income.

He says: "The decision to live in Costa Rica was made after my third trip. I began to scout out a piece of land with the idea of building a home. When a friend bought a few acres north of San Ramón, I threw in with him, buying a one-half-acre plot for my house. I decided on a prefabricated Swiss chalet–style log cabin that seemed to fit me like a tailored suit. While only 750 square feet, it has a commodious loft and plenty of beautiful land all around it."

He says: "My transition to 'Tico provisional' was not all that smooth. Without the generous help and advice of friends I made along the way, it might not have happened at all. One piece of advice I would give to anyone thinking of coming here is: Meet a lot of people—both expats and Ticos—make friends with them, and follow their advice. I know it's a cliché, but there is no sense in reinventing the wheel."

Tom manages to get by just fine on $671 per month (his Social Security check), but only because he owns his home, thus eliminating rent. His monthly expenses, such as electricity, water, and telephone are very low. Public transportation allows him to get by sans automobile. Tom says, "My budget doesn't leave much for nights out on the town or rollicking good times. But after two years, I'm convinced I made the right decision." At this point, Tom is looking about for an inexpensive car.

At the conclusion of our visit, Tom said, "I often sit on my upper veranda in the morning—looking out over a vista my friends in California would pay a million dollars for—and I ask myself: 'Tom, what the hell did you do right to deserve this?'"

As we drove away from his charming little home, we couldn't help but wonder: How would Tom be making out in Los Angeles, California— instead of Los Angeles, Costa Rica—in his struggle to survive on $671 a month? Yes, he could make it, but on what level of dignity?

COSTA RICA **SOCIAL LIFE**

Please understand, I've never promoted the idea of retirement in Costa Rica on the basis of cheap living. The attraction here is *quality* living: an adventurous, interesting life in a superb climate, with exotic tropical surroundings. The icing on the cake is affordable costs.

When asked why they decided to live in Costa Rica, most people begin by describing Costa Rica's gorgeous weather and magical tropical surroundings. They'll rave on about favorite beaches, mountain retreats, and cloud forests, and eventually they'll mention the affordable cost of living. But oddly enough, when you ask them to pinpoint the most important factor in making the decision to relocate to Costa Rica, most people admit that lovely surroundings are only part of it. After a while, pretty, exotic scenery becomes like new wallpaper—you get used to it. When you pin most people down, they'll admit that they like the many friends they've made and their social lives here.

It turns out that North Americans who live in a foreign country—any foreign country—tend to cling together, to form close social groups, to reach out to draw newly arrived English-speakers into their midst. This is partly because they feel isolated from their non-English-speaking neighbors and crave all the friends they can possibly attract. Since the pool of

English-speakers is limited, each addition to their circle of friends is valuable. People with almost nothing in common—who wouldn't even nod at each other back home as they passed on the street—become great pals in a foreign setting.

I've found this to be true no matter which foreign country we've researched. Expatriates in Mexico, Spain, Argentina, and Portugal affirm this close camaraderie among fellow English-speakers. Foreign residents usually explain their love for their new surroundings by saying, "Everyone is so friendly here! I have more friends and companions than I ever had in my hometown. There, we barely knew our neighbors. Our friends were mostly people we worked with." Almost as an afterthought they mention the exotic surroundings or affordable living costs.

Think about it: Let's say you're moving from Syracuse to Scottsdale. You'll enter the neighborhood as total strangers. If you want friends, you have to begin from scratch. That's not easy; it takes a certain personality type to quickly cultivate a compatible circle of friends from a field of aloof strangers. It takes a certain amount of exposure (parties, social events, and so forth). In Costa Rica newcomers are sought after. You'll probably have an invitation to a dinner party before you sign the home sales agreement.

This doesn't mean that you needn't work at making friends in Costa Rica. You must go halfway. If you wait for expatriates to knock down your door and drag you out to dinner, you may give the impression of wanting to be a hermit. We have those here, too.

MIXING WITH TICO NEIGHBORS The usual strategy for newcomers is to seek out a place where most neighbors are fellow countrymen who speak English and are available to guide them through the process of fitting into their new surroundings.

But not everyone feels this way. Before Laura and David Streek of Cambridge left England for Costa Rica with their two young daughters, they decided they wanted their Costa Rica adventure to be more than the usual thing.

Laura said, "We looked forward to integrating into the community and society of a new country where we could lead a simpler, warmer life spent mostly outdoors. We wanted our children to experience a new culture and learn a new language." They discovered a village they liked on the Pacific Coast and decided to try living there.

Instead of joining the foreign community who lived in tasteful and comfortable homes with lovely views of the ocean, the Streek family rented an older Tico-style house, right in the center of the village. Little stores flanked both sides of the house, and goal posts of the village soccer field were across the street. The grade school where their children attended classes was located near the sidelines of the soccer field.

Their neighbors were mostly Ticos, with a scattering of North American and European émigrés from Switzerland and Holland, some of whom were operating small businesses in the village. They immediately set about making friends. They found it surprisingly easy. Before long, the family felt comfortable with their surroundings and became acquainted with enough of their neighbors to have a party.

Laura said, "We decided to have an open house one weekend, which begged the question: Where else in the world could you have moved to, not knowing a single soul, and within two weeks have met enough likable people to have a house party? We spent a happy afternoon of flower arranging, stringing fairy lights, and setting up the music system in readiness for the night's festivities.

"Soon after sundown, with the house sparkling in the twilight and music drifting out into the balmy air, people began to arrive. Before long the party was in full swing, with guests bringing pots of chili, dips, tortillas, crates of beer, and gifts. The porch was filled with young Ticos and gringos alike drinking beers. The salon held the food, and young children danced the salsa with the more-than-willing grown-ups. The kitchen and back rooms bustled with the usual party activities. The garden was the only place one could find to sit under the stars and enjoy a conversation with new friends."

In many countries, something like this could never happen. Class lines are too rigid. But Ticos have a strong sense of equality and think nothing of joining multicultural celebrations. Instead of meeting foreigners with an awestruck bowing of the head—as is the custom in many Latin American countries—Ticos look strangers in the eye, shake hands, and sometimes even invite the strangers to visit their homes. That probably wouldn't happen in your hometown, would it?

The Streek family have since returned to England, to their hometown of Cambridge, but I am confident that they will always look back with fondness on their interlude in paradise. They will remember the Tico and gringo friends they made while in living in the village. The children will

always have the advantage of being bilingual, with a Tico accent to their Spanish.

Even if your Spanish is far from fluent, communication flows. Most Ticos have learned about as much English in high school as you learned Spanish in high school. (They have also forgotten as much English as you've forgotten Spanish!) Yet both sides have fun talking, learning new phrases in the other's language, and becoming friends.

Making friends among the Tico community is a rewarding experience. However, you should resist the temptation of moving to a totally "non-gringo" community, far from other English-speaking neighbors. The fact is, most newcomers *need* a circle of English-speakers to round out their lives. They find that even though communication skills with Ticos are okay, many common elements of understanding are lacking. After a while there's a craving to talk politics, to discuss movies, or to reminisce over the "good old days." You'll receive blank stares from your Tico friends when you start speculating about the Chicago Cubs' chances for the pennant or whether Senator Phoghorn can be reelected. In short, the average newcomer to Costa Rica needs both gringo and Tico friends. Happily, this is possible. Newcomers are attacked with aggressive friendliness.

CLUBS AND **ACTIVITIES**

There's no excuse for being lonely in Costa Rica: too much to do, too many people to meet, too many places to go. Take some Spanish classes, attend a meeting of Republicans Abroad or Democrats Abroad, do some volunteer work, learn to play tennis or bridge. You'll meet more friends than you've dreamed of, and you'll live the rich life you moved to Costa Rica to find.

The biggest mistake some make is not keeping active. Some new-comers will take a drink or two when things get too quiet for them; next thing they know, they're drinking too much. If you haven't already acquired interests to keep you busy in your new location, open the *Tico Times* to the "Club Directory" section and look at the broad range of invi-tations. (If you can't find a group of friends who are involved in your favorite activity, chances are your favorite activity is illegal, immoral, or boring!) Volunteer work is another satisfying way to make friends and become involved in fun activities; this can be much more satisfying than sitting around a bar until closing time.

An example of a volunteer project, one in which my wife and I are cur-rently involved, is the establishment of a library in a village in Guanacaste. Local expatriates contributed funds to purchase several shelves of refer-ence material as well as books that are fun to read for adults and that will enhance the local children's interest in education. When enough money was donated, we expanded the library by renting a building separate from the school and opened the facility to adults as well as children. Within about six years, the library accumulated enough donations to build a beautiful new building on land donated by the village. We now have art programs for children, ten new computers for teaching marketable skills to teenagers and adults, and fiction and nonfiction shelves in both Spanish and English for gringos and Ticos. Just a slight exposure to worthwhile projects like this increases one's social circle immensely.

SINGLE **WOMEN**

We've interviewed numerous single women and single mothers who are very happy with their move to Costa Rica. We also know just as many single women who tried Costa Rica and found they couldn't stand living here. My observation is that women tend not to enjoy Costa Rica's social scene as much as men. My wife explains it this way: "Men love sitting in bars and trading stories or sitting in a fishing boat in the hot sun. Women socialize much differently and are easily bored with this scene."

Single women will soon discover that many Costa Rican men tend to fancy themselves as prototypes of the "Latin lover." As a Brazilian friend once explained: "When I was young, my father took me aside to tell me the facts of life. He said, 'My son, in this world you must understand one thing. You *cannot* expect to go to bed with every woman you meet. But, of course, you must at least *try!*"

That's the essence of a "Latin lover." The stereotype is a playboy supporting one or more mistresses and continually trolling for more conquests. To a small extent this could be true among the more affluent Costa Rican business types (same as anywhere else in the world), but the average eligible Tico bachelor, the type most single women will meet, doesn't earn enough to even dream of supporting a mistress. He has a tough time scraping together enough money to keep gasoline in his car's gas tank.

Curiously, according to foreign women I've talked to, every one of the men who try to date them seem to be either "single" or "divorced." Convenient, no? Of course, while divorce in Costa Rica is not exactly uncommon, a married man pretending to be single or divorced *is* quite common. Is this any different from San Francisco or Baltimore?

It's much more common for serious relationships to develop between gringo men and Tica women than the other way around. There are some specific reasons for this, as we'll see later on. Yet I've seen several successful romances bloom in the other direction, when a foreign woman and a Costa Rican man find their niche together. I don't know the statistics, but I'd wager that the divorce rate in these cases is lower than the average in the lady's home country.

This brings us to the question of Costa Rican males being "macho" and their women being obsequious and subservient—the stereotype most of us have of Latino culture. In my personal experience, and in my opinion, when this condition is found in Costa Rica, it is confined mostly to those living at poverty level. Pretty much the same as in the United

States. From my observations over many years, I staunchly maintain that machismo is neither part of the Tico male personality nor of Tico culture. Yes, I realize that some Ticos beat their wives (that happens in Omaha and Orange County as well), and I recognize that some Costa Rican husbands cheat on their spouses (and vice versa).

A bit of advice for foreign women who happen to find an attractive single, marriageable male: Before you consider marriage, check out your intended rather closely. Consider whether you could end up living on an economic level to which you're not accustomed. Make it crystal-clear that you do *not* expect to have a Latin lover for a marriage partner!

SINGLE **MEN**

"After the divorce, the first thing I thought about was coming here to get away for a while. There's something romantic about the name 'Costa Rica,' and I needed something to cheer me up after all my problems. I just knew this would be a great adventure." This was a typical reply when I would ask a single man why he moved here. A common follow-up statement was, "Actually, I planned to stay for only one month, but before I knew it, I met this nice-looking lady, and now I'm married again!"

I've known a dozen or more fellow countrymen who married Costa Rican women. When I asked an ex-New Jerseyite why he married a Tica woman, he responded: "The thing is, Costa Rican women are different in many ways. It's not just that they are pretty and maybe younger. That's not what it's all about. We come here looking for something we feel we lost somewhere back along the years. What we find is a woman who treats us as though we are special and are twenty years younger. They don't nag or complain if we're not perfect. In my case, I found a friend who does whatever she can to make me feel at home and wanted."

This is not a one-sided proposition. Marriage has attractive advantages for the Costa Rican woman as well. The new groom is expected to provide not only for his new wife, but also support the children from her first marriage. He also finds himself responsible for his wife's family. When Mámi needs a new refrigerator or when Pápi wants new false teeth, the husband is expected to help pay.

GRINGO GULCH Single gringo males tend to congregate in an area of downtown San José that I call Gringo Gulch—around the odd-numbered *avenidas* and odd-numbered *calles*. A concentration of inexpensive hotels and gringo bars here attract a large number of single or divorced fugitives from northern climes. They hang out in these bars of more-or-less ill-repute, where they drink Pilsen beer and exchange lies about their romantic conquests, financial successes, and the injustices of their divorce settlements. Most habitués of Gringo Gulch are transient and ephemeral. Within a few weeks they either move on to discover the real Costa Rica or return home with exaggerated tales of their trip.

The majority of these Gringo Gulch habitués are of Social Security age, looking for that one last go-round. Surprisingly enough, some actually find it. Many women who visit the gringo bars aren't necessarily prostitutes. Often they're simply working women hoping to meet a wealthy foreigner to marry, someone who will "take them away from all this."

Prostitution is legal in Costa Rica. But a word of caution to would-be gringo Don Juans: Be careful after dark, and avoid the *zona roja* (red-light zone) as the evening gets late. Some street girls here are fairly good thieves. Your wallet can disappear quickly while you are basking in sweet talk from one of these women. Their scam is pretending to be overwhelmed by a man's sex appeal. While several enthusiastic girls hug and caress the delighted gentleman, others are helping themselves to the contents of his pockets. It's almost always a nonviolent robbery, the victim doesn't realize he's been had until he tries to pay for his next drink.

Although an occasional visit to the downtown San José gringo bars can be entertaining, it's all too easy to make hanging out here your social life to the exclusion of all else.

If you're single and are looking for someplace to go and people to meet, simply open the *Tico Times* to the "Calendar" section. You'll find a page and a half of listings: classes, art exhibits, concerts, lectures, dances, theaters, political clubs, sports, and every possible activity you can imagine—great places to meet people and make quality friends. There's no excuse for being bored in Costa Rica.

GAYS IN **COSTA RICA**

We've interviewed several gay couples who have lived in Costa Rica for some time, asking about their acceptance by rank-and-file Ticos and expatriates. Others have written to me, describing their congenial relationships with Tico neighbors. Most experiences have been positive. There does seem to be a certain amount of disapproval of public displays of affection between gay couples, as if it's okay to be gay, only don't flaunt it.

The indignation demonstrated on some levels in some other parts of the world is rarely encountered in Costa Rica. People here seem to accept both male and female homosexuality as an ordinary fact of life.

CHAPTER FIVE

LIVING IN
COSTA RICA

Used to be, we could easily distinguish between "first-world" nations and "third-world" nations by the standard of living and the type of government. First-world countries enjoyed individual freedom, democracy, and, most important, a viable economy where people lived dignified lives and enjoyed economic security.

Third-world countries were none of the above. More often than not in Latino countries, the ruling elite would be a group of wealthy families with a well-armed military enforcing order, using terror to keep citizens in line. Workers lived from hand to mouth, barely existing. Meanwhile, wealthy families became ever more affluent. Thankfully, over the past twenty years, conditions have changed for the better in most Latino countries in this hemisphere. Some, such as Argentina and Chile, have achieved living standards not too much below those found in North America. Costa Rica will probably never progress that far, but the potential is there.

Costa Rica never went through the repressive conditions described above. It started out as a democracy and has never experienced a military dictatorship. The overall standard of living in Costa Rica is admired and envied by neighboring countries. Costa Rica is different. After all,

it's a place where you can drink the water and eat the food without risking your life. Where your conscience isn't continually assaulted by beggars and abject poverty. Furthermore, it's a place where the government isn't run by a bunch of uniformed thugs.

For these reasons, we North Americans find adjusting to Costa Rican living conditions rather easy. Of course, there are differences in lifestyles, but instead of being traumatic, in most instances the variations are charming. Whether *you* will enjoy living in Costa Rica depends on your approach to life and your expectations. If you expect people to conform to your ideals and you want conditions to be exactly as they are in your hometown, you are bound to be disappointed. Costa Rica is, after all, a foreign country. That's exactly why so many gringos choose to live here. We enjoy living in a foreign country.

In this chapter we'll look at some everyday living conditions that make Costa Rica different.

COURTESY **AND CUSTOM**

Costa Rican social behavior is a curious mixture of old-world, European formality and a special Tico style of relaxed interaction. You shake hands politely when being introduced or when meeting an acquaintance on the street, women as well as men. Women may also greet other women friends with a kiss on the cheek; with close friends a woman may do the same with a man, but only if they know each other well. Exaggerated hugging and kissing, while common in the United States, is not approved of here. Men, when greeting truly close friends, will give an *abrazo*—a quick hug and pat on the back—or perhaps lightly clasp the friend's wrist or forearm instead of shaking hands.

"Getting down to business," as we North Americans are apt to do, without any preliminary greeting and small talk is considered somewhat rude in Costa Rica, but not terribly so. Costa Ricans know how we North Americans are, so they never make a big deal out of it; they realize that "business" is the custom in our countries. To be polite, you might spend a few moments inquiring about someone's children or spouse, or perhaps give a compliment about the person's clothing, the weather, or anything else you might think to say before talking business. Doing so gets things off to a smoother start.

Costa Ricans have a delightful habit of issuing off-the-cuff invitations to visit them at their homes for dinner or for cocktails, but you should always wait for the invitation and not just drop in. An exception to this is when someone moves into the neighborhood or when you move into a new home. Then it's considered polite to knock on the door and introduce yourself.

A crucial point to remember: In social or business transactions, Ticos just cannot handle confrontation. Unlike the people of some countries, where arguing, shouting, and mock displays of anger or emotion are the accepted norm, Costa Ricans are appalled at such behavior. It's considered not only rude but also degrading. Confrontation is foreign to the culture.

I know a New Yorker who lost an excellent gardener when his gringo temper flared momentarily. Chuck's employee had planted some flowers in the wrong place. As usual when making a point, Chuck raised his voice and waved his hands in the air to signify his displeasure: "No, no! Not here! I wanted them over there!" The astonished gardener loaded his tools in his wheelbarrow and left the property, never to return, despite pleas from the homeowner's wife, who tried to explain: "That's just Chuck's way. He doesn't mean anything by shouting."

LATIN **AMERICAN TIME**

A difficult notion to understand is the way Latin Americans view time. When invited to a social event in the United States or Canada, it's considered ill-mannered to arrive late. Not so in most parts of Latin America. Should you receive an invitation for dinner, say, at 7:00 P.M. and actually arrive at that time, you are likely to embarrass the hosts. She is probably in the shower, and he still at the office. Guests are expected to arrive late. It doesn't matter, because the 7:00 P.M. dinner isn't served until 8:00 or 9:00 P.M., anyway.

When keeping appointments with businesspeople, you can arrive at their offices fifteen minutes late without worrying about it. You'll probably have time to catch up with the latest goings-on in the world by reading *Newsweek* and *La Nación* while waiting for your appointment. Still, after several decades of exposure to Latin American time, I've never understood it and never will. When invited for a social gathering at 8:00 P.M., I

always ask, "Is that eight o'clock Tico time or eight o'clock gringo time?" The reply is usually a sheepish grin and, "Better make that nine o'clock." Most Costa Ricans share this cavalier view of time—not, however, to the extremes found in Mexico or some other Latin countries.

On the other hand, my personal experience with my Costa Rican employees is that they're usually on time. I'm always surprised to see them arrive at the job early, start to work on time, and—after a morning and an afternoon break—go home on time. Maybe this is because I pay higher than the going wage scales, but I suspect that the Costa Rican work ethic is unusually positive, at least for Latin America.

HOUSEHOLD **SERVANTS**

The notion of housemaids and gardeners seems a bit wild for most of us when we first move to Costa Rica. (The last time we hired a cleaning lady in the United States, she charged $16 an hour and wouldn't do windows.) But in Costa Rica servants are affordable. With the going wage for domestic servants about $250 a month—including all benefits—it makes sense to hire a housemaid and a gardener, at least on a part-time basis. Ticos are generally hardworking and honest, so if you can afford $2.00 an hour or so, you can have someone working around the house who won't complain about doing windows.

Most North Americans report that they pay more than minimum wage; doing so keeps their employees happy and loyal. Although servants are affordable, you must be aware of the laws covering their benefits. By law, not by custom, you are responsible for things like vacations, Christmas bonuses, Social Security, and severance pay. Wages are indexed twice a year, according to inflation. You are responsible for knowing about the benefits and paying them on time. These rules are discussed thoroughly in chapter 12. Don't hire a servant until you've read the rules! One way to avoid the problem of being legally incorrect when hiring servants is to contract with someone who specializes in supplying help on demand, sending them to your home and charging you a higher rate for it, but taking care of the taxes, insurance, and other legal details. Technically, the domestic help does not work for you but for the contractor.

COSTA RICA **FOOD TREATS**

Basically, you'll find two types of restaurant menus in Costa Rica. One menu will be not much different than in restaurants in Baltimore, St. Louis, or San Diego. Most menus look pretty much the same. Steaks, fried chicken, and shrimp seem to be almost obligatory on every menu.

But for really authentic Costa Rican food, you need to go to Tico-style restaurants where they serve *comida tipica* (typical dishes). *Comida tipica* is basic home cooking as found in Tico homes throughout the country. This cuisine relies on simple ingredients such as rice and beans, free-range chicken, and tasty, lean pork flavored with plenty of garlic. One of my favorites is *aroz con pollo* (chicken with rice) piled high on a dish, steaming with the savor of cilantro and diced peppers. It is often served with shrimp and calamari instead of chicken. Try the *sopa negra* (black-bean soup), topped with chopped green onions, crumbled white cheese, and a fresh egg poached in the thick broth, plus a dollop of *crema fresca* (a thick cream).

You might be disappointed with Costa Rican beef steaks, however. They don't exactly come from Black Angus; more likely from one of those large, homely creatures from India, called Brahmans. Tico restaurants routinely mix beef hamburger meat with one-third pork to give some moistness and flavor. That's not to say you can't find good beef, you just have to go to a good butcher shop or order a rib-eye in an expensive restaurant.

In the larger cities, you can find interesting dining places, ranging from elegant French restaurants to superb pizzerias. Some excellent Chinese restaurants will surprise you with dishes that are quite different from the Asian cuisine you are used to back home. Their style of cooking is a cross between traditional Oriental and tropical American. Some terribly mediocre Chinese restaurants are also to be found (ask friends for recommendations). In Alajuela we found two excellent restaurants within 2 blocks of each other, one serving Argentine food (called Como en Casa) and the other authentic Peruvian cuisine (called Inti Raymi). Don't let the humble facilities scare you off, these are great restaurants. (Ask anyone in Alajuela for directions.)

One very common Costa Rican food—served everywhere for breakfast, sometimes for every meal—is *gallo pinto,* which inexplicably translates as "spotted rooster." This is a mixture of cooked rice and black beans—sometimes mixed with cilantro and chopped onions—fried together until the rice turns a purple color. Mixed with eggs and topped with *salsa Inglesa* or *salsa Lizano,* it makes a filling breakfast—nutritious but boring when served at every meal.

In small restaurants away from the city, a typical menu item is a *casado:* a large plate with beans, rice, fried *plátano* (a green cooking banana), and some sort of meat, chicken, or egg. (*Casado* means "married man"; why the meal is called this is a mystery.) *Olla de carne* is a tasty meat stew with vegetables such as chayote, squash, yucca, and *plátano.*

Another favorite is empanadas: fried dumplings filled with meat or cheese, often sold by children, who carry them around in galvanized buckets. A *tortilla Española* in Costa Rica is an omelet made with chopped potatoes or yucca root. Mexican-style corn tortillas are popular in the countryside and are also called tortillas; these are far more common than the egg-and-yucca variety.

BOCAS A delightful custom in Costa Rica is the serving of *bocas* (free appetizers) with drinks in bars: They might include fried shrimp, a chicken dish, barbecue, or some more exotic specialty. They aren't served as frequently as they used to be, especially in bars mostly patronized by gringos, since we don't expect them. But Tico bars usually sustain this custom, so when you see someone else being served a treat, don't hesitate to ask. You may have the chance to sample a raw turtle egg—bars are just about the only places where you can legally find them. They are served one to a shot glass, with a little hot sauce. You do a bottoms up, and chew it to taste the yolk. Some people love 'em; my wife wouldn't touch one with a pointed stick. Note: some bars have *bocas* but no longer give them away. You have to pay a small amount, 50 cents or a dollar, but they are worth it!

Other treats are small dishes of chicken and rice, or perhaps a chicken drumstick or wing, a piece of fried fish, or some *chicharrones* with yucca. You are sometimes given a choice of *bocas*, other times it is whatever the cook happens to be preparing. *Bocas* aren't just for serving in bars. We are often invited to expatriates' homes for a "*boca* cocktail party." On the Pacific Coast, it's often a traditional way to celebrate a gorgeous sunset. Guests are expected to bring their favorite *boca* to share with other guests. When you have no way to make *bocas* (if you are a tourist staying in a hotel, for example), a bottle of Centenario rum or a bottle of good wine is a good substitute, or if you prefer, a takeout pizza cut into small pieces. Friends compete for new and unusual recipes for tasty *bocas*.

GRATUITIES Restaurants are supposed to add a 10 percent service charge to the bill—then it's up to customers if they care to leave something extra. Some restaurants cheat and don't give tip money to employees, so leaving an extra 5 percent tip on the table after paying the bill ensures that your waitress at least gets something—and guarantees special service next time. Away from the city, many restaurants don't add tips to the bill; it's customary to tip 10 to 15 percent in these cases. Barbershop and beauty-salon personnel expect a 10 to 15 percent tip. My last haircut cost 1,500 colones ($3.00) and I tipped 300 colones (60 cents).

At Christmastime it's customary to give something to the newsboy, supermarket attendants, and garbage collectors. By law you give a Christmas bonus to the maid, gardener, and other employees. This is one month's pay, prorated on the number of months worked. Since this Christmas bonus is not a gift or a tip but is required by law, an extra Christmas present to special employees would be considered thoughtful and generous.

If you are a guest in someone's home where there are servants, it isn't necessary to tip them unless they've done something special for you, such as laundry, ironing, or running errands. If a friend lends you the services of her maid, it's customary to tip and to pay for her taxi or bus fare home. Hotel chambermaids like to be tipped just as they do back home.

COOKING **AT HOME**

For those staying for longer than a vacation, an apartment or house with a kitchen is a wonderful way of enjoying Costa Rican cooking and experimenting with the unusual tropical ingredients available in the markets. Around the San José area, every neighborhood has at least one supermarket, supplemented by weekend *ferias* (open-air markets). Every neighborhood also has its little *pulpería* (convenience store), where you can buy items you forgot at the other markets.

Major supermarket chains are: Auto Mercado, Periféricos, Pali, and Mas X Menos. By the way, the "X" in *Mas X Menos* is pronounced as it would be in a mathematical equation: In English we would say "two times two," while Costa Ricans would say "*dos por dos*." Since the Spanish word *por* can also mean "for," the literal meaning of the store's name, *Mas por Menos*, is "more for less." (Yes, I know, it would be less confusing if they simply followed American custom and called all supermarkets "Safeway." Or even "Piggly Wiggly." But this is, after all, Costa Rica.)

Open-air markets are held on weekends, the major ones being Saturday in Escazú, on the south side of the main square; Saturday in Pavas, about 5 blocks from the main shopping center; and Sunday in Zapote, next to the Bull Ring. Heredia's farmers' market, also on Saturday, is perhaps the best known of all, with local families selling produce grown in their backyards. Heredia's main market, open daily, is a wonderful place to browse for food, clothing, tools, furniture—anything you can imagine.

Costa Rica's selection of fruits and vegetables is sometimes bewildering for us North Americans. In addition to delicious pineapples, strawberries, melons, and other produce we recognize, you'll find *chayotes*, *pejebayes*, *palmitos*, *plátanos*, and other strange-looking items that will soon become standard parts of your menu. A common substitute for potatoes, the yucca root, in my opinion, tastes much better than ordinary spuds. Exotic tropical fruits such as *guayabas*, *tamarindo*, and *carambolas* are exciting to experiment with and make delicious *refrescos* (blended drinks). One of my favorite *refrescos* is made by blending fresh cacao nuts (the source of chocolate) with *horchata* (a rice-flour and sugar drink). My wife prefers a *batida* of fresh papaya, milk, and ice, whipped to a milk-shakelike consistency.

Some fruits are so exotic they border on fantastic: With shells, spines, and barbs, they look like something from a science-fiction book cover. Especially interesting is the *marañón* fruit, the source of the common cashew nut. The nut itself grows at the end of an edible orange or yellow fruit that can be eaten raw or, more often, made into a *refresco* by blend-ing it with sugar and ice cubes. The cashew nut itself is encased in a rub-bery shell that is primed with cyanide, making it bitter and somewhat poisonous. We have to marvel over the wonderful way nature designed this fruit as an efficient way to disperse its seeds. In the wild, monkeys, parrots, and other creatures pluck the fruit and carry it away to be con-sumed. When they finish eating the sweet fruit, the bitter-tasting seed is discarded, dropped on the ground to produce another tree.

Costa Rica is a cattle-growing country, and beef is plentiful, although as mentioned earlier, not the same quality as we are used to in North America. But the quality of pork and chicken here is excellent, mostly because they are raised differently. Instead of being tightly penned or caged and force-fed to put weight on the animals, they usually run loose, foraging for food as well as being fed at the farmhouse, and living natu-ral lives. The flesh is more natural, and leaner, with a firm texture. Eggs are delicious, having a brighter-colored yolk and a better flavor than we're used to up north. The eggs often come from free-range hens instead of egg factories.

With an ocean on both sides, Costa Rica, of course, enjoys a wide selection of seafood. And since shipping distances from either ocean involve just a few short hours, the sea harvest arrives fresh. Almost any kind of fish and shellfish you can imagine is available, plus some you can't imagine. You might want to try some of the shellfish and conch that thrive only around the Costa Rican shores. My favorite is a shellfish known as *cambute*, similar to conch shellfish found in the Florida Keys. Like abalone, the *cambute* has to be pounded before cooking, and it tastes very much like the almost extinct abalone.

Imported foods can be somewhat expensive. Partly because of shipping costs and partly because of foreign-exchange differentials, North American and European products can be costly. Central American substitutes are often as good and locally grown—fresh foods are always much better than canned or packaged food.

GREAT **COFFEE**

Some of the best coffee in the world grows on shaded mountain slopes in Costa Rica. These exceptionally rich-tasting beans are in demand by coffee wholesalers, particularly those who boast that their products are "mountain grown." To substantiate such a claim, at least 60 percent of the coffee has to come from mountain farms in places like Guatemala, Colombia, or Costa Rica. Curiously, Costa Rican coffee is exceptionally low in caffeine; sellers have to use high-caffeine (and less expensive) beans from Brazil and Africa to bring the jolt up to what coffee drinkers expect. In Costa Rica you have the advantage of brewing coffee from 100 percent Costa Rican beans. If you need more caffeine, drink another cup! We sometimes purchase coffee beans directly from the roaster and take them home while they are still hot. The use of instant coffee (a barbarous practice) hasn't caught on here. A *café con leche* with just a dash of sugar makes a wonderful starter for breakfast and is great for washing down savory *gallo pinto* and warm tortillas.

Costa Ricans have an interesting way of making coffee that gives a characteristically rich flavor to the brew. Instead of using a percolator or an automatic coffeemaker, Ticos use a wire or wooden stand holding a cloth strainer bag, shaped like a sock, that hangs over a waiting cup. They place two teaspoons of coffee into the bag and pour boiling water over the grounds, letting it drain into the coffee cup below. For each additional cup of coffee, another teaspoon of ground coffee is added. The result is a flavorful, velvety drink that grows richer with each cup made. The grounds aren't discarded until the sack is full of grounds or until the end of the day, whichever happens first. "The aroma and essence of the coffee is much better if it isn't boiled," explained a Tico. "We call our coffee making system a *chorreador*. It brings out the flavor without acid bitterness. This method requires more coffee grounds, but since coffee is inexpensive here, we use nothing but the best."

FURNISHING **YOUR HOME**

At one time, when foreign retirees received their residency papers, they had a one-time right to import household goods duty-free, and the right to bring in an automobile every three years and thus avoid enormous customs taxes. This was a valuable consideration, since high import duties in those days made electrical appliances, televisions, video recorders, and the like very expensive in Costa Rica.

To the dismay of incoming *pensionados,* this benefit was repealed fourteen years ago, in 1992. The anguish and wailing over the loss of these privileges rocked the North American resident community to its heels. After a series of appeals, the courts decided that the new laws would *not* be applied to those who already had *pensionado* status or those whose applications were pending. This was a good solution, because newcomers knew beforehand that free import benefits were no longer on the table, yet old-timers retained their benefits.

Duty-free imports on household goods aren't nearly as important today as they once were. The supply of gringo-style furniture used to be limited by the capacity to produce it, so it was cheaper and more convenient to ship your used stuff from Miami than wait several months for the factory to fill your order at exorbitant prices.

Today supply has caught up with demand; you'll have no problem finding a wide variety of furniture at reasonable prices—usually for less than you'd pay back home. The amount of money you'd have to pay just to have that bedroom suite and living-room furniture shipped from Topeka or Toronto would pay for furnishing your home in Costa Rica with brand-new merchandise. Furniture stores have great selections, and you can visit small, family-operated factories and have pieces custom-made for about what you'd expect to pay for retail back home.

Household appliances such as refrigerators, washing machines, and TVs can be purchased from local dealers without waiting for months, as was the situation before. Also, import taxes on these appliances have dropped dramatically. For example, last year my wife and I built a new home and bought a washer and dryer for almost the same price as they would have cost in California. Our Tico neighbors, by the way, were astounded that we would waste money on a dryer when we could simply hang the wash on a line and let the sunshine dry it in an hour for free. But being spoiled gringos—too impatient to wait for the sunshine and too often forgetting about the drying clothes until after the next rain shower wet the clothes down again—we felt we couldn't live without an electric dryer.

Yes, it hurts not to be entitled to *pensionado* discounts, but Costa Ricans have been paying full price for years. What's so terribly unfair about having to pay the same for goods as your Costa Rican neighbors do? You can be sure this special treatment was a source of irritation and resentment among the Costa Rican community. Perhaps they didn't blame foreigners for paying less, but they did fault their government for taxing them more.

TELEVISION **AND OTHER MEDIA**

A few years ago, in order to watch baseball or football games, you had to wait for a videocassette to be mailed from the States. Today there are six cable TV services in the San José area alone, plus satellite dishes throughout the country. Costa Rica's modern television system offers six channels, some of which can be received in remarkably out-of-the-way places. On our San José cable system, we enjoyed abundant programming direct from the United States: two TV stations from Denver, one from Atlanta, and one from Chicago. Several international channels delivered programs coming from South America, France, and Germany as well. We found that watching CNN, CBS, and NBC nightly news on our cable TV made up for not having a daily newspaper delivered to our door.

Note that I describe our TV cable system in the past tense; where we live now, on the Pacific Coast, cable is unavailable and normal reception is confined to two weak channels. (That's the price you pay for living away from the big city.) The answer for those who need to watch CNN, the World Series, and Home Box Office movies is satellite-driven DIRECTV, with an almost unlimited choice of channels. Reception is as good as it gets, and monthly charges are about what you would pay in the States.

In San José and most of the surrounding cities, you'll find stores selling English-language paperback books and magazines. In addition to the essential *Tico Times*, you can buy daily editions of the *Miami Herald* Latin American edition, the *New York Times*, the *Washington Post*, and the *Wall Street Journal*. These papers are a bit expensive—they arrive by airplane—but at times North Americans become starved for a big-city daily newspaper. However, it's easy to keep up with major newspapers and very likely your hometown newspaper via the Internet. Every morning with my coffee, I read the front pages of the *New York Times*, the *Washington Post*, and the *San Francisco Chronicle* (including the comics). Several Costa Rica daily newspapers are online, so I browse *La Nación, Diario Extra*, and the *Tico Times* for Central America news.

In San José a dozen theaters show first-run and recent English-language films, mostly from Hollywood. Tickets cost about a third of what they cost back home. The dialogue is almost exclusively in English, and Spanish subtitles are printed over the lower part of the screen. San José boasts nine legitimate theaters, mostly in Spanish, offering entertainment for those who are well along in their study of the language. One ongoing production is about the history of coffee in Costa Rica, tracing its arrival from Arabia, plus legends and beliefs about the wondrous substance. It is half in English and half in Spanish, with discounts for Costa Rican citizens and *residentes*. Two small theater groups produce plays in English.

Two folklorico troupes regularly present traditions from various parts of the republic, one at the Herradura Hotel and another at the Melico Salazar Theater. Also, there are regular concerts by the National Symphony Orchestra. Sponsored by the government Ministry of Culture, Youth, and Sports, many visiting musicians from other countries add to the quality of the presentations. At the time of this writing, more than 25,000 Costa Ricans filled the National Stadium in San José's La Sábana Park to hear Luciano Pavarotti in concert. The facility was filled to capacity.

MONEY **MATTERS**

Costa Rica's currency is the colón. As with many other foreign currencies, the colón's value fluctuates against the U.S. dollar according to supply and demand. For years rates have remained fairly stable, being adjusted upward with inflation, and the currency has not been over- or under-valued. For example, in 1992 the rate was 138 colones to the dollar; four-teen years later, in fall 2006, the colón's value was about 520 to the dol-lar. That's a devaluation rate of about 12 percent a year—not much, considering some banks pay as much as 18 percent interest on colón cer-tificate-of-deposit accounts. Most financial experts predict that the colón will remain stable, with devaluations paralleling inflation. During the lat-ter part of 2005 and first half of 2006, there appeared to be some infla-tionary pressure, which was reflected in adjustment of the currency exchange rate.

Some people feel uneasy when inflation continually deflates a nation's currency. The important point is whether the exchange rate between Costa Rican colones and U.S. or Canadian dollars is in line with reality and not arbitrarily set by the government (a practice that continu-ally leads to disaster in other Latin American countries). Many people, even some economists, tend to assume that when the exchange rate is stable, inflation is under control and all is well. That's not necessarily so. When exchange rates are steady yet prices of goods and services rise in the host country, your dollar loses value every day. A currency holding its own against the dollar isn't necessarily a sign of a healthy economy. It could be an artificial manipulation of currencies that masks serious problems.

Yes, mild inflation has been going on in Costa Rica for decades, always slightly higher than the inflation rate in the United States. But since the colón adjusts for this inflation as prices and wages rise, there's no appreciable change for those who own dollars. For example, prices and wages in Costa Rica today are twice as high as they were eight years ago, yet we North Americans receive twice as many colones for our dollars as we did eight years ago. For those of us with dollar incomes, it's a wash. There's no foreseeable reason to expect that exchange rates will vary in any significant way in the future, other than a steady adjustment to world currencies, totally in line with reality.

DEALING IN DOLLARS When bringing foreign currency into the coun-try, be sure to inspect each bill carefully for rips or tears. Banks refuse to accept any foreign currency if it's torn ever so slightly. Never mind that a

1,000-colón bill you get from the bank teller might look like a dog's breakfast; if that $50 U.S. bill you have isn't pristine, you'll end up taking it back to the States with you. One scam is for a waiter or shopkeeper to take your good $50 bill, then return with a torn bill and ask you for something smaller, hoping you won't notice the tear. The bill is okay, but you'll have to take it home to spend it.

A continual problem is the importation of counterfeit $100 bills from Colombia—so many that shopkeepers sometimes refuse to accept big bills. One place where you might get stuck (so I've been told) is at a gambling casino because in the unlikely event that you win big, the house tries to get rid of the phony bills they previously got stuck with by giving them to happy gringo winners.

COSTA RICA **BANKING**

For a variety of reasons, most expats maintain their home bank accounts when they move to Costa Rica. For one thing, the U.S. government will not direct-deposit Social Security or pension checks to a Costa Rican bank, and you certainly don't want those checks floating around Costa Rican post offices. Furthermore, your checks will be tied up for weeks until the funds are available. With your money deposited in a U.S. or Canadian bank, you can use your ATM card almost anywhere in Costa Rica to withdraw cash as you need it. Some expatriates don't even bother with Tico banks. Local businesspeople who know you will usually accept your home-bank checks. They know they're good and they don't worry about a long wait because there's always a large balance in their bank accounts anyway. Our local grocery store cashes our checks for $100 any time we need money.

In many ways Costa Rica is a modern country, but for some inexplicable reason a visit to the bank is an *Alice in Wonderland* experience. It takes forever to do a simple transaction such as exchanging dollars or traveler's checks into colones. Although each bank handles things a little differently, it occasionally involves standing in one line where the clerk checks your passport, examines the bills or checks, fills out forms in triplicate, and pounds everything in sight with a rubber stamp. Then you move to another line and wait until a second clerk fills out more forms in quadruplicate and does more rubber-stamping.

To be fair, Costa Rica's banking system has been improving over time. Bank procedures are becoming more streamlined. Usually bank transactions can be done in one line, yet the wait in line can seem like forever. One thing to remember: Lines are going to be much longer on days following holidays, when banks have been closed for a day or so, and on the days when pensioners receive their Social Security checks. Some banks provide separate lines for pensioners, which helps considerably.

Our Costa Rica home is located in a somewhat isolated community, not big enough to have its own branch bank, yet Banco Popular maintains an office there, which is open two days a week. Hours are from 9:00 A.M. to 3:00 P.M. People start lining up at 8:00 A.M., hoping to cut down the waiting time.

One day the office didn't open at 9 o'clock. We waited. The clock passed 9:30 and still nothing happened. The crowd grew restless and someone asked one of the bank clerks, "Why don't you open?"

The clerk replied, "We are having a problem with the electricity." He had an embarrassed look on his face. Then he said, "Actually, we forgot to pay the electric bill. As soon as the bill gets paid, they will turn on the electricity." The government electric company denying service to a government bank. Only in Costa Rica!

Banks are also where you can usually pay traffic tickets and utility bills and sometimes make Social Security payments for your maid and gardener. Since each transaction requires a flurry of forms, rubber stamps, and calculations, you can count on spending a lot of time in Costa Rican banks. Because of the time-consuming process of dealing with banks and government bureaucracy, some Ticos make their living by standing in line for you or by knowing whom to contact and when. They are called *tramitadores* (from the verb *tramitar,* meaning "to transact," "to take legal steps"). Your friends and neighbors can recommend a reliable *tramitador* to make your life easier. Many people become close friends with their *tramitadores,* dining with them and exchanging presents at Christmas.

Criticize the banking system as we do, the fact is that government banks are financially sound. A few years ago BancoAnglo, one of the big three Costa Rican banks, was forced to close its doors because of mismanagement and reckless speculation. The situation closely paralleled the savings-and-loan debacle at that time in the United States. Costa Rican investors didn't panic; they simply took their passbooks to one of the other national banks and exchanged them for new passbooks from that bank. Nobody lost a nickel. By the way, the Costa Rican bank officials responsible were immediately arrested. Now just consider how many U.S. savings-and-loan wheeler-dealers were even *scolded,* much less shown the inside of a well-deserved jail cell.

Costa Rica went one step further: The government decided that those who borrowed money and didn't pay it back were equally guilty. The borrowers claimed that they *lost* the money, but it was surprising how quickly many "bankrupt" businesspeople *found* millions of dollars to repay their loans rather than go to prison. Is there a lesson here?

Not all banks are government-owned. Several private banks deal with the public, usually in a much more efficient manner, at least as far as the amount of time you spend in line in front of a teller's cage. But there are two problems with private banks. One is that deposits are often backed only by the bank's reserves. In some cases, limited government funds are available in the event of default. The second problem is that some private investment companies that appear to be banks are outrageously fraudulent, their reserves siphoned into private accounts in the Bahamas. Before you invest in a private bank, investigate its past performance and talk to your neighbors about its reliability. If the bank just opened last March and the main branch is a post office box in Haiti, you just might be suspicious.

Until recently only nationalized government banks were permitted to offer checking accounts in both dollars and colones. Now private banks have equal status with government institutions in this respect.

Bank accounts can be in either colones or dollars. An unpleasant and basically unfair bank practice is holding dollar checks from foreign banks for up to twenty-two working days before crediting them to your account. (This was supposed to change as a result of the bank reform laws of 1996, but the last time I checked, they're still holding checks for several weeks before crediting them to the account.) Another quirk is that the banks often do not have enough dollars on hand to cash a large check. You might have to accept a cashier's check instead of cash. This is okay if you are making a local purchase with the money, since the party to whom you are giving the cash will probably deposit it in his or her account anyway. But should you need several thousand in cash for a trip home, you'd better plan ahead.

INTEREST RATES In mid-2006 a nice rate of interest was being paid on time deposits of colones, from 10 to 13 percent. (Dollar accounts pay about the same as CD rates in New York.) While 10 to 13 percent sounds like a terrific return on your investment, you must consider the inevitability of the colón losing value against the dollar. You are gambling that the colón will devaluate less than expected, in which case you come out somewhat ahead. If the rates fall at the expected rate, you'll do fine. But if for some reason the colón's value falls more quickly than the expected 10 percent, you could lose money. In 2005 and 2006, the rate of inflation rose somewhat.

Private investment funds are famous for failures and outright fraud. The situation to be leery of is extraordinarily high interest rates. Until recently, some funds were paying 3 percent per month to investors; that's 36 percent per year! Many expats were living on the income from their savings; $100,000 invested brought in $3,000 a month—a tidy income here in Costa Rica! Tragically, the bubble burst when the largest investment company became snarled in a government investigation, and the other companies also folded, skipping out with investors' savings. Some hold out hope of recovering at least some of their money, but their chances look very slim.

CRIME AND **PERSONAL SAFETY**

I'm always amused when friends visit us in Costa Rica and express dismay when they see wrought-iron bars on our windows. "Is crime so bad here," they ask, "that people must live behind bars?" This question surprises me because bars on Costa Rican windows seem as logical and natural as window screens in Atlanta or storm windows in Cleveland.

Maybe that's because my family moved to Mexico City when I was a youth, a place where homes traditionally have bars on their windows, so I suppose I grew up with the custom. The fact is, in every Latin American country—from the Río Grande to Tierra del Fuego—a home isn't considered complete without a set of decorative wrought-iron bars. To me a Latin American home looks naked without them, like a Cape Cod home without shutters or a Southern mansion without a portico and columns. When the first Spanish colonists came here five centuries ago, they brought iron bars with them. Roman settlers brought window bars to Spain 2,000 years ago; for all I know, the Romans picked up the custom from the Greeks, or maybe the Egyptians.

My wife and I recently spent a few weeks traveling in Spain, southern France, Italy, and Malta. I made a point of observing the various residential neighborhoods we encountered in our journey. Without exception, every home we saw had either bars, heavy shutters, or both. After all these centuries, security is still fashionable in Europe.

Do window bars deter professional burglars? Not really. Not any more than door locks keep out burglars back home. Bars and locks simply keep out honest people. However, they discourage amateur burglars and remove temptation from neighborhood kids. Frankly, I feel quite snug and secure with bars on my windows. By the way, I personally refuse to sleep with the metal front door locked. Why? Partly because after having lived for years in California, another place where earthquakes are commonplace, I don't want to have the metal door jammed should the house twist. I have a fear of being trapped in a house, unable to get out for days, unable to buy cold beer. Seriously, this is also an important issue for wooden houses that could catch fire. You don't want to be rummaging around looking for your keys while the smoke and flames are getting closer! An ordinary door lock on the wooden door is easy to flip open.

NOT CRIME-FREE! Like any other place in the world, Costa Rica has crime. That shouldn't surprise anyone coming from the United States, where crime and personal safety have become a high-priority concern. Take a look at some U.S. neighborhoods: The bars you see on windows and doors clearly aren't meant to be decorative; they are grim attempts to protect occupants from violent crime. The alternative to bigger and stronger bars is moving to a safer place with lower crime rates, perhaps rural Kansas or small-town Costa Rica (that's our solution).

I personally see crime as another one of those annoyances we have to put up with if we want to live here—a nuisance, like potholes. To avoid destroying my car, I have to drive carefully to miss potholes. That's an annoyance. To avoid crime, I have to be careful where I park my car and where I keep my wallet. That's an annoyance. So far I've rarely been affected by crime, but potholes have eaten several of my tires.

Of course there's crime in Costa Rica but it's of a different nature than that in the United States. It doesn't seem fair to compare the two places in the same paragraph. While Costa Rica suffers with ordinary nonviolent petty crime, the United States must deal with frequent brutal crimes, which are uncommon in Costa Rica. Criminals don't just rob up north; they savage and maim as well, just for laughs.

The overall rate of burglaries in Costa Rica is much lower than that in the United States. However, a much higher percentage of break-ins are performed on foreign-owned homes. Burglars know that the average expat home has a nice VCR, a TV, a microwave, and maybe a stereo. Here again, a little precaution is in order. Besides a protective set of bars, it's worthwhile to contribute to the neighborhood *guardia,* the watchman who patrols your neighborhood on foot or by motorcycle. In some neighborhoods, every block has at least one. Because of these watchmen, most middle-class neighborhoods are often as safe as similar places in the United States, where a police car cruises by maybe once a day. In rural areas you seldom find *guardias,* but there are fewer burglaries, so it evens out.

Another big difference is the lack of rampant drug addiction among Costa Ricans. You won't find an army of desperate addicts forced to steal several hundred dollars each day to support a habit. Costa Rican law discourages drugs by handing out a jail sentence of eight to twenty years for anyone involved in drug dealing. Drug use is considered extremely serious, and mere possession of drugs can be interpreted as evidence of drug dealing. By the way, these laws apply equally to native Costa Ricans and gringos. That doesn't mean Costa Rica is drug-free, either. A real problem is when young gringo surfers partying on the beach share crack cocaine with the local kids. So far it hasn't gotten out of hand, but it is unsettling, to say the least.

From time to time the downtown section of San José is bothered by the appearance of gangs of street urchins, called *chapulines,* who rob pedestrians by grabbing wallets and jewelry. *Chapulines* literally means "grasshoppers," describing the way the kids jump on a victim and keep him or her off balance while one of them goes for the wallet. I believe that incidents of this nature have been somewhat overstated. (I personally know only one friend who has been victimized.) The fact that such episodes make headlines in San José newspapers suggests that such incidents can't be all that common. However, the problem all but disappeared when stricter laws were passed, with stiff sentences for juvenile offenders who previously avoided punishment because of loopholes in the law. Not long ago a San José judge handed out sentences of up to twenty-five years in prison to a band of *chapulines.*

It's best to take basic precautions when wandering about the center of San José—or any other big city in the world, for that matter. To be fair, having a wallet lifted or a gold chain stolen are crimes that plague tourists not only in Costa Rica but anywhere tourists go. Furthermore, this kind of crime can usually be avoided by taking reasonable precautions. Residents and long-term visitors infrequently haunt bad areas of downtown San José after dark, and they know how to avoid pickpockets, and the like.

MISCELLANEOUS **INFORMATION**

GOLF COURSES When I first started writing about Costa Rica, golf courses were almost nonexistent. This disappointed many tourists who feel that a vacation isn't complete without a few rounds of golf. For

GOLF COURSES

- **Cacique del Mar.** Playa Hermosa, Guanacaste; eighteen holes, par 72; members and guests only.

- **Cariari Golf Club.** General Cañas Highway, near San José; eighteen-hole championship course; hotel guests, club members.

- **Costa Rica Country Club West.** In the San José suburb of Escazú; opened 1944; nine holes; members and guests only.

- **Four Seasons Hotel** at the Papagayo Peninsula. 18-hole golf course. Guests and members only.

- **Golf La Ribera public driving range.** In La Ribera de Belen near the water park Ojo de Agua.

- **La Roca Beach Resort & Country Club.** North of Caldera on the Pacific Coast; eighteen-hole, par-72 championship course; members and public.

- **Los Reyes Country Club.** San Rafael de Alajuela, near San José; nine holes; members, guests of certain hotels.

- **Los Sueños Marriott.** Playa Herradura. Eighteen-hole, par-72 championship course; hotel guests and public.

- **Marriot Hotel Golf Course.** Nine-hole course reserved for hotel guests.

- **Meliá Conchal Golf Club and Resort.** Playa Conchal, Guanacaste; nine holes, with another nine holes scheduled; par-72 championship course; hotel guests and public.

- **Monte del Barco.** Resort north of Liberia, Guanacaste; eighteen holes; members and public.

- **Parque Valle del Sol West.** San José suburb of Santa Ana; nine holes; additional nine holes could be added; public at present.

- **Rancho Las Colinas Golf and Country Club,** near Flamingo, overlooking Playa Grande in mid-Guanacaste, is the newest course in Costa Rica.

- **Rancho Mary La Cruz.** A half hour north of Liberia; nine holes with another nine holes planned for the near future. It will be an eighteen-hole, par 72; members and possibly the public.

- **Tango Mar.** On the tip of Nicoya Peninsula; nine-hole, tough executive course, par 31; hotel guests only.

- **Tulin Resort.** South of Jacó Beach; eighteen-hole, par 72; members and public.

golfers looking for a place to spend a long time or to retire in Costa Rica, the near absence of golf was a severe drawback.

Why the scarcity of golf courses? It's partly a matter of economics. During the rainy months, when golf course maintenance is limited to cutting grass, tourists are few. In the dry season, when lots of tourists are here, sufficient water might not be available. Another factor is that golf is not a Tico tradition. The main sport here is soccer, a team sport, with strenuous running, kicking, and body contact. The excitement is contagious, with everybody cheering wildly for his or her team. Ticos have difficulty understanding golf as a sport. What they see is a few lackadaisical people fooling around with clubs. Someone hits a ball, then rides a sluggish cart to where the ball lands, and then whacks it again. Nobody cheers. Nobody gets excited. There aren't any spectators. It doesn't make sense to Ticos. To them soccer is more like a real sport.

Since only a few Ticos play golf and without enough tourists and year-round gringos to play golf, investors were hesitant to build new courses. For years the Costa Rica Country Club nine-hole course and the Cariari eighteen-hole layout were about the only golf courses in the country, and both were private. So if you were addicted to golf, you were restricted to living in the Central Valley, and you had to join a club.

Because of the increase in long-term foreign residents and the large increase of tourism, the situation is changing. As of summer 2006, fifteen golf courses were in operation. Some are for members and guests only, but eight are open for public play. Several more golf courses are under construction.

Developers are enthusiastic about golf's future here. As tourism increases and more and more full-time gringo residents are moving to Costa Rica, more courses will be opening. Following is a partial list of golf courses open or due to open soon in Costa Rica.

GAMBLING CASINOS For those addicted to the sound of a roulette ball bouncing along the wheel or to the riffling sound of cards being shuffled, you'll find no lack of action in Costa Rica. Most gambling casinos are in the San José area, with casinos in hotel lobbies. Sometimes it seems like a miniature Las Vegas. Occasionally gambling casinos are found upstairs over nightclubs or restaurants.

While I sometimes like to gamble, I also like to have a chance of winning. I have the distinct feeling that gaming in the average Costa Rican

casino is not really gambling, merely donating to the profitability of the establishment. House rules make it highly unlikely that you will break even, much less win. The games aren't standard ones that can be easily understood, even though they might seem similar to poker or blackjack. Play is similar to Las Vegas or Reno, but the rules and payoffs are differ-ent—sometimes confusing—stacking the odds in favor of the house.

Another disquieting thing about gambling in Costa Rica is that there is almost no government regulation. I doubt very much that the house cheats. It doesn't have to cheat, since the odds are so much in its favor, but there is little or nothing to prevent cheating from happening.

Having bad-mouthed Costa Rica gambling casinos, I now have to admit that several friends disagree with me. They claim that the odds and your chances of winning are pretty much the same here as in Las Vegas or Atlantic City. I'll suspend further judgment until such time as I win something.

HOLIDAYS Sometimes it seems as though every time I go to the bank to conduct business, it's closed for a holiday. Costa Rica celebrates more than a dozen national holidays and uncounted numbers of local fiestas that call for closing the bank. Watch the *Tico Times* for announcements of upcoming holidays, and plan your official business accordingly. The country's biggest celebration starts a couple of days before August 2, when thousands of people walk along the highways in a pilgrimage to

Cartago to honor the national saint, the Virgin of Los Angeles. Drive cautiously at this time.

- January 1: New Year's Day
- March 19: St. Joseph's Day (patron saint of San José)
- Easter Week: Thursday through Sunday
- April 11: Juan Santamaría's Day (national hero)
- May 1: Labor Day
- June 29: St. Peter and St. Paul's Day
- July 25: Anniversary of Annexation of Province of Guanacaste
- August 2: Virgin of Los Angeles Day (patron saint of Costa Rica)
- August 15: Mother's Day
- September 15: Independence Day
- October 12: Columbus Day
- December 8: Feast of the Immaculate Conception
- December 24 and 25: Christmas Eve and Christmas

RELIGION Costa Rica is predominantly Catholic but also has a sizable Protestant population. In the village near our home, I would estimate that 30 percent of the residents are Protestant, yet everyone seems extraordinarily tolerant and accepting of other religions. Yes, there can be rivalry between Protestants and Catholics in local politics, with the priest trying to get as many of his parishioners appointed to town councils and committees as possible and the Protestant preachers doing quite the same. However, I feel it's more of a prestige thing, because the pressure is low-key and everyone works together—at least on the community projects in which I've been involved. Priests often wield political influence in a community, which can dismay some Americans—until they recall that fundamental Christian leaders refuse to accept a church-state separation back home and are continually hip-deep in local and national politics.

Common-law marriages are frequent in Costa Rica, especially in rural areas, and are regarded as perfectly normal. Couples often live together their entire lives, raising children and grandchildren without any thought of formalizing their relationship. (This practice was originally due to the scarcity of priests in small communities to perform weddings.)

All in all, folks seem to be quite casual and tolerant when it comes to religion. Nobody seems to care what religion you may have or may not have, and church attendance seems to be very casual, similar to many U.S. and Canadian communities. People here are much more tolerant than in the U.S. South's Bible Belt. It's interesting to note that while abortion is illegal, birth control doesn't seem to be an issue here. Posters in government health clinics urge the use of contraceptives, and my understanding is that they're readily available at most drugstores.

THE **POST OFFICE**

Costa Rican mail service is clearly not up to the standards we expect at home (such as they are). Let's face it: In a country where streets rarely have names and houses lack street numbers, home mail delivery can't be expected to be "reliable." When a package or letter actually arrives, it's best described as a "miracle." We waited six months in vain for our first checking-account statements. Then one day, out of the blue, they all appeared at once. Instead of complaining, I was astonished that the mail carrier actually found our house. The address on the envelopes read, "300 meters north from Amistad Park, 100 meters to the east, and 25 meters to the south." (But which house?) The poor guy probably carried these bank statements with him every day for months, just in case he deciphered those directions and figured out which house we lived in. Unfortunately, the statements arrived after we'd sold the house and closed our checking account, having decided that having a checking account wasn't all that convenient.

That's why most folks rely on post office boxes, known as *apartados*. This means a trip to the post office every couple of days, but at least there's a chance your mail might be waiting for you. My post office box in the village near our Guanacaste home costs about $10 a year. I understand the cost is considerably higher at other post offices, and boxes can be in very short supply. In this case your mail will wait in general delivery for you to collect it.

For a while there was a problem with mail being stolen by employees within the postal system. The general impression was that most thefts occurred in the main post office in San José rather than in the smaller substations around the country. It's been some time since newspapers have reported thefts, so presumably a campaign by the government was successful in rooting out the culprits. Not too long ago, the postal system was privatized, but as far I can tell, it hasn't made a lot of difference. The same employees are working in the same offices, and things look normal.

I still would prefer using one of the courier services or certified mail if anything important or urgent needed to be sent.

Mail for international communication is a waste of time. Airmail between Costa Rica and the United States or Canada involves ten days each way. That means at best a twenty-day turnaround between the time you send a letter and the time you receive the reply. A practical way to avoid this delay is by using e-mail or a fax machine. Now that Internet access is available almost anywhere in the country (there are Internet cafes popping up everywhere), the most practical communication method is e-mail.

COURIER MAIL SERVICE Another way to beat the system is with one of several Miami–San José postal services that offer same-day delivery by air courier to and from Costa Rica. Mail going either way gets there almost as fast as if it were mailed in the States. This is the only practical way to subscribe to magazines or newspapers at domestic rates and hope to receive them the same season they were published. If you live in the boonies, your mail service company can often forward your mail by bus for pickup at the bus terminal.

Among the most popular services: Aerocasillas (P. O. Box 4567–1000, San José, CR; 506–255–4567; fax 506–257–1187); Star Box (5177 NW 74th Avenue, Miami, FL 33166; 305–257–3443; fax 305–233–5624); and Trans-Express "Interlink" (4437 Hollywood Boulevard, #B, Hollywood, FL 33021; 954–296–3973; fax 954–232–3979).

International air couriers have set up offices in San José to compete with DHL, who used to be about the only game in town. They are the most reliable and safe way to send something important and feel sure it's going to get there. They are: DHL (290–3010), UPS (257–7447), and FedEx (255–4567). Plus a few I've never heard of: Skynet (232–5678), Jetex (293–5838), and TNT (233–5678). *NOTE:* These are the numbers to dial from within Costa Rica. For help calling Costa Rica from the United States, see "Dialing Costa Rica," later in this chapter.

A new service by the post office (Correos de Costa Rica) is called EMS Courier. Supposedly this is an international courier service and has offices throughout Costa Rica where you can pick up mail or packages. The telephone number is 221–2136; fax 221–1737, e-mail ems@correos.go.cr.

TELEPHONE **SERVICE**

You'll often hear people grumbling about the Costa Rica telephone company (ICE), saying that they can't wait until the system is placed in private hands. But I suspect most complaints come from people who haven't experienced the substandard and expensive telephone service available in most third-world countries. The fact is Costa Rica has one of the best and most efficient telephone systems in all of Latin America, with almost 1.5 million phones, for a population of only four million. And this doesn't include cell phones. There are almost a million of them in service, with long waiting lists for more connections. The cellular fad is an astonishing change in communications. Many Tico families have a cell phone for each family member. The best part is that you can dial any place in the world from your home and connect just as though you were calling across the street. Try that in most third-world countries!

Privatization enthusiasts believe that once the government is taken out of the telephone equation, rates will drop. Well, check this out: Basic telephone service is around $6.00 a month, with 150 free minutes (no long-distance charges anywhere in the country). Additional minutes are 8 cents (U.S.) a minute. Cellular telephone service is also a bargain compared with most other countries. Basic service starts around $7.00 a month, which includes 60 minutes of free use. Does anyone really believe that a privatized Spanish or German telephone company can cut rates below these levels?

Infrastructure improvement is apparent every year; with more and more isolated communities receiving not only telephone service for the first time but fiber-optic lines designed for high-speed Internet connections. Ten years ago making a phone call from the Guanacaste beach area where we live required driving to the center of the village and seeing which of the three public phones had the shortest waiting line. If we saw teenagers huddled around one of the telephones, we'd go on to the next. Occasionally, we'd find all three phones hijacked by giggling teenagers, and we knew we'd have a long, long wait.

About five years later, our lives began to change. ICE telephone trucks arrived and workers began laying wires (underground, to keep falling trees from messing things up.) Suddenly, *everybody* has telephones. Teenagers have cell phones in their pockets. Instead of driving from

house to house to find out where Juan Fulano the gardener might be working, so you can hire him to work tomorrow, you simply dial his home and leave a message with his wife. Better yet, call his cellular phone.

Most Ticos are very much against privatization of their telephone service. Every time the legislature considers privatization, the public responds with protest marches and vociferous resistance. For good reason: They well know that in other countries when the government turned over their tax-supported infrastructure to foreign corporations, it was the end of improvements and the beginning of poor service and drastic rate hikes. Private enterprise is seldom willing or able to invest the money for new phone lines or improving service to rural communities and outlying towns and villages as the Costa Rican government has done. Once privatized, a foreign company concentrates on collecting phone bills and raising rates. That's simply what corporations do: reduce costs, increase income, and maximize profits.

Sometimes newcomers encounter an unexpected cancellation of phone service. Back home we are accustomed to waiting for bills to come in the mail, then writing checks and mailing them out. In Costa Rica it doesn't exactly work that way. Unless you live in the city, every month you have to remember to go to wherever phone bills are paid. This could be a grocery store, a stationery shop, or some other local business. Phone bills are rarely paid at the same place you go to pay your electric bill, your garbage collection, or your house insurance—that would be much too easy. In the city you may receive a bill by mail, but you have to personally go somewhere to pay it. Many supermarkets can accept phone-bill payments. You don't simply mail a check, not with the Costa Rican postal system!

I have a friend who owns a small village variety store and collects telephone-bill payments for the area. She speaks almost no English but manages to do okay with gringo customers. However, a couple of times I've had wild-eyed gringos come to me crying, "Please help me, John! I just paid my bill, but that woman canceled my account anyway! She said '*Está cancelada!*'" I calm them down by explaining that the word *cancelada* does indeed mean "canceled" but it was the bill that was canceled, not the service!

When we lived in the city, a telephone employee used to come around to our condominium every month and leave the bill with the watchman. We had to remember to go to his guardhouse at the proper time to pick up the bill, or there went our telephone again! Then we had to remember to take the bill to a nearby supermarket to cancel the bill before they canceled our service. This is why some people hire *tramitadores*—people who remember to do all these chores and who earn money by standing in line. Understand, telephone service improves as time goes by; conditions could be different by the time you read these words.

CELL PHONES **AND PHONE CARDS**

At the moment of writing, you have to be a citizen, a legal resident, or have your home in a corporation *sociadad anónima* to get cellular phone service in Costa Rica. This could change in the near future. There used to be long waiting lists, but it's getting easier to get cellular service every month. You may have to prove you bought your phone in Costa Rica to get it activated. Most cell phones bought outside the country won't work here anyway.

Some U.S. companies, such as Cingular and T-Mobile, have roaming plans accepted by the telephone system in Costa Rica. The catch is that it costs $1.99 a minute to use them within Costa Rica and $2.98 a minute for calls to the U.S. and Canada. The same charge applies when receiving calls from home, so you might hesitate to answer your phone, just in case the caller is a gossipy friend who wants to tell you all about her shopping trip. Calls to and from other international countries are $3.98. Hardly worth bringing the phones into the country. In the meantime, some travel agencies and others will rent cell phones to tourists. Advertisements can be found in the tourist papers and the *Tico Times,* or on Internet at: www.cellphonescr.com or www.costaricarentacellphone.com.

One of the Costa Rica phone company's modernization projects has been to convert pay phones to accept phone cards instead of coins. The problem with that is when you have to make a call on a public phone that doesn't accept coins, you have to go somewhere to buy a phone card. These cards are sold in grocery stores, drugstores, and some restaurants, and they're inexpensive. I like to use Servicio 197 phone cards, which can be used on any telephone by dialing 197 and then the special phone number on the card. This works with all phones, public or private. The phone cards are available in denominations of 300, 500, or 1,000 colones. For international calls, Servicio 199 cards work the same way and are available in 3,000- and 10,000-colón denominations.

DIALING **COSTA RICA**

To reach an AT&T international operator, you dial 0–800–0114–114, no coin needed. MCI is 0–800–012–2222; Sprint is 0–800–013–0123; Canada Bell is 0–800–015–1162; information is 113. An English-speaking operator will accept your credit- or calling-card number or place the call collect to foreign countries. If you have a phone in your home, direct dialing is not only easy but also the most inexpensive way to place an international call. The telephone directory lists codes for each country. You dial the country code, and then dial the number you wish to reach. For example, to dial the United States from Costa Rica, first dial 001, then the area code and local number. To call Costa Rica from the United States, dial the prefix 011, then the country code 506, then the local number (there are no local area codes in Costa Rican telephone numbers).

Be aware that some international collect calls can be ripoffs. I've heard horror stories of $100 for calls of fifteen minutes. The bills are collected on the U.S. end, not by Costa Rica. I recommend using the Servicio 199 card, as described above.

Emergency calls can be made by dialing 911, just as you do back home. The fire department is 118; highway police, 117; the Guardia Civil, 127; and an ambulance (Cruz Roja), 128. To report a problem with your telephone, dial 119. For electrical problems dial 126. To receive or send Western Union money orders, go to the office at Calle 9, between Avenida 2 and 4 (283–6336).

THE WORLD **OF THE INTERNET**

The computer age has arrived in Costa Rica. You'll find stores selling the latest hardware and all the software you could possibly want, at prices similar to what you would pay back home. Wisely, the government keeps customs duties low on items such as computers and accessories, the idea being to encourage the cybernization of the nation. The government is eager for the country to get on the e-mail and Internet research band-wagon and is offering free computer access (for Ticos and residents) at larger post offices.

E-mail convenience in Costa Rica is nothing short of miraculous. Pre-viously we had to depend on expensive telephone calls and faxes to keep in touch with the States, or we wrote letters that took a month for a reply. Now with e-mail, you can touch base daily with family and friends or do business, sell and buy stocks, all with a click of the mouse. The downside is that your family and friends can forward stupid jokes and chain letters that will cause seven years of bad luck if you don't immediately forward the message to your few remaining friends who still open your e-mails.

The only legal Internet service provider in Costa Rica is the govern-ment-owned Radiográfica Costarricense S.A., more commonly known as RACSA. The server offers a $15-a-month, unlimited Internet connection to families and noncommercial users. This service can only be used from the specified home connection. You pay for the phone-connection time, but the cost is minimal. Regular commercial connections start at $30 per month.

It's very easy to open an account; you don't even have to go to a RACSA office. Just about any computer store has the applications and can set you up with an account and a password while you wait. You'll have to post a $15 deposit and you have to bring a copy of your telephone bill. Keep in mind that this account can be accessed only from the home phone number listed on the telephone bill.

If you bring a laptop with you, a RACSA Internet card is very conven-ient, allowing you to go online anywhere you have a phone connection.

This is handy when you're only going to be in the country for a few weeks and don't want to sign up for long-term service, or when traveling around the country with your laptop computer. The cost of the card is $10 for a ten-hour card or $20 for a twenty-hour Internet card. You simply dial 134 and when you connect, enter the password on the back of the card. These cards can be purchased from RACSA in downtown San José and in some computer stores around the country.

Another handy and little-known way to access Internet in Costa Rica is through a "900 number." All you need is your computer with a modem and phone line. The cost of the service is 7 colones a minute, which amounts to about 90 cents U.S. for an hour-long connection, about the same as a RACSA card. Just dial (900) 365–4632.

Once the computer dials the number and receives a welcome display, the customer accepts the conditions of the service by pressing any key or keys and then the <ENTER> key. Next, press the <F7> key and soon you will be able to surf the Internet.

As pointed out earlier, the government has a monopoly over all radio and telephone communications and is jealously holding on to the lucrative Internet business. The service is occasionally erratic and sometimes frustrating, but it is the only game in town. From my viewpoint they do as good a job as can be expected and service is improving, step by step. The biggest problem is a shortage of high-speed Internet connections, which many need in order to conduct business back home while they live in Costa Rica. At the moment, cable connections are available through AMNET (www.amnetcable.com) and Tica Cable (www.cabletica.com), in a cooperative effort with RACSA. Currently the cost is about $80 a month (for up to two computers), but the speed isn't comparable to DSL or most U.S. cable services. It's only 246/128k BPS, but still quite an improvement over ordinary 56k (and less) phone lines.

CHAPTER SIX

THE MESETA
CENTRAL AND BEYOND

Where in Costa Rica should you live? If you were to take a poll among North Americans who live here—either part-time or full-time—you'd find a virtual tie. They'd be evenly split between the continual spring climate of the central highlands and the year-round tropical summer climate on either side of the country.

Each group cannot understand why others would possibly want to live elsewhere. The highlands, with an altitude of between 2,000 and 3,000 feet, offer a year-round spring climate. People who live here love it. Those who live in the tropical coastal areas enjoy their year-round summer climates—who could ask for more? Costa Ricans themselves are also divided about which is best: tropical or temperate. As proof of this division, about half of the Tico population lives in the higher reaches of the country. We'll start the discussion off with the country's temperate climate, where half of the country's North Americans choose to live.

Costa Rica's central highlands are marked by a low mountain range that starts near the Nicaragua border and marches south, where it crosses the border into Panama. This range is known as the "Cordillera,"

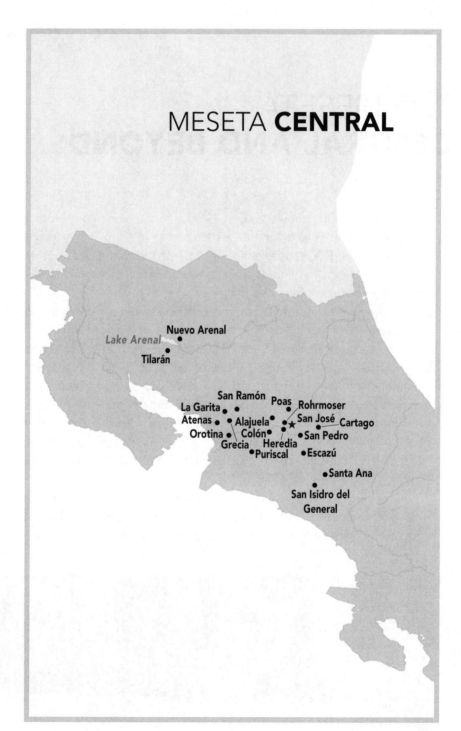

MESETA **CENTRAL**

Nuevo Arenal

Lake Arenal

Tilarán

San Ramón

Poas

Rohrmoser

La Garita

Atenas

Alajuela

San José

Cartago

Orotina

Colón

San Pedro

Grecia

Heredia

Puriscal

Escazú

Santa Ana

San Isidro del General

a picturesque complex of ridges, valleys, peaks, and tablelands that are perpetually covered with green vegetation and teeming with wildlife. The mountains vary from rounded promontories to the rugged peaks of the Talamanca Range, dominated by 12,600-foot Cerro Chirripó. Valleys and rolling tablelands are interspersed between steep hills and volcanic formations, providing fertile agricultural space.

SAN **JOSÉ**

San José, the largest city in Costa Rica, is nestled in a wide depression about halfway down the Cordillera, at an altitude of 3,750 feet above sea level. The city of about 300,000 inhabitants is surrounded by dozens of satellite towns and villages and by small cities such as Heredia, Alajuela, Escazú, and Cartago perched at various elevations on the uneven plateau. About 15 miles wide by 40 miles long, this break in the mountains is known as the Central Valley, or in Spanish, the *Valle Central* or *Meseta Central.*

From just about any point in this area, you are treated to views of mountains and extinct volcanoes that form a half-bowl around the Central Valley. Towns and villages surrounding the capital have grown to the point that it is sometimes difficult to tell exactly where one ends and another begins. Although greenery and small farms are abundant, much of the Central Valley blurs into a loose suburban complex.

Why so many prefer the Meseta Central is a question answered in two words: superb climate. This is the land of perpetual spring. Daily high temperatures are almost always in the 70s—creating newspaper headlines on occasions when the thermometer climbs into the mid-80s. Low temperatures are always in the 60s. Because Costa Rica is so close to the equator, temperatures vary little between summer and winter.

Even this weather doesn't please everyone; some prefer temperatures in the mid-80s; others feel more comfortable in the mid-70s. Fortunately, in Costa Rica it's possible to "fine-tune" your weather simply by moving a few kilometers in one direction or another. Since temperatures and weather patterns are determined by altitude in the tropics, just a few meters higher or lower in elevation make a difference. A fifteen-minute drive from anywhere on the Central Valley brings you to a slightly different climate, with more or less rainfall and warmer or cooler temperatures.

It seems as if each town or community here brags of having the "best climate in the world." Each is perfect for at least some folks. Alajuela is proud of being a few degrees warmer than San José, while Escazú is happy about being a few degrees cooler. Poas boasts about being even cooler than Escazú, and La Garita brags about its rating by *National Geographic* of having one of the three best climates in the world. The wonderful thing is that all these choices, however slight, are freely available to you. (The weather chart in chapter 2 illustrates this diversity of weather.)

METROPOLITAN SAN JOSÉ When their airplane approaches the country's international airport, visitors are treated to the sight of a broad green valley flanked by steep, volcanic mountains that seem to be forever topped with fluffy clouds. The city of San José spreads out below, thinning to a scattering of towns and villages that eventually merge into a lush green countryside. From the air one can see homes and tidy farms lining roads and highways, showing patches of cultivated fields intermixed with wild tropical vegetation.

After passing through the easy customs booths in the modern terminal of Juan Santamaría Airport, travelers make their way toward the city of San José along a modern, divided four-lane highway. Those expecting to see the usual Central American panorama of dingy buildings, shacks, and junkyards will be surprised by tastefully landscaped grounds of light manufacturing facilities, fancy hotel complexes, offices of international corporations, and other evidence of business prosperity. A large Intel computer-chip facility is a proud addition to San José's high-tech ambience. I've heard people proclaim in surprise, "Why, it almost looks as if we are in Europe!"

The closer one gets to the center of San José the denser the population becomes, and the less it looks like Europe. Suddenly, the highway becomes a boulevard when it curves toward downtown and past Sábana Park. The city starts appearing more as you might expect of Central America. By the time the average newcomer reaches the heart of downtown San José, entirely too many vehicles creep along narrow streets, past hundred-year-old buildings mixed with a few modern ones. Dense crowds of pedestrians swarm past a confusing agglomeration of small shops, vendors, and street stands with blaring music. Typically, a feeling of disappointment sets in as the newcomer thinks, "Is *this* the beautiful Costa Rica I've heard so much about?"

This first impression of Costa Rica can be a lasting one for those with limited vacation time in downtown San José, with an occasional day trip to nearby tourist attractions. When you hear people remark that they were extremely disappointed in Costa Rica, you can pretty much bet that their visit was a one-day stopover on a cruise ship. Cruise ships here disembark at shipping ports where the scenic attractions are industrial warehouses, tank trucks, and storage sheds. This doesn't create a terribly nice impression, so the cruise director quickly loads passengers onto buses and zips them away to San José for a four-hour visit and then back to the ship in time for dinner. It's little wonder that cruise ship visitors can't understand why people praise Costa Rica.

However, it's all in the eyes of the beholder. I for one absolutely love visiting San José. The city becomes more attractive to me with each visit. We live hours away from the city and get excited every time we plan a shopping excursion to San José. We look for reasons to drive or fly to *San Chepe*—as Ticos humorously refer to San José—to schedule an appointment with our lawyer when the business could just have well be done by telephone. (By the way, *Chepe* is a child's way of pronouncing José and, thus, a nickname.)

Those who live here soon learn to appreciate San José for its many cool cultural events. No other place in Central America—or even most cities in the United States—offers as many opportunities for opera, plays, museums, art galleries, symphonies, and foreign artists of all kinds. Once you learn where the good restaurants are found, you'll look forward to visiting often. Those who only know downtown San José can never appreciate San José's suburbs—places like Escazú, Santa Ana, Rohrmoser, Heredia, San Pedro, and all the delightful neighborhoods nearby.

San José, the capital and business center of Costa Rica, is a comfortable place to live despite its large population. Although downtown streets throng with shoppers and automobiles, neighborhoods a dozen blocks away can be tranquil residential areas. San José doesn't suffer from the widespread slum zones that plague many U.S. cities. You'll find modest neighborhoods, to be sure, and a few run-down areas but not the starkly depressing ghettos so apparent in some large U.S. cities. There is a slight smog problem in the downtown streets, mostly caused by belching diesel trucks, buses, and taxis. Continuous cross-breezes keep the atmosphere superclean, except in the immediate vicinity of a bus or truck. Some residents disagree with my underemphasis of San José smog. But having lived in Los Angeles and visited places like Athens and Rome, I just don't trust air I cannot see.

For some reason, people from all over the valley feel a compulsion to do their shopping in downtown San José. This is partly from habit and the fact that shopping is something of a social event. By the thousands, crowds of shoppers amble along the streets and avenues, checking out window displays, making purchases, and gossiping with friends. Most could shop in their own neighborhoods, but it's more fun this way, and here is where you will find those scarce items you need. So many pedestrians pack the main downtown avenue (Avenida Central) that the city was forced to turn part of it into a pedestrian mall.

Although some neighborhoods in San José are suitable for expatriate relocation, most North Americans are predisposed to congregate in the more costly areas on the edge of the city or in neighboring suburbs. This is understandable, since we tend to be much more affluent than Costa Ricans and can better afford upscale neighborhoods. The western edge of San José attracts a large number of foreign residents, particularly around the Sábana Park area (Sábana Sur and Sábana Norte), the upscale neighborhood of Rohrmoser, and some areas of Pavas. Better supermarkets, nicer restaurants, and amenities such as tennis clubs and attractive parks make this a very livable part of the city. The *Tico Times* classified section frequently lists homes and condos for sale or rent in Pavas and Rohrmoser. Rents for condos or apartments typically start around $400, and homes can go as high as $2,000 a month for a supernice place. Still farther out, toward the airport, is Cariari, a luxury area with a golf course and country club.

Directly across the valley, the towns of Escazú and Bello Horizonte match Rohrmoser for elegance and expensive housing. Just to the east of downtown San José, Barrio Escalante is an affordable neighborhood of stately older homes. This was the "in" place for wealthy Ticos years ago and is now in the process of adapting to middle-class families. Still farther out on the eastern edge of the city, Los Yoses and San Pedro supply moderate to expensive housing, with some of San José's most exclusive neighborhoods. San Pedro provides a university atmosphere, with many rentals available at student-budget levels. For the height of luxury housing and opulence, some neighborhoods around Curridabat cannot be topped. One area, known as "Embassy Row," has some stunning homes as well as many foreign embassies.

By shopping around you can usually find housing that will fit your pocketbook and lifestyle. Remember that ads in the *Tico Times* are directed toward North Americans who can afford to pay more. For less expensive places, check the classified ads in *La Nación;* that's where Ticos find their rentals. San José has several apartment complexes renting furnished places by the day or week that make excellent "base camps" while one is looking for permanent quarters or trying out Costa Rica as a place to live.

FINDING YOUR WAY Searching for an address in and around San José and its suburbs can be an exercise in frustration; few buildings have street numbers, and no one pays attention to them when they do. Even worse, many streets have no names, or at least no street names posted on the corners.

Suppose you are looking for the García residence, whose address is listed as "From Caballo Blanco 250 meters west, 300 south." To understand where this house is located, you need to know the location of a store called Caballo Blanco, then go 2½ blocks (250 meters) to the west and then 3 blocks (300 meters) south. At that point, you need to ask someone which house belongs to the García family.

This confusion isn't restricted to residences: Businesses use the same system. On maps, advertisements, and business cards, the word *calle* is often abbreviated as "c," *avenida* as "a," and *central* as "ctl." The distance between two points is usually stated in meters (abbreviated with an *m*). But to make it even more confusing, people occasionally give directions in *varas* instead of meters. A *vara* is an ancient measurement of 33 inches (in English it is called a *pace*), which was in common use before Napoleon's introduction of the metric system in the early 1800s.

Examples of address insanity: The address of the Hotel Presidente would be "c ctl, a 7–9," which translates as "on Calle Central between Avenidas 7 and 9." The address of the bus terminal for Alajuela is "a 2, c 12–14," meaning "facing Avenida 2, between Calles 12 and 14."

Directions and addresses can be vague to the point of impossibility. This is particularly true away from the orderly grid of north-south, east-west streets. An address might be described thus: "From the gasoline station, go 100 meters north and 75 *varas* to the east." Which gasoline station? My favorite address is on a real estate agent's business card. It says "50 meters south from where the Mas Por Menos supermarket used to be."

It doesn't do any good to complain; Ticos understand the system perfectly and actually become confused when you use logical addresses. Often when I take a cab downtown, asking to go to "Avenida Segundo and Calle Primera," the driver responds with a puzzled frown. When I add "Teatro Nacional," his face lights up with understanding and away we go.

FROM THE CITY **TO THE MOUNTAINS**

Although many foreigners live in the city of San José, the majority prefer the smaller communities surrounding the city. These towns range from expensive to moderately priced places to live. For some mysterious reason, at least six small towns in the country have the same name—San Isidro—which adds to the confusion of finding your way around. San Antonio is another favorite place-name that is scattered about like leaves in the wind.

As discussed elsewhere, the explanation for identical names is that during colonization, communication was extremely difficult between communities even though the actual distances between them is not far when using modern transportation. People couldn't possibly confuse their San Antonio with another when it took four days' travel by oxcart to get to the other San Antonio.

ROHRMOSER Rohrmoser is at the upper end of the housing market in the immediate San José area and is Escazú's main competition for upscale residences. For some folks there is no competition—Rohrmoser wins hands-down. Here homes and condos consistently command rents and sale prices higher than elsewhere in the metropolitan area. Unlike Escazú, Rohrmoser looks more like a modern city suburb; it has sidewalks and boulevards instead of mostly narrow roads and streets with dirt shoulders. (For some, an advantage; for others, lacking charm.)

Homes and apartment buildings here are much newer, with some condo development and home construction still under way. Started by a German developer (thus the name), Rohrmoser begins at the end of Sábana Park and runs along both sides of Rohrmoser Boulevard until it reaches the ultramodern shopping center of Plaza Mayor. From that point west, Rohrmoser sits on the northern side of the boulevard, with the town of Pavas on the eastern side. The U.S. Embassy, incidentally, is in Pavas, on Pavas Boulevard, a place of dozens of popular restaurants and shopping.

Many North Americans live in Rohrmoser, but the largest percentage of your neighbors will be Tico professionals who like the convenience of being close to the business center of the city. My wife and I used to live in Rohrmoser and enjoyed the peaceful ambience. I could take a taxi to downtown San José in just five minutes (traffic permitting). We would stroll from Rohrmoser Boulevard to Pavas (some 4 or 5 blocks) to dine at one of the many great restaurants and return late at night, with absolutely no feelings of insecurity. One reason we felt okay about this was the presence of watchmen on almost every block. We had full confidence in the integrity of our neighbors because most were doctors, professors, attorneys, and the like. Then one day we saw on television that a very nice home a couple of houses away from us had been rented to a gang of professional bank robbers from Venezuela. The bandits had been living there for some time while they committed a string of robberies. They were on the "most wanted" list of the OIJ (Tico equivalent of the FBI). The culprits dressed well, kept their front yard tidy, and paid their rent on time—they couldn't have been *all* bad.

ESCAZÚ Several of the more traditional communities that attract expatriate residents run in a direct line from San José westward, beginning at Escazú—only 15 minutes from downtown San José—to the town of Puriscal, about one hour from the ocean. Nestled at the base of magnificent ancient volcanic mountains, Escazú has always drawn the affluent and those seeking tranquillity away from the city. Three mountains hover over Escazú. The tallest is Cerro Rabo de Mico, at 7,770 feet; the most spectacular is Pico Blanco, at 7,250 feet, with a dramatic, sheer rock face that has challenged the skill of many a mountain climber.

Only 8 kilometers from San José and fifteen minutes or less driving time, depending on traffic, the town of Escazú used to be somewhat removed from city hustle and bustle. Residential streets on the edge of town ascend the mountainside bravely, presenting an even better view with each gain in altitude. Needless to say, the town no longer has a "village" atmosphere. It is now a city.

Originally, Escazú consisted of three separate villages: San Miguel de Escazú, San Rafael de Escazú, and San Antonio de Escazú, each having its own church and patron saint. The red-domed church in San Miguel de Escazú was constructed in 1799 and has survived numerous earthquakes since. Some of the older barrios are famous for quaint old adobe buildings that are painted with a traditional two-color motif. The design is a 3-foot colored stripe painted along the bottom of the home, which was believed to ward off evil spirits and witches. I have to admit that I've encountered few evil spirits or witches during my visits here.

The villages expanded until they formed one city with a population said to be 40,000. San Rafael is the commercial zone, with an astounding collection of businesses, restaurants, and nightlife. Traffic along San Rafael's main streets is exceptionally heavy, with shoppers and businesspeople driving automobiles at a snail's pace in traffic.

Trendy restaurants of all descriptions abound, including European, barbecue, Chinese, and even a Cajun restaurant for the yuppie trade. Yet a block away from the main streets, neighborhoods are as calm as they were twenty years ago. As San José grew and spread out, artists and those in search of serenity began moving to Escazú. No longer the peaceful retreat of yesterday, the area retains a reputation as an artists' colony as well as a retirement center.

Escazú's higher elevations are ideally suited for those who think that San José's climate is too warm. Many residents consider the weather here to be as close to perfect as you can get, with mild temperatures hovering in the mid-70s to occasional low 80s every afternoon of the year. It is also high enough that the occasional light smog that sometimes touches San José remains far below. For these reasons, a large number of North Americans choose Escazú and surrounding towns as their place of residence. This is where the U.S. ambassador's residence is located. Two famous country clubs provide the area with golf, tennis, and a focal point for the society set. Escazú is the center of much of Costa Rica's expatriate social life.

Escazú and its environs have a sophistication that makes them stand out among San José's suburbs as a prestige address. Although the area admittedly has some of the more expensive places to live, modestly priced homes and apartments are also available throughout the community. Those who choose to live here say they wouldn't think of settling any-

where else. Places where expatriates meet include the Cafe de Artistas (live jazz the second Sunday of the month with brunch) and a bar-restaurant with the non-Tico name The Pub.

"We have the best of all worlds," explained a couple who owns a small house on the slope of Pico Blanco. "We live in the country with a gorgeous view of the city below, yet we are just five minutes away from stores, restaurants, or whatever we need." They pointed out that although they are close to San José, they rarely go there on other than essential business. Well-stocked supermarkets, shops, doctors, dentists, and a first-class health clinic serve the community's needs quite well.

You'll find no real "foreign colony" in Escazú. Expatriate gringos tend to spread throughout the community, interspersed with Ticos and other foreigners. Although some prefer to live in "sealed-in" developments—compounds with high walls and twenty-four-hour guards—more folks live in ordinary homes or town houses. Those who choose to pay more for the security feel it is worth it, since they can comfortably leave their places unoccupied for months at a time while they return home for visits. Others rely on neighbors and friends to take care of things while they are gone.

SANTA **ANA**

The first edition of this book described Santa Ana as a "growing village," 6 kilometers from Escazú, separated by fields of sugarcane, rice, beans, and hillsides of coffee. Roadside stands sold braids of garlic and onions, garden-fresh vegetables, and jars of rich local honey. (Despite Africanized bees' nasty reputations, they produce high-quality honey and more of it than ordinary bees.)

Today you'll no longer see farmland between the towns. The most important crops today seem to be condominiums, homes, and gated communities. Santa Ana has become a small city instead of a growing village. For all practical purposes, Santa Ana and Escazú are one today.

The altitude here is slightly lower than either Escazú or San José, making it slightly warmer and drier. A number of small rivers cross the rolling valley, and rounded mountains provide a scenic backdrop. All roads converge upon a central area, giving Santa Ana a true downtown center, casual yet somewhat sophisticated. High above the town, on the mountain Cerro Pacacua, a 20,000-acre forest preserve and bird sanctuary keeps nature ever present in the local ambience.

A few generations ago—before it became an easy thing to drive to the beach for vacations—San José's wealthy families maintained summer homes in Santa Ana. This was the place to spend weekends and school vacations, a place for the upper crust to host parties and entertain lavishly. This old tradition left its traces on today's community, with many nice homes scattered about the area. Many rather attractive developments, complete with swimming pools, gardens, and twenty-four-hour security, are found here.

This is the place for polo matches and international equestrian competitions. Seasonal festivals bring an impressive parade of horseback riders, who ride their high-stepping steeds along the streets to the central plaza where the main celebration is under way. (Don't try to drive along the parade route on festival day; horses have the right-of-way.)

Santa Ana has a deserved reputation as a working artists' colony, with a number of writers and amateur artists present as well. The town is famous for ceramics, and production of excellent pieces is a major industry, with almost thirty workshops and 150 local people engaged in the art. Excellent restaurants, first-class supermarkets, and shopping of all descriptions are at hand, eliminating the need to go to the crowded world of downtown San José for odds and ends. Yet when such travel is necessary, it's but an easy drive along one of the country's few stretches of genuine superhighway. What is probably the largest and most elegant shopping mall in the country sits along the divided highway between Santa Ana and Escazú. It's called the Multi-Plaza and is worth a visit.

Every community seems to have an especially popular hangout where expats gather to socialize over a few drinks, lunch, or dinner. The Tex-Mex restaurant in Santa Ana seems to be the place for this. English is spoken here by a ratio of 10 to 1, and the place always seems to be crowded. Another popular place, on the road between Escazú and Santa Ana, is called the Rock and Roll Pollo (chicken).

CIUDAD **COLÓN**

Located about fifteen minutes beyond Santa Ana and twenty minutes from Escazú, Ciudad Colón is the next to last of San José's western suburbs. The town is the site of the University of Peace, sponsored by the United Nations, offering graduate courses in peace studies. A growing number of expatriates lives here, a close-knit group that welcomes newcomers. The town is very neat and inviting. As far as we can tell, there haven't been any condo developments started in Ciudad Colón, but with population pressure moving from Santa Ana, condos and gated communities seem inevitable.

The word *Ciudad* means "city," but that word hardly describes Ciudad Colón. This is a small community where folks stroll to the town center for shopping or to have lunch with friends. One of the restaurants we've enjoyed is a vegetarian restaurant called Earthly Delights (even though I'm normally a vegetarian only between meals). There's a sense of peace and personal safety Ciudad Colón. Yet, although the setting is rural, it is certainly not isolated. The enormous and elegant Multi-Plaza Mall is but a short drive, and Escazú not much farther. Frequent bus departures from Ciudad Colón take you to the heart of San José for heavy-duty shopping and browsing the interesting downtown areas of a real ciudad.

Of all the Central Valley retirement locations, I suspect that communities from Santa Ana west to the town of Ciudad Colón and on to Puriscal have a great potential for development and property appreciation. The reason for my belief: The government has plans for extending the divided highway from San José through Ciudad Colón that will someday hook up with the Pacific Coast Highway 34. This present highway, by the way, is one of the few made of cement instead of the usual mixture of asphalt, gravel, and oatmeal—or whatever they mix with asphalt to make a dissolvable road surface. The pavement has endured without damage—not even a tiny pothole—for more than twenty years. Surely the government transportation bosses will someday realize the value of cement highway construction as opposed to disappearing asphalt surfaces.

Anyway, when the highway is extended to the Pacific, this will dramatically cut the driving time to the popular beach communities of Jacó and Quepos. With Pacific beaches just an hour's drive from Cuidad Colón, the convenience will make the area even more attractive as a place to live, and real estate could become an even better investment.

According to news accounts, a contract was signed in early 2006 to start construction. The highway will be built by a private concession and will collect a toll of about $3.00. Well worth it to shave two hours off the trip to the beaches. When I mention this news to my Tico friends, they shrug their shoulders and say, "Don't count on that. We'd be delighted if they'd just fill the potholes on the roads we have!"

PURISCAL

A few kilometers beyond Ciudad Colón, you'll find a delightful mountain town called Santiago de Puriscal, a self-contained community of about 10,000 inhabitants. Puriscal is in the process of being "discovered" by an ever-increasing number of expats who enjoy the perpetual spring climate here. It's a pleasant alternative to the heat and humidity of Caribbean and Pacific beach communities, and above the smog of San José and the Central Valley. Elevations in this area range from 2,600 to 3,900 feet (792 to 1,189 meters), with homes perched on a series of ridges with spectacular views in all directions.

A massive church anchors the center of town, with a lovely park spread out in front. The church is especially interesting because it is partially in ruins, as the result of an earthquake years ago and shifting ground beneath the church. The park in front of the church is a relaxing place to wait for friends and to meet expatriate newcomers.

Santiago de Puriscal offers a surprisingly wide selection of business and commercial services. Probably because it is farther from the urbanized areas closer to San José, central Puriscal has the look of a much larger city. You'll find three supermarkets, several hardware stores, banks, even several Chinese restaurants. We had heard that Puriscal is widely recognized as making the best *chicharrones* (fried pork treats) in the country. During a recent visit we tried them, and we swear they are the best we've ever tasted!

If there's something you need and can't find in Puriscal, a good highway links Puriscal to San José in forty minutes, or a fifty-minute express bus ride. Actually, many Ticos commute to San José daily to work, preferring to live in a peaceful community, away from traffic and bustle. A bonus of living in the Puriscal area: Now that there's a paved road to Orotina, Puriscal residents are a little more than an hour's drive to the Pacific beaches.

ALAJUELA

Near the major airport, one of the less expensive yet pleasant places for foreigners to live is Alajuela. Situated on the western edge of San José, this small city is convenient to the airport and a twenty-minute bus ride from downtown San José. Clean, modern buses run every few minutes during the day, stopping at the airport on the way to and from San José. (If you have a small amount of luggage, this is an inexpensive way to get downtown from the airport.)

Your first approach to Alajuela can give a misleading impression. The highway comes in on a higher level than the town, providing an unfortunate panorama of tin roofs in every direction—some new, some rusted, some painted red to resemble tile, but mostly of corrugated iron or aluminum. Now, in the United States a tin roof usually implies cheap construction, structures such as storage sheds or temporary buildings. But as explained in chapter 2, this is earthquake country; those picturesque tile roofs can be deadly when they collapse. You may see occasional tile roofs, but you can be fairly sure that underneath all that pretty tile is a heavily reinforced substructure. Since the temperature never gets hot or cold, the insulation value of a heavy tile roof is beside the point.

Alajuela's focal point is a large park in the center of town (called the Parque Central, of course), a pleasant place shaded by tall trees, with chessboards built into some of the cement benches that surround the park. If you would like to meet North American retirees to ask for information about Alajuela, this is the place to come; sometimes there seems as much English spoken here as Spanish. This is the place to find out about housing rentals, who is leaving for the States, who has a car for sale, and who can recommend a gardener or a maid. In the evenings a mixture of classical and pop music can be heard from the park's bandstand, where professional musicians entertain a couple of times a week.

Alajuela was the home of Juan Santamaría, the young hero of the final battle against the American buccaneers under General William Walker. Every year on April 11, the town celebrates Juan Santamaría Day with a jubilant parade through town, a public fiesta, and dancing in and around the Parque Central. On one corner of the square, a museum dedicated to the hero is located in what used to be a jail. About two blocks west of the park is the Public Market, the perfect place to find the freshest veggies and choicest cuts of meat.

A good way to become acquainted with the expatriate scene in Alajuela is to visit restaurants and cafes in and around Alajuela center that are frequented by gringos, who drop in for an afternoon snack or a cold drink. If you spend enough time drinking coffee in one of Alajuela's more popular cafes, or sunning yourself on a park bench, you'll likely meet every gringo in Alajuela.

Alajuela is an excellent example of moderate housing costs, for both sales and rentals, in the Central Valley region. Prices are neither as elevated as they can be in upscale areas of Rohrmoser or Escazú, nor are they depressed as in poorer working-class neighborhoods. Neighborhoods here are middle class: Newcomers will feel comfortable, and neighbors can tell you exactly who lives in which house on the street. The expatriate community is scattered throughout the better sections of Alajuela and not very concentrated in any one location. The same is true of Heredia, the following location.

HEREDIA

When we first visited Costa Rica, Heredia was a small provincial capital of about 10,000 persons. Today the population is difficult to estimate. Heredia has expanded to meet Alajuela's growing sprawl until they've essentially joined into one large town, with nothing but a city-limits sign to indicate where one ends and the other begins. Situated northwest of San José on the sloping hills of the Barva and Poás Volcanoes (extinct, of course), Heredia's higher elevation provides a cooler climate and more rainfall, which keeps things looking green and fresh even in the dry season. Rural areas farther up the sloping hills toward Barva are renowned for quality coffee production. Small and medium-size coffee farms are scattered here and there, a few owned by foreign residents. Others own homes with orchards of citrus, avocados, and tropical fruit instead of coffee. Most places enjoy breathtaking views of the valley below.

The center of Heredia, like Alajuela, features a large, friendly Parque Central complete with weekly band concerts. This park is shaded by stands of enormous mango trees and has the usual park benches for informal meetings and gossiping. Like the Parque Central in Alajuela, Heredia's park has a large church at one end—a cathedral, actually—that has watched over the quietness of the square for more than 200 years.

The center of town is somewhat congested, but that doesn't stop expatriates from meeting at their special restaurant on a corner of the square, browsing an English-language bookstore called The Literate Cat, or taking care of banking and other errands on the plaza. One resident points out that "Heredia isn't exactly a 'culinary mecca,' yet you can find some nice restaurants nearby besides the McDonalds, Taco Bell, and Kentucky Fried Chicken that cluster around the plaza."

La Universidad Nacional, the country's second-largest university, is located not far from the plaza. A private school, Universidad Interamericana, and several language schools that teach Spanish to North Americans also exert an influence on life and commerce here. Many exchange students from the United States and Canada take classes here and become part of the expatriate scene in Heredia.

Heredia's famous market is large, featuring quality meats and exceptionally fresh vegetables, fruits, and greens of all descriptions. Much of the market's exotic produce is grown by local residents in their backyards. Saturday is market day, and selections are bountiful as well as fresh-picked. People from all over the valley come here for their weekend shopping. The market is near the Parque Central and dates back more than one hundred years. Like most other cities on the Central Valley, Heredia homes don't have street numbers. But instead of saying "150 meters north," it's customary to say "150 meters *arriba* (uphill) " because the town slopes uphill toward the north. "Two hundred meters *abajo*" would, of course, mean 200 meters to the south, downhill.

Continuing *arriba* is the town of Barva, location of the large coffee producer Café, where many tourists visit for a tour of a coffee plantation. Up the slope toward the extinct Barva Volcano, many lovely homes are tucked away among the tropical vegetation that crowds the side of the narrow highways.

From Heredia's northern edge, hills and mountains rise steadily toward the Poás Volcano. All along these foothills, winding roads travel past beautifully maintained homes, alternating with evergreen forests, small farms, and verdant pastures. This is one of our favorite parts of the Valle Central (we almost bought a coffee farm here a few years ago). As roads climb higher into the mountains, temperatures become progressively cooler, allowing prospective home buyers and renters to make precise adjustments to their environment by buying farther uphill or downhill.

An interesting place to check out is nearby San Isidro, a small village to the east of Heredia. A number of foreigners have made their homes here. They point out that the village is small enough that they can interact with villagers and get to know everyone in town. They enjoy the rustic, rural ambience—a place where oxcarts are still used for everyday farm chores.

Incidentally, those foreigners who own rural parcels and who spend half the year in Costa Rica and the rest of their time in their home country are sometimes willing to rent their property in their absence to ensure that someone will keep an eye on their place and protect it from vandalism. Some attractive rental deals can be worked out in these instances.

OTHER **TOWNS AND VILLAGES**

To the south of Heredia and Alajuela, several smaller towns and open countryside sprinkled with small farms and beautiful homes draw Ticos and foreigners alike who want to escape the city's crush. The road from Heredia to Turrucares is particularly striking, with lovely, high-quality homes interspersed with small, neatly kept farms and residences. Our taxi driver, who was renting his cab and services by the day, drove us there and pointed out some of the prettier homes along the way. "I was born in this area," he said proudly. And then, with a hint of sadness in his voice, he added, "Of course, it is too expensive for me to live here now."

GRECIA The picturesque town of Grecia is often described as one of the cleanest places in Costa Rica. Positioned northwest of San José, Grecia is situated along the edge the Central Valley with beautiful mountain landscapes in the background. It is in the process of being "discovered" by a growing number of expatriates. Conveniently located about thirty minutes from the airport, the Grecia turnoff from the Inter-American Highway is marked by a monument that tries to resemble the ruins of an ancient Greek temple. The town center is reached via a picturesque road that traverses sugarcane fields, high-quality coffee plantations, and small farms. The views are spectacular, overlooking deep valleys and lofty mountains in the distance. Grecia is noted for wide streets and prosperous-looking middle-class neighborhoods.

The center of Grecia features a lovely square in front of one of the country's most interesting old churches. Called the Cathedral de la Mercedes, the deep-red Gothic-style church was assembled from metal pieces imported from Belgium back in the 1890s. Imagine, if you will: Every piece of wrought iron used to construct the church was hauled over the mountains by oxcart from the Caribbean port of Limón, a tedious two-week journey!

A favorite place to meet local expats is the central square located in front of the church. You'll usually find some of them there most weekday mornings, sitting on benches or having coffee in the cafe across the street. Near the plaza is a large central market that, in addition to the usual collection of veggie and meat vendors, has a wonderful Tico restaurant serving some of the best *comida tipica* we've ever tasted.

English-speaking residents here vow that this is one of the friendliest and safest places in the country, and I tend to believe it. As I've driven the roads in the area, I've noticed a surprising exception to the rule of bars on windows; many homes, especially those up in the hills overlooking Grecia, do not have bars. There doesn't appear to be any one particular enclave where gringos live; they seem to be dispersed about the landscape, sometimes on small plots of land near town or in Grecia itself. Some prefer one of the nearby villages such as San Rafael, San Roque, Tacares, or any number of similar locations.

ATENAS AND LA GARITA More to the west of Grecia and only ten minutes farther from the airport, Atenas and La Garita are charming little towns with rural settings and neat town centers with wide streets. These towns sit along the alternate highway that winds down through Orotina, toward the Pacific beaches not far away. Both towns are clean and prosperous looking, with luxury properties interspersed with modest-priced, livable homes. There are adequate community services, including a health center, ambulances, schools, banks, boutiques, and supermarkets. The expatriate population here is said to be around 300 residents.

Atenas and La Garita are gaining popularity with those who want pleasant weather but want to avoid the Central Valley traffic congestion. Residents here are famous for claiming to have the "best climate in the world." They point to an article in *National Geographic* as evidence. Of course, "best climate" is a matter of personal opinion, but there's no question that it is a bit cooler and fresher here than in the Central Valley. Some properties farther up the hill, where the highway crests for its downward, twisty run to the ocean, offer some spectacular views of the Central Valley. A few locations not only overlook the San José city complex to the east, but to the west they have a view of the Pacific Ocean.

Right now, traffic on the highway heading to and from the beaches can be heavy, especially on weekends, when San José residents make their pilgrimages to the Jacó. But this doesn't affect the quiet streets of the towns. When and if the superhighway past Ciudad Colón to the Pacific is completed, the Atenas–La Garita area will make exceptionally desirable places to live. With the new freeway, Atenas will be 30 minutes from Jacó, ten minutes from the International Airport, and twenty minutes from San José. Since Atenas–La Garita is somewhat more affordable than some other desirable areas, you can find moderately priced homes on good-size parcels of land with wonderful views.

SAN RAMÓN An often overlooked possibility for relocation, San Ramón has just as much going for it as most other Central Valley locations. A pleasant and well-maintained city of about 20,000 inhabitants, San Ramón sits almost halfway between San José and the port city of Puntarenas. The exit is just off the Carretera Interamericana that joins San José with the Pacific coast, 22 miles (35 kilometers) from the airport and 30 miles (48 kilometers) from San José. The altitude here is a bit higher than nearby Grecia and Atenas and it's therefore slightly cooler. Hot, sweltering days are almost nonexistent.

Local residents like to call San Ramón "the city of presidents and poets" because several of Costa Rica's famous political and literary figures were born or had long-time residence here. These include three former presidents, the most famous being José Figueres Ferrer—a champion of democratic reform who abolished the military—and several celebrated poets and novelists. In keeping with San Ramón's cultural past, there is a campus of the University of Costa Rica here, as well as a regional hospital.

This is a place where you can experience the genuine, low-key Costa Rica that you'll not find in busy, tourist-oriented towns. The pace here is slow. The central market seems to be the heartbeat of the city. There is also a huge weekly market. San Ramón is a place where neighbors stop to gossip on the street or meet in the central park around the old church. There is no hurry. At the present time, there is only a small contingent of expatriates living in the city of San Ramón. Most prefer to buy property in the picturesque rural areas within a few kilometers of the city center.

When I asked one resident about the cultural advantages of living in or near San Ramón, he replied: "Well, let's see . . . San Ramón is an hour closer to the Guanacaste beaches. Also, there's a three-screen movie theater, plus a Longhorn Tavern (Casona del Cerdo) featuring great BBQ ribs, cut-with-a-fork *Lomito,* and real corn on the cob, yellow and sweet!" (All of that, plus two kinds of homemade draft beers—what more could anyone ask?)

The North American population here is not overwhelming, by any means. One resident estimated less than fifty expats in and around San Ramón. "Not nearly as gringoized as Grecia and Atenas, where they have regular gatherings at the park and such," he added. The recent opening of a new store/office/club in downtown San Ramón has created a gathering place. It's called the Solo Bueno, or in English, "Only the Best." It offers an Internet cafe, used English-language books, mailboxes, and a real estate office. The owner says: "Seems like whenever gringos come to town, they drop by to see what's happening, have a cup of coffee, check e-mail, or pick up a paperback."

CARTAGO Costa Rica's first capital city, Cartago is famous for its rich history. Colonial buildings and ruins dating back to the sixteenth century are reminiscent of an era when Cartago was the center of the country's breadbasket region. Nearby rural villages, with ancient adobe buildings and colorful wooden houses provide glimpses of the region's vibrant past. Sitting at the base of majestic Irazú volcano, the town of Cartago has an elevation of almost 5,000 feet (1,524 meters) above sea level. This provides a much cooler environment than the rest of the Central Valley.

Cartago used to be a major stopping place on the now-defunct San José–Limón railroad line. While waiting for the train to resume its slow crawl to the coast, we used to stroll around the nearby market and feast on steaming empanadas while we waited for the train's whistle to announce the continuance of its journey. We liked the town at that time, wondering why it wasn't being "discovered" by gringos looking for an "authentic" Costa Rican relocation haven.

Costa Rica guidebooks seldom mention Cartago except to note the ruins of an ancient cathedral dating back to the sixteenth century and the slightly newer cathedral that houses Costa Rica's religious icon, the Black Virgin. Also of interest is the fact that Cartago was Costa Rica's first capital city. Cartago is one of the obligatory places to take visitors—close enough to San José's suburbs for an afternoon's visit to the historic monuments, a lunch at a Tico restaurant, and then home before nightfall. But that's where tourist interest in Cartago ends.

I feel that things are starting to change. Bearing out my observation that North Americans feel at home almost anywhere in Costa Rica, the city of Cartago and surrounding communities are attracting a few newcomers. This idea isn't exactly new: Some expat residents have lived here for more than twenty-five years. Only ten or so expatriates live in Cartago itself, while at least fifty live in or around the nearby suburb of Paraiso. There you'll find one of those new Mega Supers, as well as a newly constructed shopping mall.

An expat resident from Ohio who lives with his wife in Taras (at the beginning of the road to Irazú Volcano) said, "I was surprised that so many expats say that they live here mainly because of the climate. I always considered it to be cool, and my Tica wife says it's cold. Also, the rainy season here is probably a little wetter than in San José."

Cartago doesn't seem to have a "hangout" where gringos go for morning coffee like some other towns do. For the most part you run into them in the various shopping centers or on the downtown streets. They will tell you that they enjoy the quality of life in Cartago and that the people really do accept expats and make you feel good about where you live.

ALSO IN THE **TEMPERATE ZONE**

The following locations do not exactly lie within the Central Valley, but they do have similar climates. These are places for those who don't care to put up with the heat and insects of the jungle, yet they are close enough to salt water that you can usually drive down to the beach for the day and return to sleep under a blanket that same night. Temperatures here are wide ranging, with places like Arenal being very cool and San Isidro del General being rather balmy.

SAN ISIDRO DEL GENERAL At first glance, this town would seem to be a rather unusual place for North Americans to choose as a place for residence or retirement. There is nothing spectacular about San Isidro del General; it is an ordinary, small Costa Rican city. It's neat and orderly, with the ubiquitous mountain views common to most other parts of the country. Few vacationers visit San Isidro, and those who have passed through the town may get it mixed up with one of the half-dozen other San Isidros in the mountains. But those North Americans who have discovered San Isidro's secrets love living here. The climate is considerably warmer than that of San José, which suits some folks just fine, and the pace far slower.

Located on a wide ridge, not far from the high peak of Cerro Chirripó, the town enjoys a continuous breeze that keeps the air clear and aromatic with flower-blossom perfume. Daytime temperatures are pleasantly warm for my taste (maybe hot for some folks), and evenings are tempered by cool air flowing down from Chirripó Peak. Although San Isidro is not as serene and idyllic as some other Costa Rican towns, once you are away from the main square—and the inevitable cars, motorcycles, and trucks circling in search of a parking space—the pace slackens to a very peaceful stride.

Like most older Costa Rican towns, San Isidro features a main square in its center, the usual well-kept park. Since the park is the social gathering place for local residents, it isn't surprising that members of the North American community use it as their social focal point as well. The open-air restaurant of Hotel Chirripó faces the park, and at any given time you can count on at least some of the tables being occupied by English-speaking patrons.

Real estate and rentals are exceptionally inexpensive here. Since it is off the ordinary tourist routes, with no beaches and lacking in discos and other flashy attractions, San Isidro is likely to remain inexpensive. On one visit I talked with an American who had just completed building a small, two-bedroom home and was eager to find a tenant. He was offering to rent it for almost nothing just to have someone to take care of it while he returned home.

Several North Americans have taken advantage of the climate and low-cost real estate, living on small farms on the outskirts of town or along the highway toward the beach at Dominical. The views along this road are absolutely spectacular, with neat, prosperous-looking farms and picturesque homes in the mountain valleys below looking like toys along a model train set.

LAKE ARENAL DISTRICT The northern portion of the Cordillera mountain chain, until recently ignored by North Americans, has one of the better potentials for expatriate population growth in the northern regions of Costa Rica. Certainly that's my opinion and one shared by other North Americans who are buying property around Lake Arenal as quickly (and quietly) as they can. Those who know about Lake Arenal would love to keep it a secret, but truth will out! The character of this region is so different from that of other parts of Costa Rica that it's difficult to believe you are in the same country.

The Lake Arenal district is in the upper end of the same mountain chain, but that's as far as the similarity with other highland areas goes. As I understand it, the mountains dip lower at this position in the chain to form a low break or window in the Cordillera. This interruption in the mountain ridges permits a reversal of wind patterns, allowing strong easterly winds to bring moist air off the Caribbean with an abundance of rain.

There is no such thing as a dry season in the Arenal area; it's a year-round wonderland of greenness and lush vegetation. When I asked one long-time resident how much it rained, she replied, "On average, about fourteen months out of the year."

Before the government started building the dam that created the wonderfully scenic lake, the region was lightly populated. Still, about 2,500 people had to be relocated to make room for the 72-square-mile lake. The project required several thousand workers and support people and took sixteen years to complete. Roads were cut into the area, opening it up to Costa Rican settlers who started farms and small villages. After the lake was created, many workers elected to stay on in the company housing that was built during the construction stages. The population here seems to be growing daily, including numerous foreigners who have "discovered" the Lake Arenal region.

To get here via paved road, the quickest way is by turning off the Inter-American Highway at Cañas, an extremely hot and dusty place during the dry season. Were it not for the ample irrigation water coming from Lake Arenal, Cañas would be more like a desert than a rich agricultural region. An air-conditioned auto and lightweight clothing are necessities here. Yet just 18 kilometers away by a tortuously winding road, the air conditioner is shut off and car windows rolled down to take advantage of the delightful fresh air.

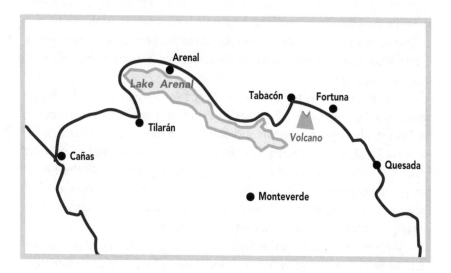

TILARÁN By the time you reach the little town of Tilarán, only 14 miles (23 kilometers) from Cañas, a sweater might feel comfortable when the sky happens to be overcast. The countryside changes from pool-table-flat to steep-sided hills; colors change from dusty dry to emerald green. The road climbs gently now, as vegetation seems to become fresher with every curve, past fat cattle grazing fetlock-deep in richly grassed pastures and, where land hasn't been cleared for cattle or agriculture, some astonishingly heavy stands of tropical forest.

A surprisingly nontropical-looking town—with wide streets, neatly maintained homes, and prosperous businesses—Tilarán has become the home base of a number of expatriates. The climate is temperate and springlike due to a continuous eastern wind that drops moisture on Tilarán even during the dry season. Local residents publish their own newspaper, in English and Spanish, which promotes ecology and recycling projects for the nation.

A few miles east of Tilarán, the view of Lake Arenal bursts upon you, one of the prettiest lakes in the world. The fact that it is artificial fades in importance when the overall effect is considered. Windsurfers claim this is the second-best place in all the world to enjoy their sport. What the first place is for windsurfers, I don't know, but it surely can't be any more beautiful than Lake Arenal.

Almost all residents in this area live on or near the drive that skirts Lake Arenal. The paved portion of the road has a scattering of European-type homes, chalets, and an occasional commercial unit such as a *pulpería*, those community store-tavern combinations so common in rural Costa Rica. Many homes were obviously constructed recently, evidence of a developing region.

Several charming little villages and occasional inns or small hotels are spaced along the highway between Tilarán and Arenal. The road is paved and is usually in pretty good condition. A few miles east of the town of Nuevo Arenal, the road turns into graded clay and occasional stretches of blacktop. The condition of the road is never predictable. At the beginning of the dry season, after bulldozers scrape the road into a smooth surface, fill in the gigantic potholes, and sometimes cover it with a bit of gravel, the route feels like a superhighway to drive.

When the road is okay, the distance from Nuevo Arenal to Arenal Volcano seems like nothing, with a wonderful view of the lake and thick tropical vegetation lining the road. Other times the road is an absolute nightmare. Entire sections of the road can be missing. Water and mud can bury a four-wheel-drive up to its windshield, and other horrors. I believe the problem is that the steep mountain slopes along the north side of the route come down from rain forests above, bringing water and mud sluicing down onto the road. What doesn't get washed away gets covered with mud. The lesson here is to make inquiries about taking a shortcut from Fortuna to Tilarán. When the road is good, it is very, very good; and when it is bad, it is horrid.

NUEVO ARENAL   The town on the lake is called Nuevo Arenal or, more often, simply Arenal. This is a surprisingly prosperous-looking place, with neat little houses interspersed with expensive-looking ones. The town sits high on the sloping bank of Lake Arenal, and most homes and businesses are situated to take advantage of the lake view. Streets are well paved, and more are in the process of being paved in anticipation of a population explosion. Parts of town have an oddly unfinished look, as newly paved streets and vacant lots mix with an occasional house. The center of town has the inevitable soccer field with spectator benches curiously pointed toward the street, away from the field, as if the soccer team is so bad that locals would rather watch the traffic, scarce as it is.

Arenal obviously was a development planned by the government during the dam's construction phase. Many of today's homes here are left over from that era. Unlike the traditional Latin American residential style—built close together and against the sidewalk to allocate space for interior patios—some Arenal homes have real lawns, reminiscent of small-town U.S.A. This adds to Arenal's strange, non–Latin American look.

Because of the area's beauty, the temperate-tropical combination climate, and the low cost of real estate, the Lake Arenal region is undergoing a buying frenzy. Buyers from Canada, the United States, and Europe are furtively looking at property and investing. Germans, Swiss, and Italians appear to be the biggest sharks, biting off chunks of the land as quickly as they can. They try not to appear eager as they snap up bargains, and they do their best to keep this place a secret, lest hordes of other foreigners descend upon paradise and ruin their plans of being the only ones here.

It's not surprising that prices are going up on property around Arenal. It's a very desirable area. Still, it's hard to conceive that inflation could be anything like that along the Pacific beaches. Another favorable circumstance: Since this is lakefront property, it doesn't fall under the complicated and restrictive laws that regulate ownership and construction on beachfront parcels. Here waterfront property is owned outright instead of being leased from the municipality. However, be aware that the water level in the lake fluctuates from dry season to wet season as water is drawn off for irrigation and hydroelectric power. Your waterfront lot could end up with a broad frontage of dry land in the dry season.

LA FORTUNA No trip to Costa Rica can be considered complete until you've visited the Arenal Volcano, which is only about 8 miles (13 kilometers) from the town of La Fortuna. Active continuously over several centuries, the volcano's northern slope suddenly exploded almost forty years ago, destroying a village and killing more than sixty people. (A geologist had tried to warn them of an impending eruption, but nobody believed him.) The nearest and best place to observe the activity is in the hot pools of Tabacón, a resort wedged into a steaming-hot river canyon at the volcano's base. You can sit on underwater stools by the bar and sip piña coladas while every twenty minutes or so, a jarring explosion shakes the swimming pool, accompanied by puffs of smoke and red-hot boulders tumbling down the volcano's steep side. (That's time to order another piña colada.)

The volcano has done marvels for tourism hereabouts. The nearby town of Fortuna has become prosperous serving the needs of the hordes of volcano visitors. New hotels, restaurants, and stores are appearing each season. Fortuna is an exceptionally neat and pleasant community, one that could well make a good place for retirement. With a new road going through San Ramón, San José is only a two-and-a-half-hour drive away.

A small town with a friendly atmosphere, spic-and-span streets, and a great climate, Fortuna has my prediction of a place that could someday have a sizable expat community. Sitting at approximately 1,312 feet (400 meters) above sea level, Fortuna is too high to be tropical, yet it's low enough to avoid chilly winds. About 10 miles (16 kilometers) from the entrance to Arenal Volcano National Park, La Fortuna serves as an ideal base for tourists visiting the volcano, popular Tabacón Hot Springs, and Lake Arenal. Not far from Caño Negro Reserve and such outdoor activities as windsurfing, fishing, and white-water rafting, it's almost obligatory to stay at or pass through La Fortuna to enjoy these facilities. The tourism potential will do nothing but grow over time, and this will bring more North American residents. The town and vicinity have a growing number of hotels, cabinas, restaurants, and travel/tour agencies. As you depart La Fortuna toward Tabacón and Lake Arenal, several new tourist facilities with terrific views of the volcano are always under construction.

A small group of foreigners are now settling into the Fortuna area. Of course, everybody knows everyone here, but to date they haven't formed any residents' club or formal organization. That will come later, when a critical mass of expatriates forms around La Fortuna. In the meantime, as one resident says, "Most of us come here to enjoy living with our Tico neighbors and being independent."

SAN CARLOS When people talk about "San Carlos," they could be referring to the northern region of Costa Rica, from below Ciudad Quesada on up to the Nicaraguan border at the San Juan River. They could also mean the small city known as San Carlos, located in the more southern portion of the San Carlos region. To add to the confusion, you won't find the city of San Carlos on the map, because officially it is called Ciudad Quesada. However, for some reason unknown to me, Ticos always refer to Ciudad Quesada as San Carlos.

San Carlos offers another example of Costa Rica's microclimates. With a lower elevation than the Valle Central, the region is warmer than the San José area and receives more rain during the dry season. Yet it doesn't have the heavy rainfall of the nearby Lake Arenal area. Agriculture is a year-round activity, with citrus, macadamia, and other orchard crops as well as numerous *fincas* (ranches) with horses and cattle tended by expatriates.

These lands were once tropical forests, which during the past decades have been transformed into cattle pastures and fruit plantations. The exceptionally rich farmland here has attracted a number of gringo farmers and would-be agriculturists. San Carlos's agricultural zone devotes almost 70 percent of the land to raising cattle. The area produces first-quality milk, beef cattle, and agricultural products. Expatriates have set up on small to moderately large spreads; some experiment with refor- estation. Some people have been planting teak, even though some experts claim that teak needs definite dry seasons alternating with wet periods to force the tree to produce oil and densely grained wood. Time will tell, because it takes many years before teak is ready to harvest.

Ciudad Quesada, or San Carlos, or whatever, is the main center of services and commerce for the Northern Zone. This prosperous-looking city-town was settled in 1840 when the Quesada family moved here from San Ramón and founded a village. As is the custom, the center of town holds a central park and the ubiquitous Catholic church. Nearby is the customary central market full of colorful stalls selling fruit, vegetables, herbs, and locally made leather products and crafts.

ACOSTA A few years ago, the Ministry of Tourism came up with the idea of promoting "rural tourism" as an economic-development project for communities with limited tourist attractions and no hotels or other tourist facilities. The idea is to attract certain types of tourists, those who aren't looking for golf courses, beaches, discos, and the traditional tourist glitz that draws many foreigners to Costa Rica. This special kind of tourist will be curious about the everyday life of the Ticos: who they are, what would it be like living in a "typical" Costa Rican village. Since these isolated communities rarely have hotels suitable for tourists, local residents organ- ize to turn their homes into bed-and-breakfasts and welcome visitors. Since the community goes all out to make visitors welcome, it occurs to me that retirees might be received even more warmly as permanent eco- nomic benefits to the area. A small handful of expatriates are living there. A Web site describing the program is found at www.costaricanrural tourism.org. (However, I have to say that they are very slow in answering queries, but the region is worth a visit anyway.)

Finding this idea intriguing, I decided to investigate by making a trip to one of the designated rural tourism areas, an area known as Acosta, the general name given to a half-dozen villages in the mountains south of San José, about an hour's ride by bus from the center of the city. An excellent road snakes its way upward, winding through small villages and past some very interesting homes. The drive is spectacular, with deep valleys and ravines, lush vegetation, and spectacular views of San José and the Central Valley way down below.

The largest village is San Ignacio de Acosta. It's difficult to know the population, because none of the people I met there could make an estimate that agreed with anybody else's. There's a lovely church and a large, landscaped park. The surprising thing is the high quality of the housing. It was explained to me that at one time the Tico government was making low-interest loans for quality housing, and many people took advantage of this and upgraded their homes. The setting is overwhelmingly beautiful. San Ignacio de Acosta is perched on the top of a rounded mountain, with an astonishing view of other villages so far below that the houses look like toys. San Luis de Acosta is about five minutes away, looking down the other side of the mountain into other valleys. Coffee farms are interspersed with forested land and small farm homesteads. Except for the main roads and some town streets, all roads are graded gravel, some in excellent condition, others not so great. The climate is superb, one of the best in the country, at least for those who like year-round springlike weather. The temperatures are seldom over 75 degrees or below 65 degrees. Air-conditioning and heating are unknown here.

I was welcomed enthusiastically as a visitor and was given a room in a private home, where I was treated as one of the family. I joined with the family in the local fiesta celebration and was very impressed. In my opinion, a place such as Acosta is a retirement option for certain types of North Americans: those who speak at least some Spanish or those who are willing to learn. Acosta would be appropriate for those who do not require a large circle of English-speaking friends. The local Ticos are exceptionally friendly and open. I feel that before long, a retired couple could easily be involved with the Tico society, with friends and volunteer activities keeping them very busy.

CHAPTER SEVEN

COSTA RICA'S
PACIFIC COAST

The western side of the country is characterized by wet summers, dry winters, regular surf from the open ocean, and a much larger population of foreigners. Although most come from North America, a considerable number of Europeans are moving into the area. Many come from Germany, Switzerland, and Italy; other nationalities are well represented as well. Some expatriates operate successful hotels, restaurants, and other tourist-oriented ventures that the business-friendly Costa Rican government makes possible.

Costa Rica's Pacific Coast can be divided into three basic geographic sections: the Nicaragua border to the end of the Nicoya Peninsula area, the beaches from Jacó to Uvita in the center, and the Golfo Dulce–Osa Peninsula area to the south. Each area has its boosters who will assure you that there is no place in all of Central America as nice as their favorite location. I've seen them all, and I can say that making a choice among them would be difficult indeed.

A nice feature of most of these tropical beach areas is that they are easily accessible from the Central Valley—within a few hours' drive by bus or automobile, almost no time at all by airplane. Some locations

Panama
Playa Hermosa
Potrero
Flamingo • Liberia
Brasilito
Conchal
Playa Grande
Tamarindo

Lake Arenal

Junquillal
Playas del Coco
San Juanillo
Ostional
Nicoya •
Nosara
Playas de Nosara

Puntarenas

Sámara   Carmona •
Carrillo   Naranjo •
Paquera •

Tambor
Montezuma
Malpaís Cabo Blanco

NICOYA **PENINSULA**

require longer driving times than others, but as pavement replaces gravel roads, travel times will decrease.

Eastward from the ocean's surf, rolling hills of forest and farmland spread inland and up the mountain slopes, becoming steeper and more picturesque with each kilometer. Much of this land is wilderness, traversed by occasional dirt roads that become quagmires in the rainy season. Despite isolation and transportation difficulties, foreigners find these rustic sections exceptionally desirable places to live. As the government gradually paves the roads along the coast and into the interior, more and more settlers are swelling the ranks of North Americans and Europeans who live here and operate businesses. With easy access, property values ought to increase dramatically.

GUANACASTE **REGION**

A number of important beach locations on the North Coast attract Costa Ricans and foreigners alike for vacation, retirement, or business opportunities. These beaches are easily reached from San José in three to five hours by car. The main highway is paved and in generally good condition but can be agonizingly slow when you are stacked up behind a string of slow trucks on their way to or from the Pacific docks. Slow as this stretch may be—about 10 miles (16 kilometers) or so—you will be glad you have to go slow, because there are some shoulder drop-offs that could be dangerous if you drive carelessly. The secret to driving this section of the highway is not to be in a hurry. Relax and go with the flow. Enjoy the spectacular and ever-changing scenery of the Inter-American Highway.

Rainfall amounts are lower here than anywhere else in the country. Unlike most of Costa Rica, here the dry season is truly dry, with almost no rain falling from January to May. This is similar to much of California, but in reverse. That is, in California it almost never rains between May and October. In Guanacaste's dry season grass turns parched and yellow and many trees lose their leaves, often replaced with a gorgeous display of colorful blossoms. Around homes or along inhabited beaches, however, you'll see more evergreen trees and broadleaf plants because they've been deliberately planted and cared for.

PLAYAS DEL COCO **AREA**

A quickly developing complex of *playas* (beaches) begins at Playa Hermosa and Playa Panama, stretching south through Playas del Coco and ending at Playa Ocotal. A nice beach in this complex and one with development potential is Playa Hermosa. Hermosa means "beautiful" in Spanish, and Playa Hermosa lives up to its name. This is a lovely place, with a curving shoreline of clean sand and a peninsula that shields it from the open ocean and dangerous riptides.

Playas del Coco, however, is the most commercially developed of all these beach communities. Since the pavement ends in the center of El Coco, tourists tend to stay here rather than braving annoying stretches of washboard gravel roads to get to nearby beaches. Coco's scenery consists of the horseshoe-shaped Coco Bay with islands in the distance and steep hills and cliffs on either side.

This is probably not the place in which you'd want settle down, not if you are looking for a "typical sleepy fishing village" (as I've seen it described in a recent tourist publication). Actually, I don't believe Coco ever sleeps—it offers some of the wildest nightlife in the country. The town boasts over two dozen bars, discos, and nightclubs that rock all night, every night. There are also two casinos.

There can be no question about Coco's potential for business, retirement, or long-term living. Several very successful American-owned enterprises operate here, and more are probably on the way. But if I don't sound particularly enthusiastic about the place, it's probably because this is where I locked my keys in my rental car and struggled for two hours in the hot sun before figuring out a way to get inside without breaking a window. A good car thief could have done it in less than twenty seconds.

A few kilometers to the south, Playa Ocotal manages to maintain a village atmosphere despite also hosting a deluxe tourist resort. The accommodations are tasteful, blending in with the natural surroundings. The village is on the shore of Bahía Pez Vela (Sailfish Bay), and the fishing is said to live up to the name. Each time we visit, we see a noticeable increase in housing, making this another viable retirement option.

FLAMINGO **BEACH**

The next beach complex to the north is just a few kilometers away and is probably the most popular residential complex on this part of the Pacific Coast. New paved roads have opened the area to increased settlement. This array of beaches starts with Playa Pan de Azucar and continues south to Playa Tamarindo, including the beaches of La Penca, Potrero, Flamingo, Brasilito, Conchal, Playa Grande, Tamarindo, and Langosta.

By far the prettiest beach is Playa Flamingo. A wide, curving stretch of white sand with startling blue waves that turn to white-capped rollers before crashing loudly against the shore creates one of the loveliest scenes imaginable. Hotels here cater to affluent tourists who can afford to fly in from San José and spend $150 a night for rooms. Tourists on ordinary budgets will find few (if any) reasonably priced rooms. Ongoing building activity may change all this.

As you might imagine, foreigners have taken over this beach and have built some very spiffy places. I consider Flamingo the "Cadillac" of Costa Rican beach communities. The hillsides display sumptuous homes, set in tropical landscaping and overlooking a gorgeous beach view. The scene is reminiscent of Acapulco many years ago when it was the playground of the Hollywood and European jet set. Needless to say, Flamingo is not the place to look for inexpensive ocean-view lots.

The beach adjacent to Flamingo is Brasilito. Instead of having a tourist-resort atmosphere, the village of Brasilito is more like a typical Costa Rican pueblo, complete with a soccer field, small bars, and restaurants. This is a bedroom community for workers employed by affluent residents and businesses in Flamingo. It's also an inexpensive place for Ticos and foreign residents on a budget to find an inexpensive cabina or room and enjoy the beach. The beach isn't bad at all; I'm surprised there isn't more commercial development and foreign settlers. For a beach community, property here is reasonably priced.

The next village is at Playa Conchal. The Spanish word *Conchal* refers to the shells on the beach. In fact, the entire beach is composed of tiny, water-worn shells instead of sand. This area has attracted numerous expatriates in the past few years. This is another place with a large resort, spread over 2,400 acres of lush land, including a golf course and 350 rooms. Several really nice housing developments are also found here, including gated communities, all near the beach.

Just over a mile (2 kilometers) north of Flamingo, the tiny fishing village of Potrero has a handful of foreign residents. They're building along the beach toward Flamingo, eventually to become an integral part of one community. The village itself is much more laid-back and relaxed than Flamingo, with some residents' homes built on the hillside overlooking Potrero's exceptionally gentle beach. This is a place where you can hire a local fisherman to take you out in his *panga* to fish for dorado or parga.

REGIONAL **DEVELOPMENT**

The entire west coast of the Nicoya Peninsula is slated for eventual tourism development by the government's tourism ministry (ICT). Of particular interest, with short-term plans in the works, the stretch from Sámara north to Tamarindo is drawing a great deal of attention. Two circumstances account for this recent flurry of building activity. The first is the recently completed bridge over the Tempisque River, which cuts at least an hour's driving time from the trip from San José. The second is the possible paving of the road from Sámara north to Tamarindo. (We're not holding our breath.) This plan sets out certain areas as high-density tourism centers, suitable for large hotels, intensive usage of beachfront, and full-service tourist facilities. Sámara and Garza are so designated. Other places are planned for residential and low-intensity tourism.

Nosara was supposed to fall into the latter category, much to the delight of local foreign residents. This is precisely what they wanted: protection of the beach and forest, yet development of low-impact tourism to boost prosperity for the natives. Unfortunately, the desire of local residents has little effect on the determination of tourists to enjoy the Nosara beaches. Not to mention the determination of developers to accommodate tourists and new residents. The region is booming, with more facilities and homes being built every year.

TURTLE **BEACHES**

An excellent example of how tourism and conservation can work hand in hand is found from Playa Grande south along the peninsula beach communities. One noteworthy turtle conservation project is at Playa Grande, just north of Tamarindo, a broad, sandy beach area famous as nesting grounds for endangered leatherback turtles. It used to be that local residents awaited the arrival of these huge, prehistoric survivors, collected the eggs in buckets as they were being deposited, and sold the harvest to bars and restaurants all over the country.

Alarmed by the possibility of the turtles' extinction, the Costa Rican government instituted a model conservation program. Local people are enlisted to help protect the nesting grounds. Guarding the beaches and guiding tourists through the nesting grounds put local people to work. Hotels and restaurants have opened to accommodate the ever-increasing number of tourists. Jobs are created for even more local residents. This boom has only begun; future ecotourism development seems inevitable.

Conservationists have expressed mixed feelings about this program. While they praise the protection of the nesting grounds, they point out that the extra tourist foot traffic causes damage when visitors inadvertently step on the hatchlings. On the other hand, the number of baby turtles killed in this manner is nothing when compared with the unborn ones that used to end up as a tasty *boca* in San José bars.

PLAYA GRANDE Turtles need a wide, sandy beach with ample portions not touched by normal high tides, and Playa Grande fills these requirements admirably. It used to be relatively unpopulated, with few human footprints to disturb the solitude. Until a few years ago, only a handful of homes and one or two tiny motels were to be found near the beach's access roads. Today development is under way. However, as part of the Tamarindo Refuge, the beach area will always be somewhat restricted in tourist development, even though the region's natural beauty and wildness are bound to attract even more people in the future.

One place I looked at was a large, tastefully constructed home with a neatly manicured lawn ending at a beach wall marking the 50-meter boundary. The owner half-apologized for the home's isolation and lack of anything to do, adding, "The hope of this little community is that things won't change. What we offer here is location, nothing else." He indicated the broad expanse of beach visible through a stand of coconut palms and said, "The whole idea here is to fit into the ecology without disturbing things, particularly not the nesting turtles and their life cycle." The house's window frames were made of wood instead of the more practical aluminum "because metal frames reflect moonlight and confuse the hatchling leatherbacks. We don't allow any lights from our homes to escape at night. For bright lights and nightlife, you have to go to Tamarindo." Since my writing of these lines, several bars and restaurants have opened near Playa Grande, and several housing developments are under way.

Local turtle-watchers report some good news: The number of turtles visiting the beaches to lay eggs in 2003 doubled from the previous year, with new turtles joining the flock (or should it be covey? Band? Could it be a herd of turtles?). The numbers still remain below what they were in the 1980s, but locals are hoping this will become a trend.

PLAYA TAMARINDO Playa Tamarindo begins where Playa Grande ends, a picturesque estuary separating the two. Tamarindo is where leatherback-turtle-watchers find hotels. Launches begin ferrying passengers across the estuary around midnight. Visitors tiptoe quietly along the beach and pause to observe the huge turtles as they awkwardly pull themselves up on the beach to bury their eggs 6 feet deep in the sand. This is an unforgettable sight; some of these turtles are said to grow to more than 12 feet

across and weigh up to 1,500 pounds! The one I watched laying eggs may have been a pygmy; she was barely 6 feet wide. Our guide claimed that during the peak of the season, as many as 350 turtles can be on the beach in a single night. What an amazing sight!

Because of excellent surfing beaches and nearby Playa Grande turtle beaches, Tamarindo has always been a magnet for tourists of all ages. The coastal region here is easily accessible by pavement rather than gravel and dirt roads, which ensures a steady stream of visitors as well as new residents who often become part of the business community. Note that in mid-2006, the pavement to Tamarindo was in horrible condition, all but replaced by washboard surface, but the government promises a resurfacing as soon as possible.

The new international airport in nearby Liberia has accelerated development, with visitors avoiding the long drive from San Jose and usually an overnight stay there. Among the airlines landing at Liberia are Delta (departing from Atlanta), American (from Miami), and Continental (from Houston).

Tamarindo's popularity with tourists and expatriate residents has transformed the sleepy village of a few years ago into a busy, highly commercial entity. The town is a textbook example of foreign development of a Costa Rican beach community, totally developed, and with a cosmopolitan mix of nationalities. Almost all businesses—restaurants, hotels, shops, bars, and so forth—are owned by foreigners: North Americans,

Italians, Germans, and French, with several other European nations also represented.

Some residents and longtime visitors lament these changes, while others appreciate the presence of upscale restaurants and quality retail and food shopping options, including a supermarket and conveniences that a mere village would lack. While some yearn for the "good old days," Rob Gibson, a Tamarindo homeowner, says: "The surroundings are still spectacular, and the relative success in protecting Playa Grande and the estuary behind it from unbridled development has been key to maintaining its attractions. The beach at Tamarindo is large and long enough to take on considerable development without losing its attractiveness. The walk to Langosta still evokes a feeling of Big."

A few years ago, a Tamarindo Tico complained to me: "We keep selling our land and moving farther back into the hills. Now we are working for foreigners on land we once owned. Before long we won't be able to afford to live in our own village!" That prediction has come true; the price of real estate makes property ownership impossible for local families, and hotels are priced out of range for vacationing Tico families. However, Rob Gibson—who speaks Spanish with local working people—observes no general sense of resentment. "Most Ticos say that tourists and part-time residents are good because they bring money and create jobs in the area. I love the practicality and lack of xenophobia among *Costarriquenses*, and if we gringos behave decently, perhaps we can keep it that way." Rob also points out that there are definite advantages to living in an expatriates' enclave. "I don't know how much my gringo neighbors would help me in a crisis, but it is nice to have so many of them around."

For those with school-age children, this is the only region outside the Central Valley with an international K–12 college-prep school. Country Day School Guanacaste is a private facility located between Tamarindo and Flamingo. It isn't inexpensive, but as one parent said, "The school is small enough for the teachers to have a one-on-one relationship with their students." There's also a bilingual elementary school, Niños del Mundo, with classes for students from pre-kindergarten to fourth grade.

PLAYA JUNQUILLAL South of Tamarindo the coast is lightly populated by foreigners or Ticos. This is partially due to the seasonal condition of the dirt roads along the coast. Most residents believe that a paved road will be built not too far in the future and that beaches along this coast might have potential for development. A series of beaches front the Pacific along this coast, some with tiny villages, others almost unpopulated. Among the beach villages are: Playa Avellana, Playa Negra, Playa Junquillal, and Playa Lagarto. These beaches are graced by large waves rolling in from the open Pacific and are very picturesque. Since I'm not an expert swimmer and know little about ocean currents, undertow, and riptides, I can't vouch for the safety of these beaches. You'll need to consult local authorities on the subject. This is a sensible practice anywhere in the country.

A place that's attracted our attention is Junquillal, a growing village positioned on one of the longest beaches on the Nicoya Peninsula. The region is known for exceptional surfing waves in the Playa Negra and Junquillal areas. Endangered leatherback and green turtles come ashore to lay their eggs in the sand. Most businesses in the area are owned by Americans, Canadians, Italians, and Germans who are trying to develop more tourism in the area. Meanwhile, residents are hoping that Junquillal doesn't develop to the same extent as the more popular beach towns. One Canadian expatriate said, "We like progress, but we'd prefer to keep the area as a serene place to come for relaxation and the natural beauty of the area."

One small hotel, right on the beach, is owned by several California couples who take turns managing the establishment as their excuse for a working vacation (presumably tax-deductible). One partner said, "It's a very small operation. We consider a month successful when we don't have to dig into our pockets to make the payroll." A few kilometers from the village center, an elaborate residential development is being purchased exclusively by Canadians and Americans. Construction quality is tops, with all amenities. Since Junquillal has a small population, major shopping and other services are available about forty-five minutes away. Recently a mini-super market appeared on the scene, providing most basic supplies.

BEACHES OF **NOSARA**

We "discovered" Beaches of Nosara (Playas de Nosara) about twenty years ago, while researching the Guanacaste beach communities on the

Nicoya Peninsula. Driving north from Sámara over a dirt road that parallels the ocean beaches, we stumbled on an almost isolated beach community inhabited exclusively by North Americans and a few Europeans. Because the road was not paved, and many rivers need to be forded, few tourists bothered to investigate the heavily forested and lightly populated community. Over these years, we've been privileged to see many profound changes to Beaches of Nosara.

Starting at the Nosara River, three lovely beaches and a wildlife reserve extend south along Playa Nosara and Playa Pelada to Playa Guiones (*Playa*, of course, means "beach"). Nosara started as an experiment in a different concept of foreign development. The emphasis was on private homes and pristine beaches rather than tourism and commercial enterprise. Along more than 5 miles (8 kilometers) of beaches, to this day only two small restaurants are located on the beach. As you stroll the ocean's sandy shores, you'll see no discos, fast-food restaurants, miniature golf courses, or any other evidence of higher culture. Just beach and jungle. At least for the first 200 meters)—after that, all bets are off. There's a possibility that in the future the government could relent and allow building closer to the beach but residents are hopeful this will never happen.

Don't misunderstand; you can find plenty of services like the above (well, maybe not miniature golf), just not on the beach. Two hundred meters (656 feet) is as close to the water as they can legally be located. So when you are strolling the beach, swimming, or sunning, there's nothing to remind you that you are not in pure paradise. The major exception to this rule is a small Tico bar and restaurant, Olga's Bar, which has occupied a patch of beachfront for the past thirty years and is therefore grandfathered (or grandmothered) into acceptance. Thirsty residents concede that they need at least one bar on the beach!

A major problem has always been that newcomers aren't as ecologically aware as the original owners. Residents and old-timers continually try to educate newcomers about the importance of not cutting down the trees or destroying the animals' habitat. Howler monkeys need regular "trails" through the treetops that they use daily to go from one feeding area to another. Since the project is set in the forest, a great deal of the Nosara project was zoned as greenbelt, forever to be public parklands, never to be developed or built upon. Until recently parklands have been sacrosanct, with development verboten. Longtime residents are deter-mined that their parklands remain protected from development. This is their insurance that their unique forest won't be replaced by lawns, t-shirt shops, and condos.

When this book first described Nosara, development was still in its infancy. Services were limited and property prices were very modest, probably one-half to one-third of more accessible beach locations such as Tamarindo or Flamingo. Then, at the turn of the new century, change began accelerating. New residents began arriving in a steadily increasing stream, looking for homes to buy or construction lots. Several new hotels and business buildings are under construction. An astounding amount of commercial construction seems to be going on everywhere. Many origi-nal residents shake their heads in disbelief at these radical changes. Oth-ers are happy, convinced that this growth will force the government to pave the road. At the present time, it takes an hour to drive a dirt road to the nearest pavement. That doesn't stop newcomers.

Despite changes in ambience and lifestyles, I'm firmly convinced that Nosara will maintain its charm and forest ambience. There is room for all.

SÁMARA AND **CARRILLO**

A welcome development for those traveling to the Pacific Coast from San José and points inland is the "Friendship Bridge" constructed by the Tai-wanese government a short time ago. This bridge replaced the cumber-some ferry across the Tempisque River. In the time it would take the ferry to cross the wide stretch of water, carrying a limited number of vehicles, a thousand cars and trucks can zip across the bridge. Travel time to the peninsula has been shortened by about an hour. This new access is hav-ing a profound impact on the development of the entire coast, with Sámara and Carrillo being affected the most.

Much of this area is already developed, particularly in and around Sámara. New hotels and condos are going in, and more expats are build-ing homes south of town, extending toward Carrillo. However, this is only the beginning. As we noted earlier, the Tourism Institute has targeted the Sámara-Carrillo area for high-intensity tourist use. We expect to see some large hotels and probably a resort going in before long. Smaller hotels, restaurants, and shops will naturally follow. If Sámara develops as did

Tamarindo, we can expect a large percentage of new businesses to be owned by North Americans. It seems to be working out that way.

The area is quite appropriate for this kind of development. Sámara and Carrillo share opposite ends of the same bay, one of the most beautiful imaginable in a country of beautiful beaches. Several long stretches of beach are flanked by a wide road fringed with coconut palms, making the beaches freely accessible to all. At the northern portion of the bay, Sámara attracts more Tico tourism from the Central Valley area at the moment (on weekends and holidays they arrive by the busloads). Toward Carrillo, more hotels cater to foreigners and are higher priced. This is where the airstrip is, which makes it handy for visitors.

All along this part of the coast, some low mountains sit back about a kilometer from the shore, and here is where many expats make their homes. The views of the bay are magnificent up here, whereas homes built at sea level have views of nothing but trees or the nearby hotel.

An item of interest about Carrillo: A short distance south of the airstrip there is a bridge over a small river where two large crocodiles lurk. Local residents regularly feed them by throwing frozen chicken carcasses tied with nylon line into the river. They then troll the tasty morsels toward the bridge to lure the monsters from their hiding places. Although the river isn't posted against swimming or wading, I would strongly recommend that you refrain from this activity. The crocodiles strongly disagree with this advice.

LOWER **NICOYA PENINSULA**

On the southern tip of the Nicoya Peninsula, a string of beaches with tremendous potential are undergoing development. The beaches run from Naranjo on the Gulf of Nicoya side to Cabo Blanco at the very tip of the peninsula, and then up along the coast via impassable roads, toward Carrillo. Most investors agree that the economic growth between Cabo Velas and Cabo Blanco could be among the best in the country. It all depends upon when (and if) the roads will be made passable.

Getting to this area from the northern part of the peninsula has always been a problem. The paved highway ends abruptly at the little town of Carmona, presenting about a 19-mile (30-kilometer) stretch of dirt road to the coast. The road paralleling the Pacific Coast dwindles to a trail from time to time, and you have to ford several good-size streams. Even rugged four-wheel-drives avoid the coastal route. An easier way is to take a ferry from Puntarenas to Playa Naranjo or Paquera, which shortens the drive considerably. It's possible that the road is currently in much better condition. Make inquiries first.

PLAYA TAMBOR The setting of Tambor is an extraordinarily calm horseshoe bay called Bahía Ballena (Whale Bay). Two long projections of forested and rocky coastline protect beaches from ocean swells. A major tourist attraction used to be the migration of whales into the bay's protected waters during the summer season to give birth. Nowadays, probably because of the increased boating and fishing activity, whales stay further offshore. Bahía Ballena's beaches of dark volcanic sand and shallow water offer perfect swimming for even the most timid of bathers. Not good for surfing but great for swimming, snorkeling, and diving. The nearby Curu Wildlife Reserve is known as a place for viewing wildlife and lush vegetation.

This is also the location of a controversial hotel-resort by the Barceló chain. I say controversial because the construction caused a maelstrom of controversy, with ecologists accusing the hotel chain of doing damage to the environment in the construction of the hotel. Oddly enough, the huge Playa Tambor resort doesn't seem to affect the atmosphere of the village of Tambor. It's the same laid-back, friendly place as before—ever popular with retired foreigners, who appreciate the conveniences that Tambor offers. You'll find golf, tennis, and a small airport with daily twenty-five minute flights to San José.

The reason tourism at the expensive resort hasn't affected the town could be the fact that the hotel and grounds are self-contained and guests seldom venture elsewhere. Interesting to note: The hotel enjoys a nice white-sand beach (ecologists complain the sand was imported from elsewhere). The little surf that Tambor beach gets is rather gentle, always peppered with little Tico children splashing and laughing.

Several gated communities set back on the hillsides are in place, and others presumably are on the drawing boards. A little farther west, the gated community of Tango Mar provides an elegant contrast to funky Playa Tambor. Tango Mar is basically a private (and expensive) resort with deluxe accommodations; it is also a retirement community featuring a small golf course, tennis courts, and a lovely beach.

MONTEZUMA Located about 19 miles (30 kilometers) down the road from Playa Tambor, the village of Montezuma is the entry point to a beautiful string of beaches. A description of "laidback" or "tranquil" would hardly describe this picturesque little village. It is widely known for its bohemian flair and reputation as a party town. Although many tourists you meet are younger, many residents are older, reliving the continuous party scene of the 1970s. Along Montezuma's main street, you'll see a continuous parade of characters such as aging hippies, tattooed surfers, and Rastafarians, plus some occasional visitors who seem overwhelmed by it all.

Just a few steps from the hustle bustle of the town center, you find yourself on Playa Grande, a great place for a walk to secluded coves, tide pools, and sunbathing. The village itself is sheltered by vertical cliffs overgrown with vines and green tropical foliage. Several streams flow down from the hills creating scenic waterfalls and natural swimming pools. Monkeys, parrots, and other wildlife are frequent visitors.

Montezuma is not only a mecca for backpackers and surfers but also a special retirement place for more mature counterculture people. (Maybe I fall into the latter category, because I've always felt right at home in Montezuma with kindred spirits my age blending into the scene.) It's not for the early-to-bed set, needless to say. Gringos who love the Montezuma scene enjoy a lively and active social life; those who covet peace and quiet will probably want to look elsewhere. Residents and businesspeople are very ecology-minded and maintain a continual campaign for clean beaches. The last few miles of road to Montezuma used to be rather bad during the rainy season; hopefully it's better now.

MALPAÍS

Malpaís is Spanish for "badlands." The region certainly lives up to its name with rugged, twisted, and bizarre rock formations breaking the surf as ocean waves crash into spray and foam. Malpaís is said to be one of the better surf destinations in Costa Rica—actually it's at nearby Santa Teresa. The settlements here are located about as far as you can drive around the tip of the peninsula. The road up the other side of the peninsula is just about nonexistent. I've heard people claim they've driven four-wheel-drives up the western edge, all the way up the coast to Sámara, but that seems reckless to me.

Along with most of the Nicoya Peninsula's tourist areas, the Malpaís area is continually growing and attracting more retirees and businesses. I can see a promising future for the region if the road is ever paved. The government is eager to develop places such as this and will surely devote whatever resources are available for roads and infrastructure.

Unlike Montezuma, the village of Malpaís can truly be described as tranquil. The area is sparsely settled, with not much in the way of a village commercial center. Rather it's a long collection of houses, restaurants, and small hotels scattered along about 2 miles (3 kilometers) of gravel road parallel to the ocean. Cabo Blanco Nature Preserve is to the south. Despite the small population, a surprising number of expats live here. They live in houses dotting the beaches, some more cliffs than beach. The area seems to be peaceful and quiet, probably as quiet as Montezuma is noisy. The last time we visited, there were a number of development sites being laid out in anticipation of new expatriate settlers.

MID-PACIFIC **COAST**

If there is any place in Costa Rica that's bound to bloom with foreign investors and retirees, it would have to be that stretch of beachfront from Jacó to Dominical and, with the newly paved road, south toward Palmar Norte.

Although pretty beaches line the entire Pacific Coast, the Mid-Pacific beaches are the most readily accessible for residents of the populous Central Valley. A short drive or bus ride makes this coast practical for overnight sojourns. A weekend home here is convenient and usable by family and friends, whereas one that requires a five-hour drive over horrible roads might sit vacant most of the year. When the main route has been paved and time-saving shortcuts completed, a drive from Escazú or other suburbs will take as little as an hour to Jacó or two hours to Dominical when the coastal highway is totally paved. Today, add an extra hour to allow for the dirt road south of Quepos to Dominical.

PLAYA JACÓ Very popular with residents of the San José region, Playa Jacó and other nearby beaches offer the most convenient opportunity to enjoy Pacific Ocean beaches. From the residential resort at Punta Leona to Playa Hermosa south of Jacó, a string of beaches bring thousands of weekenders for surfing, swimming, and partying. Since it's only about a two-hour drive from San José, it's entirely possible to drive here in the morning, enjoy the surf, and be home in time for supper. No surprise that many Central Valley residents have weekend homes here. Several hundred North Americans and many Europeans make their permanent homes here.

Jacó is the largest and most developed town along the portion of the coast (about 4,000 inhabitants) and has everything you need, from good medical care to discos and casinos. The main street is sprinkled with open-air restaurants where members of the foreign community can be seen socializing, day or evening. Since Jacó is one place where beach property can be owned rather than leased, it's possible to find a home right on the ocean, with beach and surf for your front yard.

Many if not most tourist businesses here are owned by gringos and Europeans. Some do quite well because the area's many tourist attractions bring streams of visitors in search of adventure. Every surf and nature sport, from surfing to crocodile safaris, ensures plenty of tourist business. Two eighteen-hole golf courses are open to public play here, one at Marriott's Los Sueños resort, 3 miles (5 kilometers) north of Jacó, and another about 9 miles (15 kilometers) south at Quebrada, Amarilla, the Tulin Resort.

When I asked Mike Gernazian (better known as "Gringo Mike") why so many Americans choose to live in Jacó, he replied, "We want to be close to the big city but still have the pleasure of the clean air and the beach. There are several hundred of us in the area, yet Jacó is small enough that we all know and help one another. If you need to borrow a

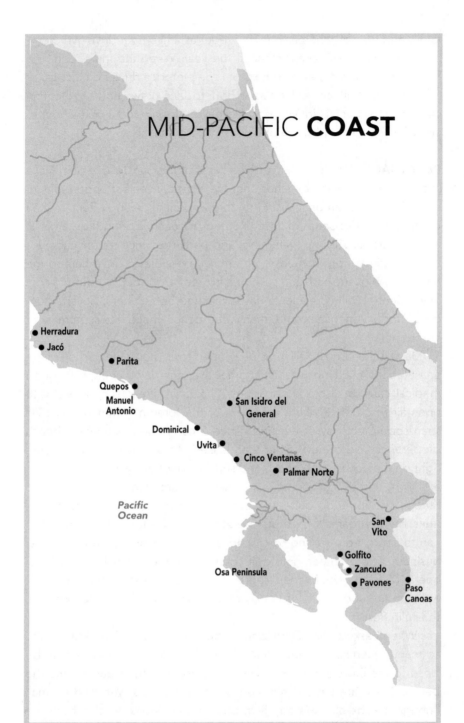

MID-PACIFIC **COAST**

- Herradura
- Jacó
- Parita
- Quepos
- Manuel Antonio
- San Isidro del General
- Dominical
- Uvita
- Cinco Ventanas
- Palmar Norte

Pacific Ocean

- San Vito
- Golfito
- Zancudo
- Osa Peninsula
- Pavones
- Paso Canoas

tool, there is always someone to help. The only spat I have ever seen is over the one copy of *USA Today*'s crossword puzzle at Zarpe's Bar (a gringo hangout). We all want to work it." Mike rents cabins near the beach and says business is booming.

PLAYA HERRADURA Playa Herradura is smaller than Jacó, enjoys gentler surf, and has more shade trees. At the moment Herradura offers economical tourist hotels and weekend homes for highland residents, both Ticos and gringos. But the town extends a promise of better things to come. For a beachfront community, Playa Herradura boasts property that is reasonable—at least compared with prices at Jacó or Manuel Antonio. Many building lots can be found within walking distance of the beach, and construction is booming. An upscale development known as Los Sueños overlooks Playa Herradura. With its large-scale marina, luxury homes, and condos, Los Sueños raises the general tone of Herradura and brings in more development. An eighteen-hole championship golf course is located in the Los Sueños complex.

About 6 miles (10 kilometers) north of Herradura (about 19 miles/30 kilometers north of Jacó), Punta Leona has an attractive private club (with day admission for nonmembers) with a complex of condos and cottages owned by retirees and weekenders from the Central Valley. Like Los Sueños in Herradura, there is a very safe feeling about these gated communities, but prices reflect the additional costs of privacy and luxury.

MANUEL ANTONIO It was the middle of February and we were sitting with a group of friends in a restaurant overlooking the Pacific. A long, palm-fringed beach stretched out into the distance as far as we could see. Behind us loomed mountains covered with rain forest, sweeping down to accent the beach, with its azure blue water and sparkling surf. The sun was at its zenith, beating directly down with dazzling strength. Two members of our group were complaining about the heat. We consulted a thermometer and found that the temperature was 85 degrees. Suddenly they broke into laughter as they realized that Baltimore, their hometown, was dealing with 4 inches of sleet and snow. Two weeks of Costa Rica's idyllic weather had turned them into indignant complainers over an ordinary 85-degree day at the beach! We all ordered a cold beer served over ice cubes (a Costa Rica tradition) and looked out over the panorama with renewed appreciation for where we were: Costa Rica's famous Playa Manuel Antonio.

What kind of name is that for a beach? According to legend, a husband, worried about his pregnant wife, placed her in a dugout canoe and headed north for Puntarenas, hoping to find a doctor to deliver the baby. But before they could go very far, the wife went into labor and they paddled ashore to camp in the shelter of a gentle beach cove. His wife gave birth to a healthy child, whom they named Manuel Antonio; the beach has been called that ever since. Travelers who have visited beaches all over the world swear that Manuel Antonio is the most beautiful of all.

The coastline north of Manuel Antonio is a long shore of golden sand that catches the full force of the Pacific's waves as they roll in from China. Then, at Manuel Antonio Park, a narrow peninsula juts out into the ocean, curving to form two protected coves on either side of the land. Here the waves suddenly become gentle, a place where you can float on your back for an hour without worrying about getting surf in your face. You'll often find a sailboat or two anchored here, gently swaying, resting on the way to the Panama Canal or the big voyage north to Acapulco.

Originally United Fruit Company banana property, the area was made into a national park in 1972 with almost 1,730 acres (700 hectares) of land, partially expropriated, partially donated. The park contains three beaches, each with its own character. The first is Playa Espadilla Norte, which sees occasional riptides, although many people swim here anyway. Next is Playa Espadilla Sur and then Playa Manuel Antonio, both quite safe for swimming and snorkeling. From the beginning the emphasis has been on preserving the natural beauty and protecting wildlife. Whiteface capuchin monkeys frolic in the trees, competing with arboreal iguanas for food. A tropical storm in 1993 ripped up some of the trees, causing the sloth population to go elsewhere, but other than that the damage was minimal.

Since Manuel Antonio's fame makes it an almost obligatory part of a tourist's itinerary, a bed-and-breakfast or room rentals can be a viable business. Rooms are likely to be rented solidly through the summer (December, January, and February) and to have low vacancy rates during the rest of the year. During a recent trip we rented an apartment from a woman who came from Florida several years prior to build a small house for herself. She added a couple of rooms for extra income during the tourist season. As the volume of tourism during the off-season increased, she added more rooms, until she now has a pleasant ten-room hotel plus two apartments across the road, all with a splendid view of the ocean. "I hadn't considered becoming a hotel owner when I came here," she explained. "It just happened to work out that way."

Over the thirty years that I've been visiting Manuel Antonio, I've seen the most profound changes of anywhere in the country. It has changed from a very rustic, low-density tourist destination to a full-tilt, full-service community. The road from Quepos to Manuel Antonio Park is jam-packed with hotels, restaurants, and other tourist accommodations. Scarcely a square meter of land remains undeveloped. Oddly enough, this doesn't seem to detract one iota of the region's beauty and charm.

DOMINICAL South of Quepos and Manuel Antonio, along the 28-mile (45-kilometer) stretch of gravel road to Dominical, you'll find occasional roads leading to the beach. We've found a few small hotels along this part of the coast, but for the most part this country is either palm-oil plantations or flat farming land. Yet starting with the village of Dominical and heading south, this part of the coast is turning out to be another of those "undiscovered" places with potential for retirement and/or investment.

Before long the Pacific Coast Highway will be paved all the way to Panama, joining the Inter-American Highway at Palmar Norte. This route will take considerable pressure off the present Inter-American Highway as well as open the region to tourism and development. Although a stretch of road south of Quepos is still gravel, it's not a bad drive in a rental car; they keep it graded (however, during the rain of the 2005–2006 wet season, parts of the road were in bad shape).

As paved roads replace the almost impassable stretches of rock-and-mud obstacle courses, ever-increasing traffic streams along the coast—tourists looking for rooms and retirees buying property. The village of Dominical and its surrounding communities can't help but flourish. As you might guess, many foreign residents prefer things the way they are; they dread the thought of developments and tourists destroying the peace and tranquillity that have been theirs for so long. As one man said, "It is funny to think that in a few years we'll be looking back fondly to the time when there were no traffic lights in Dominical."

If you want to drive on pavement all the way to Dominical, travel south on the Inter-American Highway and turn toward the Pacific at San

Isidro del General, then just follow the signs through town. Because of San Isidro's system of one-way streets, you may have to ask directions by pointing in whichever direction you are going and asking "Dominical?" Someone will steer you in the right direction.

In its own way, this road is one of the more scenic in all of Costa Rica. The narrow pavement traverses rich farming country, up somewhat steep grades, running along ridges with breathtaking views on both sides of the road, looking into deep valleys where the farmhouses are so distant that they seem like toys. Even during the dry season, the countryside is lushly green, plants heavy with foliage and banana trees shading the roadside. Although the drive is less than 25 miles, it takes about forty-five minutes. That's the way it should be, because the scenery is so spectacular that you might miss something if you could whiz along at 60 miles per hour. Also, the pavement has a way of disappearing from time to time, turning into stretches of gravel road where construction crews are still at work. The problem is not serious; just slow down and relax.

The paved highway ends at the newly paved coastal road at the Barú River, a picturesque mountain stream that empties into a lagoon at this point. A turn to the left, over the river's new cement bridge, and you find Dominical. Take the first right turn past the bridge. This is another place I've watched develop over the years, from a sleepy village to an awakening, cosmopolitan community. It is my impression that this region is one of the fastest-growing along the coast—at least as far as residential development is concerned. Excellent restaurants and other retail businesses seem to be popping up in response to the growing number of expatriates in the Dominical area.

Dominical's main street (there are only a few streets here) follows the river past several rental cabins and businesses. It ends at the beach, where another road follows the shore down to Punta Banda, also known as Roque Azul. Camping beneath a grove of shade trees is free on the edge of the broad, sandy beach of Playa Dominical. Rest rooms and showers are strategically spaced along the beach. For the most part, campers are Tico families and backpackers, but all are welcome. As with anywhere in Costa Rica, be careful of leaving valuables in a tent while you are surfing or dining in a restaurant.

Open ocean surf here is spectacular, booming across the beach, occasionally making swimming hazardous when riptides harass those not used to handling them. "You usually don't realize what is happening," said a longtime resident here. "It seems as though you are staying still in the water, yet the beach is moving away from you. We lose a couple of tourists every year to these tides, and it isn't necessary. Instead of trying to swim against the current, the best thing to do is relax and leisurely swim parallel to the beach, until the shore stops moving away. The current is only a few feet wide. Then work your way back to shore, pausing to float on your back and rest. The water is so warm and salty that you can float all day long and never get tired. There is no reason for anyone to drown in a riptide."

UVITA South of Dominical, as far as the village of Uvita (11 miles/18 kilometers distant), numerous beaches face the open ocean, some with houses or tiny farms, places that will someday become villages. One of the prettiest on this part of the coast is called Punta Dominical. A high point juts out into the ocean, with cliffs and surf reminiscent of California's Big Sur or Spain's Costa Brava. Below a small hotel, cliffs and rocks catch the full force of the ocean's strength as waves crash and send cascades of white foam flying high in the air.

Most desirable property along this coast seems to be owned exclusively by foreigners, many of whom don't appear to be particularly eager to sell and, when they do, not at bargain prices. Occasionally a beachfront property will be found at a highly inflated price. Affordable property is found away from the beach, where Ticos have land for sale. I looked at one parcel in Uvita, about half a mile from the beach, twelve acres of land with a comfortable house for half of what it would cost near Dominical. There were many fruit trees and enough pasture for keeping a horse or two.

A longtime resident named Lillian said, "We looked all over Costa Rica before settling on Uvita. We found a ten-hectare [25-acre] plot up on the mountainside. Not only do we have a gorgeous view, but there are also six beautiful waterfalls on the property. For me it's like having my own national park." She added, "We are holding it in trust for our two granddaughters, as a future for them."

A difficulty with small communities such as Uvita is a lack of enough residents to form an effective community organization. Local residents hold informal meetings but not enough attend to get much done. (Most unimproved properties belong to absentee owners.) This is due to change, however, since the pavement now connects with the Inter-

American Highway at Palmar, just a few miles south. Rapid development is under way as some prime land is now available for development.

A problem with lightly populated areas like Dominical or Uvita is the lack of sophisticated medical care. Often a resident doctor in the village can handle emergencies, but for serious problems, the nearest emergency clinic in this region is in Platanillo, about 8 miles (13 kilometers) from Dominical, or the hospital in San Isidro, some 28 miles (45 kilometers) distant. Uvita's medical needs are taken care of in Palmar Norte.

This problem of medical care was brought home to me on a recent trip. As I was driving from Dominical to San Isidro, a *campesino* (peasant) ran out into the road and flagged me down. His hand was bleeding from an accident, and he needed to get to the hospital. I had to act as an ambulance driver, not knowing whether to go top speed and risk killing us both or to slow down while my patient bled to death. He was the calm one, as he insisted on trying to show me his wound and describing in minute detail what had happened. Fortunately, we both survived.

CINCO VENTANAS The road from Dominical south to Palmar Norte (where it joins the highway going to the Panamanian border) is brand-new and a marvel compared with the old rock-and-mud nightmare trail of a few years ago. Today it is a matter of ten or fifteen minutes from Dominical instead of the hour and a half it took me the first time I made the trip. The road zips on down the coast past areas that before were seen only by four-wheel-drive daredevils.

One very interesting place we encountered last year is called Cinco Ventanas. Even though development here is rather new, there are already 1,400 properties owned by foreigners (only a few live here full-time). A fourteen-unit shopping center including a small supermarket, gasoline station, and restaurant serves the area. The majority of the foreign property owners are French-Canadian, but other North Americans are discovering the area and will be moving in as well.

The developer explained why there are so many French-speaking residents: When she and her husband started their project here, they advertised heavily in the Quebec area as an experiment. They sold building lots by mail, with the buyers being assured that if they didn't like the property when they arrived, they could either have their money back or choose another lot. Before long, most of the lots they had were gone,

bought by French-speakers." They just love it here," she said, "and since French is similar to Spanish, they have no problems with language."

Just east of Cinco Ventanas, the mountains quickly rise to more than 3,000 feet (914 meters), providing the same kind of "air-conditioning" as in Dominical, with breezes coming inland during the hot part of the day, and cool breezes flowing down the mountains at night. By the way, the name Cinco Ventanas (Five Windows) refers to some natural caverns in the cliffs by the water's edge. Residents in this area have exclusive rights to cross the private land between the highway to Playa Ventanas, a small bay with a wide beach and bordered on both sides by rocky cliffs ranging in height from 60 to 200 feet, making this one of the few "private" beaches in the country.

SOUTHERN **COSTA RICA**

For years I had heard people speak of Golfito and the Osa Peninsula. The area sounded like a place of adventure—panning for gold in forest streams, fishing for trophy sailfish, or hiking rain-forest trails. In order to complete research for this book, I resolved to spend some time around Golfito to collect information. But when I asked folks around San José who either owned property or regularly visited here, I found their answers short and vague, always skirting the subject as if trying to draw my attention elsewhere. When I spoke with a man who owned property on Zancudo Beach, his face burned angrily as he said, "Zancudo is my special place, and I don't want any damned travel writers drawing attention to it! It would destroy things for all of us!"

Obviously, our interview was over, but now I knew I had to go! I jumped in a car and was soon on my way to Golfito, the jumping-off place for the Pavones–Zancudo Beach area. The drive south on the Inter-American Highway is gorgeous. One unbelievable view after another invites a pause wherever the car can be parked safely off the pavement. Ordinarily the trip takes six hours, but by the time I stopped several times to sample pork *chicharrones*, marvel over the views, and take a nap in the shade of a banana tree, the trip stretched into an eight-hour day. When truck traffic is diverted along a completed new coastal highway, you might be able to make the trip in five hours from San José.

GOLFITO Golfito is the jumping-off place for nearby and regional expatriate communities. This is an often neglected part of Costa Rica, with scanty information provided by most tourist guides. The town of Golfito began its existence as a banana port for United Fruit Company but was abandoned when a disease damaged the banana crops and the company decided that the operation had become unprofitable. When it was a banana port, there was no incentive to develop it as a tourist attraction, although today the area is trying hard to do so.

The town itself can hardly be described as anything but picturesque. It looks like a cliché movie set of a banana-shipping port. Just a few blocks wide, the town follows the water's edge, with some houses actually standing over the water on stilts and others clinging to the cliffs and hanging out into empty space. A couple of excellent hotels accommodate the growing number of curious tourists, but many lodgings are rather ordinary to downright rustic. They are often full with Costa Rican shoppers who take advantage of the port's duty-free warehouse. From the slope of a low mountainside overlooking the town, a rain forest serves as a wildlife preserve and watershed, ensuring Golfito a pure water supply.

Golfito's main commercial street, looking delightfully ramshackle and picturesque, climbs a hill that parallels the highway and waterfront. Foreign residents patronize a couple of open-air restaurants here, as well as hardware stores, shops selling tackle and boating supplies, and several red-light bars. A surprising number of North Americans live in or around Golfito. A few actually live in town, but most have places scattered along the shores of Golfo Dulce and commute via motorboat. Ferries commute between Puerto Jiménez and to Zancudo. You'll often see expats hanging out in the restaurants in the commercial area or along the waterfront. Ask around to find out which are the favorite haunts of the day.

The government is working hard to bolster the economy in this region, trying to attract new businesses to fill the void left when United Fruit abandoned ship. One popular program that brings hoards of residents into Golfito: duty-free warehouses. Anybody, resident or tourist with a passport, can obtain a permit to enter these warehouses and purchase a wide variety of goods duty-free. To make sure that Golfito tourist facilities gain from this, buyers must register the day before—thus ensuring that they will spend money on meals and accommodations. You are allowed $500 per person tax-free every six months.

Another project that helps local commerce is a Free Trade Zone, a special place for manufacturing and exporting by Costa Rican and foreign businesses. Those operating within the zone's coverage are exempt from some taxes and customs on importation of raw materials, components, and parts. This should attract investors who would like to take advantage of the tax breaks and the availability of good local workers.

ZANCUDO BEACH   Although Golfito is the central focus of the area, many North Americans prefer to live nearby rather than in the town. Their homes and business interests are in nearby villages or on isolated bays around the Golfo Dulce. Playa Zancudo is one of the secluded communities that attracts expatriates. It's a relatively small village stretching along one sandy street with a handful of restaurants, cabin rentals, and a small hotel or two. The black-sand beach is backed by homes not far from the water's edge but concealed from the view of swimmers and surfers by the usual coconut and strangler fig trees. Zancudo is a popular place for local Ticos to come to swim on weekends. Unlike Pavones, the famous surfing beach to the south, Zancudo's beach is very swimmable, with gentle surf.

Several bars and restaurants serve as social centers, with occasional weekend dances. A stop at any of the local open-air restaurants will usually find a table or two of North Americans or Europeans discussing local news and making plans for the development of their properties. Paving the road is a common topic. Those who own homes along the beach shudder in horror at the image of the throngs of tourists, property buyers, and developers a paved highway will surely bring. They feel that since they have discovered this part of Costa Rica, it is rightly theirs, and it would be downright rude for others to crowd in. (I'm exaggerating, of course. Residents of Zancudo are as gracious as you will find anywhere). Actually, those who have businesses, who depend on tourists and new residents to make their enterprises grow, eagerly look forward to the road and the increased prosperity popularity brings. Property owners are delighted to see values of their holdings increasing.

We spoke with several folks who routinely come here for three months or longer every year. A house or a cabin with a small kitchen, right on the beach, can usually be found at reasonable rents during the off-season. By all means, stay for a couple of months before deciding to invest or build, get to know the other expatriates, and know whether you will find enough compatible friends. This will also give you the opportunity to talk with local residents and get the latest on land values and who has properties for sale.

A local resident remarked, "Everyone wants to come here in the winter months (referring to winter and summer in the North American sense). People seem to think that summer is a total monsoon. But the weather is wonderful then. It's actually a little cooler during June, July, and August. Every morning is sunny, and at least part of the afternoon is usually rain-free. Often it doesn't rain at all." The hottest month of the year is March, according to local residents, just before the rainy season gets started.

Buses and stake-bed trucks bring families from nearby towns on weekends, loaded with children eager to enjoy the beach. The waves are gentle, the water's warm, and the kids are in danger of nothing worse than sunburn. An easier way to get here is by water taxi from Golfito. Schedules vary with the tides.

The shortest way to the beach is a two-hour drive over a gravel and sometimes rocky trail. This same road splits off and goes to Zancudo's sister beach to the south, Pavones. During the rainy season this route requires a four-wheel-drive vehicle, and it's not all that great in the summer. Maps don't help much in finding either Zancudo or Pavones. I have three different maps: For all practical purposes they might as well have been of three different countries, because each has a different version of the road system, none approaching reality. It's best to stop often and make inquiries.

SAN VITO

Shortly after World War II, Luigi Sansonetti and three sons from Italy decided to investigate Costa Rica as a place for a new beginning, away from the chaos of postwar Europe. They fell in love with a beautiful valley surrounded by mountains and rain forests. Their discovery was in the canton of Coto Brus, just north of the Panamanian border, in one of the coastal mountain ranges of the southern region. At 3,200 feet (975 meters) above sea level, with cool mountain breezes and ample rainfall, this seemed to be the perfect place to grow coffee and begin life anew.

They notified friends and relatives back in Italy of their discovery and invited them to relocate here. Before long Italian immigrants were settling the town of San Vito de Coto Brus and planting coffee on the hillsides. It wasn't easy. The pioneers suffered hardships as they established their colony: hand-sawing huge trees for lumber, cutting them into boards to build houses, no electricity, little food, and having to wait for three years for coffee to be ready for harvesting. Partly by courage but mostly by stubborn determination, they survived.

Fortunately, in the early 1950s the world market for quality Costa Rican coffee was at an all-time high. Coffee plantations could not help but prosper. Their economic success is reflected in San Vito's infrastructure today and in the quality of homes and farms surrounding the town. You'll find banks, supermarkets, Internet centers, great restaurants and bakeries, taxi service, as well as a hospital and nearby airport. A charming plaza in the town center makes a pleasant place for young people to congregate and residents to relax.

San Vito's population today is around 10,000, and the town still displays prosperity, even though the coffee market tanked a few years ago. Many of the original families have moved on, but they've left their mark on today's population. Around the square and in outdoor cafes, you'll see beautiful young people with faintly olive-colored skin and strikingly beautiful grey-blue eyes characteristic of regions in Italy. You'll often hear Italian spoken. You might hear "*ciao*" instead of *adios* when someone says goodbye.

San Vito's best restaurants are Italian, as you might expect. One is the

dining room of the popular Hotel Ceibo, where lasagna, scaloppini, and other traditional dishes are served. The owner, Antonio Papili, was one of the original settlers. He was 5 years old when his family immigrated from Italy. He is proud of his heritage and it doesn't take much encouragement for Antonio and his wife Carmen to talk about the old days.

I have to admit that I had reservations about including San Vito in this book. Why? Because I made friends with some of the North Americans who've relocated here, and because some worried that publicity might cause a land rush, bringing hordes of new residents, along with some undesirables. I gained their grudging support when I pointed out that: First of all, adding a few new residents would only increase their support group of English-speaking neighbors, and secondly, the undesirables they have in mind are the types who prefer the action of beachfront discos and all-night reggae or rap music.

I am convinced that it will be some time before we'll see surfboards and party animals elbowing aside the two dozen or so expatriates in residence in San Vito. The most exciting things to do here are gazing at breathtaking vistas of the mountainous Amistad International Park and the volcano across the Panama border; visiting the nearby, world-famous Wilson Botanical Gardens; and having cocktails at homes of other San Vito expatriates.

CHAPTER EIGHT

THE
CARIBBEAN COAST

The same mountain chain that creates the delightful temperate weather in Costa Rica's highlands separates the country into eastern and western tropical zones. Because of this separation, the Caribbean and the Pacific zones have dissimilar personalities. Not only will you find differences in weather patterns and varieties of animal, plant, and marine life, but distinctive cultural differences as well. The Caribbean is Jamaican/African; the Pacific is Latin/European.

The word "tropics" implies long stretches of deserted beaches with thick jungle hovering at the edge of the sand. It means monkeys jostling branches in the strangler fig trees while parrots, macaws, and 1,000 other birds screech, twitter, and sing lyrically in the sunset. Costa Rica's Caribbean Coast has all of the above and much more.

Often referred to as the Talamanca Coast, it consists of two distinct regions. The northern half is almost uninhabited, visited mostly by fishing fanatics, tourists, and ecology students. (Incidentally, Costa Ricans usually refer to this entire coast as the "Atlantic" rather than the "Caribbean.") The southern coast is populated with a mixture of Jamaican culture and black, white, and Indian races, creating a distinct type of Tico personality.

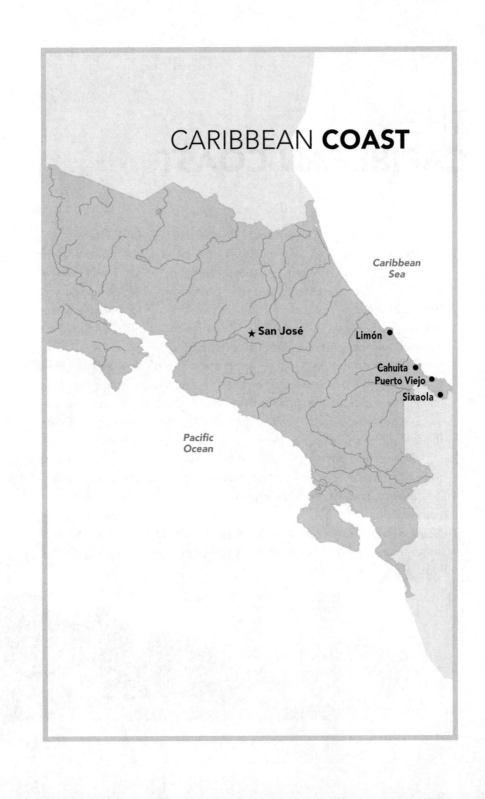

CARIBBEAN **COAST**

Caribbean
Sea

★ San José

Limón ●

Cahuita ●
Puerto Viejo ●
Sixaola ●

Pacific
Ocean

The northern inland lagoons and waterways are famous for world-class fishing of all kinds. Record-size tarpon and snook are routinely hooked in these scenic jungle rivers and inlets. The best snook angling is usually from the shore, around river mouths, with twenty- to thirty-pounders not uncommon. Fishermen also bring in jacks, mackerel, barracuda, snapper, and other species when fishing the Caribbean Coast. While waiting for exciting action, you are treated to the sight of monkeys frolicking in the trees, an occasional parrot or toucan darting among the branches, and sometimes a crocodile lurking along the shoreline. The Tortuguero area is known as an important nesting place of the endangered green sea turtle.

No passable roads enter this northern region; the only way to get here is by airplane or motor launch. My belief is that the area is far too isolated and the climate too humid for development other than ecotourism projects.

SOUTHERN **CARIBBEAN**

The southern Caribbean Coast attracts surfers, snorkelers, and reggae enthusiasts, as well as ordinary tourists and ecology buffs who want to savor the unique tropical environment. Weather patterns here are unpredictable, with no sharp distinction between winter and summer. Rain can fall at any time and usually does. Winds often blow down from the north, sometimes causing the Caribbean Coast to replicate Miami's weather. The plus side of the Caribbean weather is that things stay green and lush year-round, unlike the Pacific Coast, where it seldom rains between December and May. The downside is that this weather is always more humid, and insects tend to grow healthy and robust on this edge of the continent.

There is a tendency among North American expatriates to view this region with suspicion of crime and drug use. There have been a couple news stories of crimes that did severe damage to the tourist image. However those who live here paint an entirely different picture. They point out that these incidents can happen anywhere, and just by chance they occurred in their region.

Our experience with this area is limited to short stays and visits with friends, never staying more than a few weeks at a time. Therefore I felt it would be best to get opinions from folks who actually live here before making recommendations for relocation. We've interviewed several expatriates who live on the Caribbean Coast for their views and recommendations. One person—who prefers to be called "Expat Hatch"—lives near Puerto Viejo, and had the following to say about the eastern coast of Costa Rica:

"The Talamanca Coast (not Limón city, but from Hone Creek to Puerto Viejo, then down to Manzanillo) to me represents what ¡Pura Vida! is all about: the jungle, the beach, the environment, and the people. A unique mix that you either love or you hate. I happen to love it.

"Yes, there is the Caribbean drug corridor, but the serious things that go down remain largely invisible—just don't get involved. And yes, you may find yourself feeling even more laid-back after breathing the ganja-laden collective cloud coming from backpacker and surfer hangouts and wafting over the area from Playa Negro to Playa Cocles. But if crime were truly serious here, you wouldn't see the elderly gringo ladies who live here riding their bikes up and down the road with smiles on their faces.

"I personally believe that most of the negative hype about the Caribbean side boils down to culture shock, which seizes white folks who aren't used to seeing so much 'black' when they walk into Limón from the cruise ship docks. Things are definitely not white, clean, and tidy there. Limón is a third-world city populated by Caribbean descendants of Jamaica, Panama, and Nicaragua. If that's not what you want to experience, then don't go there, because it's not been prettied up for tourism at this point.

"But as you go from Limón down the Talamanca coast, you will meet a broad mix of people: Ticos, indigenous Indians, Jamaicans, Panamanians, Nicaraguans, and Europeans such as German, French, Polish, and Italian. It truly becomes a rainbow soup of humanity, which I personally think makes it that much more interesting.

"But *Pura Vida* does have a price here—forget making a list of twenty things to do in the day. Because you'll only get two of them done if you're lucky. Things are more primitive here. I just smile, say ¡Pura Vida! to myself and chalk it up to the universe forcing me to slow down after working seventy-hour weeks in the U.S.A. rat race for so many years. The bottom line for me is that I can sit in a hammock writing on my laptop, with the beach in front of me, the jungle behind me, and howler monkeys making awesome sounds while they meander through the trees in my backyard. *That's* why I moved to Costa Rica—not for conveniences."

LIMÓN The city of Limón, a two-and-a-half-hour drive from San José, is probably where Columbus sighted the American mainland for the first time back in 1502. Since nothing of value was found, the explorers moved on, leaving this coast to the native Indians and later, scattered villages where bananas were grown for export. Until a railroad was constructed from San José to Limón, the area was mostly ignored by those living in the highlands. Many of the settlers were English-speaking Jamaicans of African descent. Many came to work on the banana plantations and later to build the railroad.

At best, the city of Limón has always been a ramshackle affair—a tropical banana port, too large to have the charm of a small town, yet too small to offer the amenities of a real city. The population is predominately black, and the major business here is related to shipping. Not many expatriates will care to relocate here, in my opinion.

Having exposed my bias toward Limón, I must point out that there are those who disagree with me. A number of North Americans who reside in the community testify to the charm and friendliness of their African/Jamaican neighbors. Racial tensions, resentment, and animosity that are so common in some U.S. cities are virtually unknown here. The social atmosphere here is relaxed, friendly, and neighborly. In fact, Costa Rican race relations and attitudes toward citizens of color are very different from those in many other parts of the world. Because many people in Limón speak perfect Spanish as well as English (with a British-Jamaican accent), those with education are much in demand in the business world. They often find positions as supervisors or managers. They can communicate with London, New York, or Geneva (English being the lingua franca of business today), and they can deal with North Americans and Europeans who speak very little Spanish.

The number of foreigners living in Limón is difficult to ascertain. I asked a friend who lives in Limón to make an estimate and he replied, "I can't put a solid number on the expats here, but we just celebrated Thanksgiving with about twenty-five of them. We had a great dinner with turkey and all the trimmings—a full-blown Turkey Day, including watching football. I've met teachers in the Caribbean School [English-Spanish], Peace Corps people, semi-retirees, Evangelical missionaries, and ship's chandlers [people who are commissioned to buy or supply provisions for all the freighters that come into port]. We have also run into a few retired people who have been here for many years and still haven't learned any Spanish."

CAHUITA One hundred fifty years ago, the beaches of Cahuita and Puerto Viejo were uninhabited except for seasonal campsites of Miskito Indians who followed the migration of green and hawksbill turtles. ("Miskitos" are a mixture of native Indians and escaped African slaves who fled Jamaica and Cuba to settle the coasts of Nicaragua and Panama.) The newcomers named their camp *Cahuita*, which means "Point of blood trees" in Miskito dialect, because of the large number of blood trees growing on the promontory now known as Cahuita Point.

The region remained uninhabited until the late 1800s, when William Smith, an English-speaking Afro-Caribbean who came from Panama every year to fish and hunt turtles, decided to build a permanent home on Cahuita's beach. He was joined by a group of Jamaicans who originally came as construction workers on the railway from Limón to San José. In addition to working on the United Fruit Company's banana plantations, the settlers worked at subsistence farming, hunting, and fishing and small-scale cultivation of cocoa. Settlers here were pretty much self-sufficient, having had little contact with the rest of Costa Rica. (In fact, for many years the central government prevented people from the coast from traveling to the highlands for fear of spreading yellow fever and malaria.) The first road to Cahuita didn't connect with the outside world until 1976. This isolation enabled people here to preserve their African-Jamaican-Caribbean heritage and bring it intact into the twenty-first century.

Because English is the area's first language (usually spoken with a delightful Jamaican patois), this area is favored by tourists and visitors who don't want to bother learning another language during their stay. The genuine lack of racial tension here is refreshing for those of us who have been used to the self-imposed social barriers and chasms of hostility that separate black from white in some areas of the United States. I personally feel welcome here and enjoy basking in the warmth of genuine hospitality.

The village of Cahuita is a three-and-a-half-hour scenic drive from San José. It's about four hours by bus. The village's Afro-Caribbean setting has a picture-book quality. Many houses stand on stilts to discourage insects as is the custom in African and Caribbean villages. These buildings tend to be painted with bright, contrasting pigments similar to the flamboyant styles of Jamaica. Slender, colorfully dressed women and girls carry bundles on their heads with grace and enviable posture. It's easy to imagine you are in an African seashore village.

The main road follows the shore, past black-sand beaches and coral reefs to the north and past more coral and beaches of yellow sand to the south. Along the yellow-sand beach is Cahuita National Park, an 8-mile (13-kilometer) stretch of jungle complete with howler monkeys (which the Costa Ricans call *congos*), feisty parrots, and wildlife of all descriptions. A foot trail parallels the beach through a thick tangle of tropical trees, vines, and orchids. Butterflies, orange and purple land crabs, and iguanas keep you company on the hike.

Many North Americans and Europeans live here year-round, some operating successful businesses. Others regularly arrive in November and head home by May. I had the good fortune to meet a young California couple who invited me to visit their winter quarters in Cahuita. They lived in a picturesque, thatch-roofed cabin perched next to a coral reef and shaded by graceful coconut trees. Their house was very rustic, with minimal furniture, but they enjoyed their winter home immensely. Surf washed over rocks in front of the home, spilling into a small depression of smooth black coral where their children played in their own private saltwater swimming pool.

PUERTO VIEJO   The village of Puerto Viejo is 10 miles (16 kilometers) south of Cahuita by road and somewhat less by the beach trail. To make matters a bit confusing, there are two Costa Rican places called Puerto Viejo. The one here is formally called Puerto Viejo de Limón, and the other is a small river town in the northeast, near La Selva Reserve: Puerto Viejo de Sarapiquí.

This Puerto Viejo, on the southern Caribbean Coast, used to be much more sleepy than its sister village of Cahuita. Things have changed, with surfers, Rastafarians, and tourists of all descriptions now thronging through the town. Puerto Viejo has the reputation of being one of the coolest spots in Costa Rica. When discos are going full tilt, especially on weekends, you might find it impossible to find a room. Young visitors and adventure seekers, mostly from North America and Europe, throng the streets in the evening, visiting bars and restaurants throbbing with reggae music.

Yet, intermingled with the under-25 crowd, an older generation of expatriates have their own parallel scene. Dozens of retirees, residents, business owners, and seasonal visitors age 50 and way above live here,

many of their homes just steps from the main street action. They blend in with the younger generation as smoothly as cream and coffee liquor.

There's no question that the beaches here are much nicer than Cahuita, as is the case down the coast, toward the Panamanian border. Not only that, the businesses, bars, restaurants, and so forth are just steps from the beach, often visible through palm trees from the barstool where you are sitting. An additional attraction is that homes can be built within 328 feet (100 meters) of the surf, a happy condition of which many expatriates take full advantage.

WHY THE **CARIBBEAN COAST?**

People who love Cahuita and Puerto Viejo will tell you that the rest of Costa Rica is too tame for them. They prefer this movie-set tropical ambience: romantic, picturesque, and inexpensive. One bar in the very center of Cahuita features on its front porch extraordinarily powerful loudspeakers blaring Jamaican rock music day and night. The volume was such that it rattled windows a block away and peeled the paint off passing automobiles. I love to visit here, but for long-term living in the tropics, my personal preference would be the Pacific Coast. It's my age I suppose.

Others have a completely different take of lifestyles on the Caribbean. To get yet another viewpoint and perspective, I took advantage of my friendship with a couple who make their home in Puerto Viejo by asking how they made their decision.

Doug and Rosin Warren, who moved here from Arizona a couple of years ago, said that numerous other people had e-mailed similar questions about living on Costa Rica's east coast. They wanted to know the "whys" of choosing the Caribbean side rather than other, more popular sections of the country. Here's what Doug had to say about living here:

"We made our decision from the position of someone who wants to live on or very near a beautiful, tropical beach," Doug says. "We realize we're in the minority, since many more people prefer the Pacific beaches. Our viewpoint is sort of a Caribbean versus Pacific comparison, so here it is:

"We honestly believe that the southern Caribbean Coast is the best-kept secret in this entire country. The 20 miles [32 kilometers] or so from Cahuita down through Puerto Viejo and Manzanillo and to the Panamanian border have some of the most beautiful beaches I've ever seen, with white sand and palm trees, where the jungle comes right down to the shoreline. For the most part, the beaches are almost deserted. You can have a whole cove all to yourself if you want.

"On the last 5 miles [8 kilometers] of this section, from Manzanillo to the border, there's not even a road! You walk along an easy trail, right on the beach, and you see nobody. Beaches here are spectacular, clean, unspoiled—if you feel like skinny-dipping in crystal-clear, warm water, knock yourself out!

"Weather is another important factor: 70 degrees early in the morning and then about 85 degrees in the afternoon—that's all twelve months of the year! We don't keep blankets on the bed, just a couple of sheets. The downside is that there is no defined dry season. It can rain anytime, but the showers are usually short, and the rain is always warm.

"Another reason for choosing this area is the price of land. It's much cheaper than just about any place the Pacific side. Our house is 100 meters [328 feet] from the beach, sitting back in the jungle. When we relax on our veranda, we can hear the ocean, but we can't see it. On all four sides of the house, trees grow 30 to 60 feet [9 to 18 meters] high; it's lush with vegetation—all you can see is green. In the front yard we frequently see three-toed sloths, iguanas, parrots, gorgeous blue morphus butter-flies, and more. I'm the first to admit that this is not paradise, but it is damn close to it.

"We had the house built two years ago: two bedrooms, one bath, a little more than 1,300 square feet, with a huge veranda out front, a cov-ered carport, and gorgeous hardwood floors (we sort of splurged on that). Total cost of land and building was about $45,000. Try doing that over in Tamarindo, with just a minute's walk to the beach!

"Another reason we love it here: Small villages are cool places where everyone knows everyone else. When we go into the grocery store, the hardware store, or the bank, they call us by name. That's a touch you just don't find anymore. Yes, I've read about how crime is so bad on this side of the country, but I really have no idea where all that comes from! Sure, petty theft is 'alive and well' over here (as it is everywhere); we've had hik-ing boots and other items taken from our porch when we were foolish enough to leave them out at night. But neither our house nor our car has ever been broken into. (By the way, we do not have bars on any of our doors or windows. I refuse to live in a prison.) We feel perfectly safe strolling through the village at night or walking along the beach at any hour. We do it all the time; we just use common sense.

"Maybe the main reasons we chose this coast are the attitude of the people and the laid-back lifestyle. There's a very strong Jamaican 'yeah, Mon' sort of thing here; it's unlike anywhere else in Costa Rica. You almost get the feeling that time stood still on this coast. They say it looks pretty much the way it did forty years ago. On the other hand, you'll find places on the Pacific side where, if you didn't know better, you'd think you were in San Diego or Hawaii. Thank God, the big resorts and commercial developers haven't discovered this place yet.

"I will be the first to agree that this coast is not for everyone: no shop-ping centers, no movie theaters, no golf courses. But that is exactly why we live here! If we had wanted all of that other stuff, we would have stayed in the States! To sum it up in terms of my '60s generation: 'If you were a yuppie, you belong on the Pacific side. If you were a hippie, come on over here!'"

CHAPTER NINE

A HEALTHY **COUNTRY**

Costa Rica is a healthy place to live. The United Nations recently noted that Costa Rica is in first place in Latin America for the development of preventive and curative medicine, ranking with the United States and Canada among the twenty best in the world. Infant mortality is lower in Costa Rica than in the United States, and the average life expectancy is longer than in the United States. This is not happenstance: The Costa Rican government spends a great deal of money on health care.

For example, in many third-world countries, you play a game of Russian roulette every time you choose a restaurant. A dining room can look wonderful, with white tablecloths, gleaming silverware, and tuxedo-attired waiters, but the kitchen can be a virtual cesspool. Not so in Costa Rica. If a restaurant looks good, then its kitchen will probably be just as nice. I've found very few places where I would hesitate to eat, and I've never been served spoiled food. This is due in some measure to the high quality of the underground water supply but also to the Ticos' natural inclination toward neatness and order. The level of cleanliness of Costa Rican restaurants is remarkable. This is reinforced by frequent visits by health inspectors to make sure that the normal Tico cleanliness is maintained.

Another factor in restaurant safety is the relative scarcity of houseflies in most parts of Costa Rica. Since this is the tropics, you might expect to see more insects than you would in the temperate zones of North America, and you do, but in balance. For some reason you'll see remarkably few houseflies, true villains in spreading intestinal disease. In San José and other towns on the Central Plateau, you can eat outside at a sidewalk cafe without sharing your lunch with flies. This seems strange to visitors from North America's Midwest, where the fly population blooms in the summer to a plague. Yes, an occasional fly might drift past, curious as to what you are having for lunch and hoping to join you, but nothing like you expect back home in the summer.

The same thing goes for mosquitoes: In the dry season they are as scarce as houseflies. In many areas of Costa Rica, people don't use window screens. (I wouldn't advise this, because you never know what kind of critter might be attracted to house lights in the evening.) However, when in an area where dengue fever is known, mosquito repellent is essential. Mosquitoes can carry this flulike illness, which has also appeared in the southeastern United States. So far it's affected only a few parts of Costa Rica, around Puntarenas and Cañas. A continuing campaign to wipe out the particular mosquito that carries the virus is under way.

One health condition that never fails to impress visitors: You *can* drink the water. Unlike most Mexican and Central American cities, safe drinking water is the rule rather than the exception. Most smaller towns have excellent-quality water, as do most hotels, where drinking water comes from safe wells. As part of its commitment to serving the public, the Costa Rican government spends large sums of money on water and sewage treatment. All water systems, even private ones used by a only a handful of people, are strictly monitored. Every two months, at a minimum, tests are made for purity and submitted to the government agency overseeing water control.

COSTA RICA **MEDICAL CARE**

The U.S. health-care system, with its exclusion of more than forty million citizens from the ranks of the medically insured, is a major reason some folks think favorably about living in a country where health care is not only available but affordable. In a typical U.S. hospital, for example, patients

with Medicare coverage usually pay more for the deductible share of an operation than the total surgical and hospital bill might cost in Costa Rica.

Should you visit an emergency room in the United States, you have to provide proof of a hospitalization plan or a personal credit card. If you have neither, you could be told to get lost. If you have Medicare, you will find a growing number of doctors who won't accept you as a patient. When someone goes to an emergency room in any government hospital in Costa Rica, there is no mandatory charge for resident, visitor, or even someone in the country illegally. If you can pay, they appreciate it, but you will never be turned away. This affordable medical system is another of the benefits Costa Rica enjoys because there is no military or defense industry to absorb resources. Statistics show that the general level of care is equal or superior to that in the United States—and it's available to all citizens, not just those who can afford premiums.

Obviously, the level of health care and facilities cannot be the same in rural and isolated communities as in the metropolitan area of San José. Yet the government tries. To ensure that most villages have medical backup, a system of mandatory medical service sends newly graduated doctors to remote or rural settings for a one-year period. These new doctors have to work for minimum wages for this time as a way of repaying the country for the education received in state universities.

Why is quality health care inexpensive in Costa Rica? A prominent physician (in private practice in San José) explained it this way: "Here, our government considers medical care a public service and obligation, just as it considers education and highways a public responsibility. The government builds hospitals and trains medical specialists to serve the people, not as a business. But in the United States, medical care is a profit-making industry, a big business where profits are maximized to the highest point people can pay. Here, a doctor working for a government clinic earns between $800 and $2,000 a month. In the U.S.A., where doctors work for profit, $20,000 a month is more common."

The doctor went on to say, "Where there is no competition, medical specialists can charge what they like. But here in Costa Rica, we have competition between our free public hospitals and private clinics staffed with private doctors such as mine. We private doctors must keep our fees in line or we lose our patients to free clinics."

MEDICAL **BILLS**

In San José a routine visit to a private physician's office costs between $25 and $50. Specialists tend to charge toward the upper end of the scale. As of summer 2006, a day in a first-class private hospital cost less than $200. Hospital food is excellent, by the way, not the skimpy, tasteless food we're used to in U.S. hospitals, but delicious food and usually more than you can eat. That $200 rate is at one of the country's most expensive hospitals—for a private room, a private bath, and a color television, plus an extra bed and meals for an *acompañate* (a companion). It's customary for a family member or friend to spend the night in your room after an operation or when you are in serious condition, at no extra charge.

If you are willing to put up with sharing a bath with the room next door and can do without your own private phone, the daily room cost can drop to almost half. A day in a first-class hospital in Costa Rica costs about the same as a deluxe hotel room! Compare these prices with those in your community. In the United States if you can get out of a hospital for less than $1,500 a day just for the room, consider yourself lucky.

CHOOSING **A DOCTOR**

Foreign residents can "buy into" the Social Security system (*Caja*, as it's called in Costa Rica) by paying $40 to $50 a month and then going to government hospitals for treatment. However, since medical care is free, it isn't surprising to find the public system well used and crowded. When people don't feel quite up to snuff, they traipse off to the hospital to see a doctor. Of course, for emergency treatment there is no problem—you are seen immediately. But for an ordinary office visit with a government doctor, you could find yourself standing in line or sitting in the waiting room for a long while. For elective surgery, you can expect a wait of several months for your turn.

However, there is a better way: Choose a family doctor who is in both public and private practice. See him or her as your private doctor by making an appointment whenever you have a minor problem and paying for an office visit. But if something expensive ever comes up, such as a major operation, your doctor will check you into the government hospital for free treatment—by the same doctor.

Even if a patient chooses a private doctor and uses a private hospital, costs are ridiculously low compared with those in the United States. For example, in San José the typical bill for a gallbladder operation is $2,500, and for an appendectomy, $1,200 to $1,800.

Again, for those with Medicare, be aware that you're not covered outside the United States. However, those under 70 years of age can buy a health insurance policy from the National Insurance Institute (INS). The last time I checked, the premiums were approximately $500 annually per adult and $250 annually per child. Individual premiums are based on several factors, including age and health history (just like any insurance policy). Several clubs and organizations offer insurance with a group discount (usually 10 percent). Among these are the Association of Residents of Costa Rica (ARCR), the American Legion, and the Canadian Club; sometimes a property owners' association can obtain the discount. An example of medical insurance for expatriates: You can enroll through the Residents' Association ARCR, and take advantage of their special arrangement with the National Insurance Institute for about $37 to $58 monthly per family. Of course, you have to belong to ARCR, with an annual membership fee of $50 to $100 per year. (As a member of the Residents'

Association, you are entitled to many other benefits in addition to health insurance.) Some plans allow you access to any doctor, hospital, clinic, lab, pharmacy, or provider of medical goods and services of your choice. Under other policy plans, you are given a list of affiliated providers.

With a typical policy, 80 percent of medical costs are covered to about $14,000 or $20,000 per year. (This may sound low, but for Costa Rica it's usually sufficient protection.) Covered are costs of a private room, postoperative care, medicines, lab tests, X-rays, CAT scans, cardiograms, therapy, home care, and support systems. For surgical fees the policy pays 100 percent, up to the maximum set level. As is the case with similar policies in the States, you choose from among the hospitals, clinics, and physicians recognized by the plan. When you join you receive a book listing medical providers, which is updated yearly. The list offers a choice of almost 500 physicians, fifteen clinics or hospitals, and almost one hundred pharmacies. Dental and eye care are not covered. After you've been insured for a year, up to 80 percent of prescription drugs are covered.

All expatriates we interviewed swear by the quality of Costa Rican medical care. A friend recently told me: "I've had good and bad experiences with the Caja. I had an emergency appendectomy, got great treatment, speedy, all good, that would have been a whopping $300 out of pocket if I had not had the Caja (at Hospital Mexico).

"My son has had excellent care since birth for his hyperthyroid condition, and an operation he had for frozen head plates came out fine. Hospital de Niños is first-rate. But my cancer situation was different. I had a couple of small operations, then went out of the system for a third, because I felt I was not getting the kind of care I needed. My out-of-pocket for massive surgery (radical neck dissection), six hours in the O.R. at Clinica Biblica, whole thing, O.R., surgeon (U.S. residency at U Michigan and U Miami, head and neck ontological surgery specialty), anesthesiologist, two nights at the hospital, excellent service, food, care, etc., was $6,000, and subsequent radiation at a state-of-the-art outpatient center was $3,000.

"I pay about $20 a month for me and $20 for my child and his mom. I will continue to pay it forever, and save the rest of my money (of the $500 or more I would pay in the U.S.) for any other needs I or they may have. I use a local private doctor for anything the pharmacists can't cure, pay the $20 visit, and she sends the testing to the Caja. I pay for any meds out-of-pocket."

DUAL **SYSTEM**

After graduating from medical school, many Costa Rican doctors go to universities in the United States for further study and to do residencies. This is particularly true for specialists; since Costa Rica is such a small country, there aren't enough patients with the same problem to give a doctor the opportunity to see the wide variety of patients needed to get experience in his or her specialty.

I asked a physician from the United States who had retired to Costa Rica some years ago, "Why would a Costa Rican doctor who does a residency in the United States or Canada return here to work for Costa Rican medical earnings?"

"You have to understand," he replied, "that most doctors only work half-time for the government. The rest of the time, they work for themselves. Take the case of a cardiologist who charges $50 an office visit. If this doctor sees five patients a day, that's $250 a day, or about $50,000 a year, plus his salary from the government. When you consider that income taxes and the cost of living are far less here, and that high malpractice premiums aren't necessary, a huge percentage of the doctor's earnings are available for savings or investment. Even though Costa Rican doctors earn a fraction of what U.S. doctors do, they live here just as well or better, and they can live in Escazú instead of Kalamazoo!"

SAN JOSÉ **HOSPITALS**

Three large Social Security–system hospitals provide San José with round-the-clock emergency care, with regular hours for laboratories, X-rays, pharmacies, and doctors' appointments. These are the Calderón Guardia, San Juan de Díos, and Mexico. Some private hospitals are the Clinica Santa Rita, the Clinica Biblica, and the Clinica Católica, all excellent hospitals.

Next to the Clinica Biblica is the Clinica Americana, an office complex with a group of English-speaking doctors, most of whom did residency in prestigious U.S. university hospitals. The KOP Medical Clinic in Escazú specializes in treating foreigners, with a staff that speaks English, French, Spanish, and Japanese. They offer a wide range of services, including obstetrics, gynecology, pediatrics, and dermatology.

Some emergency rooms specialize; for example, Hospital Mexico specializes in heart problems, and San Juan de Díos has a burn center. All towns of any size will have a hospital, and those that are too tiny often still have a doctor or paramedic and emergency equipment.

The latest and most impressive addition to Costa Rica's medical care system is Hospital CIMA San José, which is located in Escazú. This is one of the largest, most modern facilities in Central America, offering complete clinical laboratory services, radiology (including the only open MRI in Central America), and a full range of medical and surgical specialties. The hospital is affiliated with Baylor University in Dallas, Texas.

MEDICINES AND **LIFE EXPECTANCY**

Most prescription drugs cost slightly less in Costa Rica than in the United States, but for Costa Ricans, prescriptions are horribly expensive. Note that Americans commonly spend more for hypertension and cholesterol-lowering medications and other drugs every month than the average Tico *earns* in a month! Costa Rican physicians are reluctant to prescribe drugs unless the patient absolutely needs them, such as antibiotics to halt an infection.

However, according to recent statistics, the male life expectancy in the United States was 76.9 years. In Costa Rica the life expectancy was 76.22 years. That would indicate that after spending thousands of dollars a year for the latest pharmaceuticals and availability of the most ultimate in high-tech medical treatment, the average American lives only eight months longer than the average Tico. Go figure.

REST HOMES **FOR THE ELDERLY**

Care for infirm elderly patients is excellent in Costa Rica, with the cost paid for by the government. However, I believe that this is something available only to long-term residents who become infirm after being *pensionados* or *rentistas for an extended time.*

A government facility probably won't be suitable for a foreigner because of language and communication problems. But several private full-care facilities are able to address the needs of non-Spanish-speakers. (At least one of these offers specialized care for Alzheimer's patients:

Golden Valley Hacienda in Alajuela; also in Alajuela is the Villa Comfort Geriatric Hotel, which specializes in folks who are not bedridden but who need care in everyday living.) The cost is about $1,500 a month for the services provided.

A facility in Los Yoses, the Hogar Retiro San Pedro, was given high praise recently by an American woman for the care there. Another facility is the Hogar para Ancianos Alfredo y Delia González in Heredia. This one is in the process of starting something new in Costa Rica: a residence-development of individual cottages for senior citizens who do not require full care. Housekeeping services and meals will be provided, as will recreational facilities and physical-therapy services. In addition to medical care, the facility will have recreational, hobby, arts, and travel programs for its people. Residents must be over 65 and able to purchase a cottage. A catalog can be obtained by writing to Apdo. 138 in Heredia.

If the patient is not fluent in Spanish, my recommendation is to personally check out the facility and speak to the employees to see if indeed they can communicate. Not being able to communicate your needs can be very frustrating. I have a friend who was in a facility that he had been assured was bilingual. Once he had a terrible pain in his back and called for some medication. Instead the confused aides brought him a washcloth, a glass of water, and finally some cigarettes (he didn't smoke). Management can exaggerate the facility's English-speaking ability in order to gain a new patient.

COSTA RICA **DENTISTS**

The University of Costa Rica trains medical specialists of all kinds, including highly skilled dentists, periodontists, and orthodontic surgeons. Like medical care, dental care in Costa Rica is affordable. I go to an English-speaking dentist in Pavas who has a very modern clinic. After he received his degree in Costa Rica, my dentist did postgraduate work in the United States.

When asked about Costa Rican dental prices compared with those in the United States, the dentist replied, "Depending upon where you live in the United States, dental care there can be three to six times as expensive. For example, in Costa Rica the standard price for a porcelain cap is $135. In Los Angeles the same work costs from $600 to $700. A bridge typically costs $375 here, but a similar job in Los Angeles would cost at least $1,800. I've had patients who fly here, pay for their hotel, food, and airfare, and still save money."

What about quality? "Dental work in Costa Rica is equal to that done in the U.S.A.," he replied." There is absolutely no difference in the competency of the dentists. However, the quality of dental laboratory work is usually better here in Costa Rica. Don't misunderstand, the U.S.A. also has excellent dental labs, but because they can get the work done cheaper in the Philippines, many dentists routinely send bridgework and dental caps overseas to low-cost laboratories. The quality just isn't up to the standards of Costa Rican or American labs. If I were to have caps or bridgework done in the U.S.A., I'd certainly insist that my dentist use an American dental laboratory."

Charges for dental work vary widely, depending on the part of the country in which you live and on the financial status of the dentist's clientele. You'll pay more in the more affluent suburbs of San José and less in small cities in the provinces. Many smaller towns and few villages have no dental services other than visiting dentists who are sent in by the government to take care of schoolchildren's teeth.

Along with cosmetic surgery, cosmetic/restorative dentistry is becoming a big business here, with huge savings over the cost in the United States or Canada. People have reported savings of $6,000 to $18,000 over prices quoted in the United States and Europe. They've reported satisfaction with the treatment and quality of the dentists.

PLASTIC **SURGERY**

Costa Rica has gained worldwide recognition for another of its medical services: reconstructive surgery, commonly known as plastic surgery. San José is becoming known as "Beverly Hills South" because of the number of people coming here for body renewal. Several excellent surgeons specialize in face-lifts, liposuction, breast reconstruction, and other corrections of nature's imperfections. Not only are Costa Rican plastic surgeons ranked among the best in the world, but their fees are based on Costa Rican medical standards: in a word, inexpensive.

Why would Costa Rica be so popular with those wanting to rid themselves of wrinkles? Besides affordable costs and quality surgery, it turns out that San José is a perfect place to slip away to have an operation because of its climate—never hot, never cold—which makes recuperation faster, safer, and more comfortable. Since the healing process takes three or four weeks, many patients find this a great time to learn Spanish in one of the many "total immersion" schools around the city. These schools provide for homestays with Costa Rican families and have small classes or even individual instruction if you prefer.

Another attractive thing about Costa Rica as a base for cosmetic surgery is that many folks feel embarrassed about having their friends and family know they are going to have it done. Therefore, a growing number of them vacation in Costa Rica, where they are unlikely to run into acquaintances; they have the operation; and they return home a month later, when all traces of the surgeon's handiwork have disappeared.

What does all this cost? Happily, the cost of a face-lift, a breast job, or a tummy tuck with liposuction, including surgery, postoperative care, and hospital stay, is a fraction of what one might pay for a similar procedure in the United States. For example, a complete face-lift costs from $2,000 to $4,000, plus $1,100 for the operating room and two recovery days in the hospital. The same operation in New York or Los Angeles would be $22,000, plus a lot more for the hospital.

San José's leading plastic surgeon is Dr. Arnoldo Fournier, who did his residency in reconstructive surgery at New York's Columbia University and who has the oldest established plastic surgery practice in Costa Rica. Dr. Fournier charges $800 to $1,200 for an eyelid operation when done separately. Nose surgery or liposuction to abdomen and thighs costs about $1,500 to $4,000, compared with U.S. rates of about $15,000 for the same procedures.

How safe is it? Costa Rican hospitals are excellent, with all modern equipment. Personnel are highly trained. Dr. Fournier points out, "Most of my surgery is done under local anesthetic and sedation. The patient is given some pills a couple of hours prior to the operation, and intravenous medication is given by an anesthesiologist during surgery. This is much safer than using a general anesthetic. Some patients just stay one night in the hospital and then check into a bed-and-breakfast for a few days. Others prefer to stay awhile, since hospital rooms don't cost any more than a first-class hotel." For information about plastic surgery, go to www.drfournier.com/ing.

CHAPTER TEN

THE REAL **ESTATE GAME**

The best advice about how and where to buy property in Costa Rica comes from folks who've lived in the country for some time. They can tell you how much you should pay for property and which attorney would best represent you. They also know which real estate brokers are professionals, which are beginners, and which are downright unethical. This book cannot make recommendations on business services such as real estate agencies, simply because of the impossibility of being able to vouch for reliability or character. Personnel can change; brokerages are sold; and Costa Rican real estate agents are not bound by the strict rules of ethics common in the United States and Canada. Your job is to investigate, get recommendations from other expatriates, then make your own, educated selections. When business services are mentioned, we're not endorsing their reliability but simply giving you a starting place for checking out the field. At the time I interviewed these business representatives, I was impressed by their knowledge—but that says nothing of their competence or honesty. These are judgments you must make for yourself.

When I asked a longtime resident who dabbled in real estate why prices sometimes seem to be off the wall, he replied, "I learned in my

contract-law class that the price of a thing is exactly what it will bring. This is especially true here in Costa Rica, because there are no records of buying and selling prices, no 'comparables' at all. People go by word of mouth and rumor about what a neighborhood property sold for. So one crazy buyer paying a crazy price will immediately raise prices all over the area. In the end, most buyers have a price/budget in mind of what they want to pay and can afford; in the end you'll get what you want, you just have to search hard."

Lynn Zamora from Grecia, who sells real estate, made the following comments when asked why the price-per-acre cost of bare land could vary so widely on various-size properties in the same area. Lynn's explanation: "It's a common practice here in Costa Rica to price land depending on how large the entire piece is. For example, a lot that's 600 square meters (approximately one-eighth acre) might have an asking price of $17 dollars per square meter, or $10,200 for the lot (equivalent to $81,600 per acre). To continue the example, in the same neighborhood there is a lot of 1.7 acres. The asking price is $38,000 total (equivalent to $22,353 per acre). Yet an adjoining finca of 206 acres might go for $667,000 (equivalent to only $3,238 per acre).

"There is logic to this method of pricing land. Foremost, the property with the most value here is one with the most street frontage. Therefore the more frontage, the higher the cost. The land way in the back of some large finca, far away from the paved road, is worth much less. Land that has street frontage can be divided into smaller lots for building and sold at pretty hefty prices, as seen in the first example.

"Another thing to remember: Although there's plenty of land for sale here, the great majority of the owners do not really need to sell. They might be happy to sell to some gullible foreigner for double what the land is really worth, because a neighbor once made such a lucrative sale." Then she added, "It is easy to buy here but not so easy to sell if someone bought an overpriced property or one that has a problem. And problems are not so easy to spot beforehand, especially when someone comes with an American mind-set."

I cannot stress enough the importance of being careful and having the services of a good lawyer. Do not be impressed when a property owner or salesperson flashes a *plano catastro* (an impressive, authentic-looking plat map that looks as though it could be a deed) as proof that they either own the land or have authority to sell. This is just a piece of paper: It doesn't matter if it contains an official-looking stamp. Anybody can commission a *plano catastro*. It's just a survey plat, and it proves nothing other than the land in question has been surveyed. A surveyor who worked for me said, "If you want a *plano catastro* on the local soccer field, *no hay problema*. I can make you one." That doesn't mean you own anything more than a just a worthless piece of paper.

Remember: If a deal sounds too good to be true, it usually is. If something doesn't feel right, it probably isn't. Don't let the sun and climate go to your head. Keep this in mind, and Costa Rica's a terrific place to be and possibly a great place for a real estate investment.

DECIDING **WHERE TO RELOCATE**

Most North Americans feel at home in Costa Rica's city and suburban middle-class neighborhoods throughout the Valle Central. They don't feel the need to group together, living in compounds or sealed-off neighborhoods as expatriates do in many other foreign countries. Because Costa Ricans and North Americans are similar in personality and world views, most expats feel right at home with their neighbors. Since juvenile delinquency isn't out of control in most residential areas and because neighborhood kids are generally well-behaved, Americans don't feel threatened as we might in some low-economic areas back home. For these reasons, the price range of housing in Costa Rica is very wide, with inexpensive housing available in perfectly acceptable neighborhoods and towns as well as elegant-view homes on mountain slopes and beach palaces.

Granted, North Americans do tend to congregate in the more expensive areas with nice homes, condominiums, and plush housing developments. But not everyone can afford to live in these neighborhoods, and not everyone wants to live in an English-speaking enclave. Therefore, you'll find foreigners scattered all over the Valle Central and, in fact, all around the country.

One expatriate who has lived here for nearly twenty years with his family of five said, "We live in a Costa Rican barrio with Ticos who are typical of most Costa Ricans I know. They love their families, neighborhood, and country, and [we] all work together at watching out for one another. Our home has never been broken into, and we don't live in a fortress. We have no walls, pit bulls, Dobermans, or security systems. Five minutes and a crowbar could gain entry."

Not only are foreigners right at home in city and suburban areas of Costa Rica, but they also find that they are accepted without any fuss in rural settings and villages away from the Valle Central. This is something you'll definitely not find in the rest of Central America or even in Mexico. In other cultures, a gringo family living in a native community would stand out like a pig wearing a toupee. Your neighbors would look at you as more than a little eccentric, and you would feel bewildered and lonely because the culture is so different. Not so in Costa Rica. I know many gringos who enjoy living in rather humble (and inexpensive) lodgings in picturesque villages, and their neighbors are proud that foreigners would like them so well that they'd want to be neighbors.

This extraordinary flexibility as to where it's possible to live presents a wide variety of alternatives. You can live almost anywhere you want to, and you can buy or rent a range of housing that's almost infinite.

RENTING **IN COSTA RICA**

When you first arrive in Costa Rica, you really should rent for a while to get an idea of where you want to live. Neighborhoods vary greatly in quality of shopping, access to transportation, compatibility of neighbors, and, of course, price. There are some areas where you definitely wouldn't want to live—you can usually detect "bad vibes" quickly—and there are other areas that may look great at first, but later you could be sorry you didn't know about another, more interesting neighborhood. Take your time when looking for a place to live, and ask many questions of fellow expatriates.

To get an idea of what you might have to pay to rent a house or an apartment, check the *Tico Times* classifieds for a wide range of rents. The last time I looked—in fall of 2006—houses and apartments were offered at rents ranging from $350 to $2,500 a month (and even higher). While the $2,500 place should be spacious and luxurious, chances are the $350-a-month place could be perfectly livable and just as nice as places back home that rent for twice that amount. Don't rent on price alone, however; check out the neighborhood closely.

For many Costa Rican families, the idea of paying even $350 a month is prohibitive. (Remember, that $350 is considered a nice monthly salary for many Ticos.) So if you are looking for the rock bottom in rents, check the classifieds in the Spanish-language newspaper *La Nación*. The ads in that paper are read by local people who do not have the ability to pay higher rents.

When trying out Costa Rica for livability, most people don't enter into long-term rentals or sign leases until they are certain they want to settle in for a long time. An ideal way to savor living in the country, particularly on the Valle Central, is to rent an apartment by the month or the week. Short-term rentals are particularly useful when determining which neighborhood you'd like to settle in. San José has several apartotels, small furnished apartments complete with cable TV, telephone, and cooking utensils—in short, everything you need for a trial of Costa Rican living.

Another excellent way of discovering whether you like a neighborhood or a city is to rent a room in a Costa Rican home. Because of pressure on hotels for tourist rooms a few years back, many private families converted spare bedrooms into rentals for the busy seasons. They're delighted to host North Americans on their visits, to take them into their homes and treat them as part of the family. Another possibility is a bed-and-breakfast located in the neighborhood you want to investigate. The owners can provide invaluable information about the area.

BUYING **REAL ESTATE**

Many if not most countries in the world severely restrict the rights of foreigners to buy property. Some absolutely prohibit it. Not Costa Rica. This is one country where you needn't be a citizen or go through all kinds of legal gymnastics in order to own property. If you're financially capable of buying it, it's yours.

The standard recommendation to visitors is to wait at least six months before buying property. However, many catch real estate fever within the first few days of their initial visit and end up buying something anyway. For a while the buying spree in Costa Rica diminished somewhat, but people from all over the world are still plunking down money to buy something—anything—before it's all gone. At the present time, the dollar is weak against the euro and some other foreign currencies, down sometimes as low as 30 percent under the dollar's peak rate. This makes Costa Rica properties look very attractive to Europeans who desire to move to Costa Rica and puts an upward pressure on prices. Over the past several years, the real estate market has been gradually going up at a higher rate than inflation, but from my point of view, many properties are still bargains. My guess is that the boom will continue, with predictable cycles of frequent selling followed by slack periods, just before another sellers' market.

Some people are surprised when researching home prices by the Internet or looking at ads in the *Tico Times*. Prices are sometimes higher than expected. There are plenty of places to be found at bargain prices, but you must realize that there are several levels of real estate, from the very cheap to the ultraexpensive. If you're looking for something at the lower end of the scale, Internet and English-language newspapers aren't the best places to look. When property is a real bargain, it won't be on the Internet and it probably won't be in the *Tico Times* either. The more affordable properties are usually bought and sold by Ticos, who read *La Nación* or *La Republica*, and who don't have access to the Internet. When the price is much over $60,000, most Ticos and those gringos with ordinary budgets can't buy. The advertisement for these properties goes into places where well-to-do buyers will see it, like on the Internet. The same goes for rents. A house or apartment that rents for $200 a month doesn't need to be advertised in a newspaper or posted on the Internet; word of mouth takes care of it. But a luxury place that rents for $2,000 or sells for $300,000 needs to be exposed to a different market.

For twenty years armchair experts have been saying that Costa Rica real estate is overpriced, that the market has peaked and is sure to tumble. Overpriced compared to where? Clearly, you can buy a home in Nicaragua, El Salvador, or Panama for a fraction of the price in Costa Rica. If you want to live in Nicaragua, be my guest. These same experts have been predicting the collapse of California real estate for twenty years. Yet prices keep going up, despite the fact that you can buy cheap property in places like Oklahoma, Nebraska, or Kentucky. The reason Costa Rica and California real estate keeps appreciating is a basic principle called "supply and demand." When a surplus of buyers feel they'd rather live in San José than Nicaragua, prices will be higher in San José. Should they prefer Scottsdale to Sioux City, home prices will rise to meet the demand in Scottsdale.

As an indication of how many foreigners are buying real estate in Costa Rica today, private banks have started financing sales by granting mortgages. Previously, this was unheard of. Sales had to be handled by cold cash up front. Of course, the loan will be in dollars, and the interest rates are somewhat higher than you'd pay up north. (A friend is paying 8 percent variable on a fifteen-year loan.) If you're not a resident or a resident in progress, you'll probably pay an extra percentage in interest. I hope I'm not making this sound easy, because the few people I know that have received financing had to wade through complicated applications and provide letters from their home bank and/or employer. Obviously, banks are concerned that you can and will pay off the mortgage rather than walk away and leave them with a foreclosure.

TICOS **ARE NOT NAIVE!**

Some newcomers to Costa Rica have the mistaken notion that there are two prices for real estate: the "gringo price" and the "Tico price." They sincerely believe Ticos are simple, naive country folk who will ask for less money from another Tico than from a foreigner. Therefore, they believe the trick is to have a Tico do the negotiating for them. They also believe that bargain real estate can be had because most Ticos don't know the real value of their properties.

First of all, it is more than a little arrogant for strangers to come to Costa Rica and assume that they know more about the real estate market than Costa Rican landowners, who have lived here all their lives and are thoroughly familiar with selling prices. To assume they might sell property at less than its value to another Costa Rican is very naive on the part of the prospective buyer. Money talks. When we are talking about desirable properties—those with ocean views or in pleasant neighborhoods with elegant homes—realize that virtually all of these properties are owned either by wealthy Tico families, North Americans, or Europeans, few of whom are naive or ignorant of the value of their property.

Obviously, land isolated from the city, up in the mountains, accessible by dirt road, will usually be owned by Ticos who have only a vague idea of the value of their properties. Who does know? Certainly not a new-comer to the region. If that's the kind of land you want, having a Tico bargain for you makes sense only because the landowners probably can't speak English. But it is a mistake to think that you can pick up land like this at a below-market price because these are simple people.

BUYING A **HOUSE FOR INVESTMENT**

Sometimes people will buy their dream home now, planning on renting it out until the day retirement rolls around. Usually this works out fine, particularly if they find amiable renters who are temporary and who clearly understand that when the owners need the house, it must be vacated. The key here is to be sure you have "amicable" renters, people you can trust to do the right thing. Like most Latin American countries, the land-lord-tenant laws of Costa Rica are tilted to favor the tenant over the land-lord. Once tenants are in possession of your home, getting them out can be a problem if they don't want to go. For example, all leases have a min-imum validity of three years, regardless of whether they are written for a shorter term. Therefore a one-year lease could be extended, by the option of the tenant, by another two years. Eviction is a difficult, involved process. On the other hand, the tenant can break a lease simply by walk-ing away and forfeiting the deposit (usually a month's rent). Your rent or lease money should be in dollars, not in colones, because it's not easy to increase the rents as the value of the colón depreciates.

LEGALITIES OF **BUYING REAL ESTATE**

Since Costa Rica is so small, the government is able to keep all land records in one place, at a central title registry called the *Registro de la Propriedad, or Registro Nacional.* Most people just say "Registro." All liens and attachments against a property must be registered here to be legal, and the books are open to the public simply by going to the Registro's Web site. Of course, you must have your attorney double-check the Registro before making an offer, just in case you missed something. (At the end of chapter 18 you'll find instructions for using the Registro Nacional's Web site.)

If your lawyer finds no liens or mortgages registered against the piece of real estate and has no questions about the legal standing of the owners, you can safely transfer the property to your name. Any outstanding debts or obligations that were not registered are none of your concern. But don't feel smug until you make sure that your lawyer actually registers your new property and the documents are stashed away in your safe-deposit box.

Incidentally, another valuable use of information provided by the Registro is checking the ownership of motor vehicles. You'll find the complete legal history of the automobile, motorcycle, or pickup you might want to buy. Before putting up the cash, you can see who actually holds the title to the car, whether there is a loan, and who were previous owners.

Although buying property in Costa Rica should be rather straightforward, it can be hazardous if not handled carefully. The following are some points to keep in mind. (For more details, see chapter 18.)

The first rule: Under no circumstances should you use the same lawyer who represents the seller. Find a competent, English-speaking attorney to handle the deal for you. This can be a challenge in itself. Too many Costa Rican lawyers are part-timers and aren't truly familiar with the rules. Inquire around the North American community for recommendations.

Why is this important? For one thing, your lawyer needs to make sure the person who is selling you the property actually owns it. Your lawyer needs to make absolutely sure that no liens, mortgages, or second deeds are attached to the property. The seller's lawyer has no obligation to things like this; it's up to your lawyer. Legally, an attorney can represent both sides of a transaction but if the lawyer's first client is a crook, look out. The lawyer may well be part of the scam himself. It happens.

The second rule: Never count on a verbal contract. A handshake means nothing. You may think you have a deal, but when you return with the cash, someone else owns the place and is moving in furniture. After you are completely satisfied that the property is free and clear and actually belongs to the seller, and that the seller is who he or she claims to be, get everything in writing, in Spanish as well as English.

The third rule: Do not trust the seller or real estate agent just because he or she is a fellow North American! There's something about Costa Rica that seems to bring out latent tendencies

toward larceny in some of our compatriots. An astounding number of confidence men come out of the closet the moment they arrive in Costa Rica. Most of the real estate agents who are just starting out are rank amateurs, but since they deal with people like you and me—also rank amateurs in business deals—even honest amateurs can cause serious damage.

The fourth rule: Do not be so overwhelmed by the beauty and tranquillity of Costa Rica that you pay the first price asked. Gringos and Ticos alike can display irrational streaks of optimism when valuing their properties. Foreigners, bloodthirsty for profit, can be even worse. Determining the actual value of properties is difficult because there are no "comparables" to gauge value as we were accustomed to back home, where selling prices are a matter of record. In Costa Rica everyone knows how much is *asked* for a property, but the actual sales price is a guarded secret. This is partly because property taxes and transfer fees are based on the stated selling price, and partly because of income-tax or capital-gains issues. Incidentally, my attorney tells me that although it's customary to fib a little to tax collectors about the sales price of a property, if you get too creative about your fibs, they can arbitrarily assign a value to the property, no matter how much you paid!

The fifth rule: If you're buying unimproved land, be sure you can bring electricity and year-round water to the property. (Some parts of Costa Rica suffer water shortages every dry season.) If there is no water connection, make sure that you can get a permit to drill a well. Have the soil tested to be sure it's suitable for a septic system. If sewage can't be treated properly, it will sit around, back up, and make your new home smell like an open cesspool. Furthermore, that may prevent you from getting a building permit.

Another important consideration: electricity. If you have to bring power to your place from the nearest source, it could mean paying a fortune to install power poles and electric lines. The last quote I heard was $15,000 a kilometer. The cost could be double the price you paid for that lovely parcel in the mountains. Solar-power installations are not cheap and limit which appliances you can use.

The sixth rule: Always keep in mind that brokers and sales personnel are not regulated in Costa Rica as they are in the United States or Canada. No training is required, there are no rules of ethics, no professional organization to oversee behavior or competence. Anyone can become a real estate broker simply by claiming to be one. My impression is that every third person I meet in Costa Rica is selling real estate. Ask local residents for broker recommendations. They know how to separate the honest and competent real estate agents from beginners and fast-track wheeler-dealers.

The final rule: When selling property, be wary of a listing agreement that doesn't pay you the full sales price less commission. These contracts are known as "net listings" and are illegal in most, if not all, parts of the United States and Canada, yet they are legal in Costa Rica. I've seen net listing sales where the agent boosted the sales price of property by 50 to 100 percent over the price asked by the seller, keeping the balance for the sales agent, *plus* a commission on the asking price. The agent can end up with more money than the property-owner client. Since there are no laws or regulations, this is perfectly legal. In the United States or Canada, the agent would go to jail for not properly representing his client. If the salesperson wants your listing, he or she will agree to a commission-only deal. If not, look for another salesperson.

A final suggestion: When buying property, the title is often in the name of a Costa Rican corporation, or *sociedad anónima,* which is good. If not, one of the first things you'll probably want to do is form a corporation. This may sound strange, but there are several advantages. (The section on offshore corporations in chapter 18 explains how corporations are set up and how they are used in buying property.) Although offshore corporations are sometimes used for avoiding taxes, hiding assets, and other marginal activities, there is nothing at all questionable or illegal about placing home ownership in a corporation.

The big advantage of property registered in the name of a corporation is the ease of transferring ownership. Instead of going through the expensive and complicated procedure of transferring property into your name, you simply purchase the corporation's shares, take possession of the corporate books and deed to the property, and now you own a corporation whose major asset is your house. When you sell, you simply sell the shares.

BEACHFRONT **PROPERTY**

Real estate is booming along both coasts. Prices in some areas are going wild, while other places still have bargains available. The situation is somewhat murky, because some properties that are being bought and sold have tough building and ownership restrictions that you might not be told about until you're ready to start construction. Foreigners are supposedly limited as to ownership of oceanfront property, but they manage to sidestep this law by putting their land into Costa Rican corporations.

Property owners are restricted as to how close to the beach they can build. The most important point to bear in mind is that you cannot actually own beachfront property; it must be leased from the local municipality. Make sure you're comfortable with this concept before deciding on that wonderful stretch of coconut trees and sand.

Chapter 18 discusses beachfront property in great detail, but generally, the law goes like this: The first 200 meters (656 feet) ashore, starting halfway between low-tide and high-tide lines, is the "maritime zone," and it belongs to the municipality. It cannot be sold, but it can be leased. (This lease is called a "concession.") The first 50 meters from the beach is the "public zone," which belongs absolutely to the public and is off-limits to construction of any kind.

Construction between the 50- and 200-meter points must have the permission of the municipality. Building permits are sometimes issued only for tourist-related projects. Remember, that $85,000 lot on the beach is not an outright purchase; you actually pay that money for the right to renew a lease every five years. It's yours provided you do everything right: make the lease payments, pay taxes on time, and obey all the rules.

Caution: A seller may claim that an existing building that falls within the first 50-meter mark is legal because it's been "grandfathered." That's possible, but more likely someone in the past ignored the rules and the bureaucracy hasn't gotten around to enforcing the laws. The government could force you to dismantle the buildings and restore the property to its original state, when and if it chooses to do so. Check grandfather clauses with a skeptical eye—and a good attorney.

SQUATTER **PROBLEMS**

Anyone who has followed the battles between North Americans and squatters in the *Tico Times* is aware of hair-raising stories concerning squatters and legitimate property owners. The popular name for a squatter is a *precaista*. If you're thinking of buying a piece of rural property, you need to be aware of the squatter problem. The problem is with agricultural land, not residential property.

We've all heard stories of North Americans who purchased lovely tracts of forested land with the intention of building a home someday and then, when they returned a few years later, they were surprised to find the land cleared and someone farming it.

If the property you are interested in has an extra house and a Tico family living in it, beware. Don't let the seller glibly pass this off as the "caretaker's residence." It could be a squatter's home. "This family takes wonderful care of the place!" the seller might exclaim. "They never leave the property unattended." The seller should add, "They'll never leave, period!" Make sure you see documents proving that this is indeed a caretaker employee, not a squatter. In order to be an employed caretaker, the employee must receive the legal minimum wage rate, including Social Security, and all other legal benefits. The papers proving all this must be up-to-date. Insist that your lawyer examine the proof. If someone is paid to simply look over the property on a regular basis, make sure there's a written receipt that he is being paid for this service and is not a squatter himself.

To most of us the idea of someone simply moving in on your property is outrageous. It's trespassing! It's theft! Can this really happen in a law-abiding country like Costa Rica? Aren't property owners protected by the law? Isn't all of this illegal?

Well, it turns out that to an extent, it is legal. There are laws to the effect that unowned or abandoned property is open for homesteading, just as it was in the early days of the United States and may still be in some western states. These Costa Rican laws were intended to prevent a few wealthy people from hogging land they don't use and don't need. This is precisely what happened in the other Central American countries, where 2 or 3 percent of the people own 90 percent of the good land. One reason Costa Rica is so much better off than its neighbors is that citizens have access to land. The laws are well intentioned and fair. The problem lies in how these laws are interpreted and who is doing the interpreting. Too often the bias is in favor of the squatter. (Remember, this only applies to agricultural land. Residential properties cannot be claimed as abandoned.)

Just when is a piece of land abandoned? One law, which seems clear, states that after property goes unattended for ten years, whoever has been using the land in a "continuous, open, and peaceful manner" for those ten years may apply for a title. The intruder will be successful unless the original owner has a good lawyer and a valid excuse. Another principle of law is that the squatter must show that he had reason to believe the land was abandoned. This means that someone who was being paid to watch your land can be removed if he attempts to take it over for himself. (Remember, you need receipts and canceled checks.)

Typically, the scenario goes like this: A choice piece of unattended property becomes a tempting target for a *precaista*. He'll construct a cabin and plant a crop in the hope that he won't be discovered for a year. If the occupancy is less than a year, it's considered trespassing and is handled by the Ministry of Interior and the courts. If the trespass is less than ninety days, you call the local police, and they are obligated to evict the squatters and "present you" with a paper that confirms that you are the true owner of the property. (If the police fail to act, your lawyer can do something about that.) But let it go a full year and the situation becomes a bit more serious. The owner usually has the option of paying the squatter for his expenses and "improvements" or else going to court. ("Improvements" could be cutting down all your beautiful trees and selling them to make a pasture of your forest.) When the bill is too high—you can be sure it will be padded—sometimes it's cheaper to walk away. Understand, these problems seldom occur anywhere but on agricultural land. Land zoned or used as residential property doesn't fall under the category of this law.

The solution to this problem is a matter of prevention. While you are out of the country, have a friend or a management agent drop by the property at least once every three months. At this point, a simple complaint to the police is usually enough to boot someone off your land. Be sure to keep records of expenses and improvements to the property as proof that you haven't abandoned your land. Paying someone to clear brush once in a while is good enough. Be sure to keep a record of how many hours he worked and receipts for how much you paid him. Any place where there are a lot of foreign property owners, you'll find someone who watches property as a paid service. However, be absolutely sure you know who is taking care of your property, and keep records that he is being paid. My attorney advises, "Hire someone to check on the property, and then hire someone else to check on the person checking on your property." The last thing you want to do is hire a squatter to watch over your property!

Occasionally a problem arises when a foreign resident decides to return to the United States for an extended stay and has to lay off the maid, gardener, or other employees. If the property owner isn't familiar with the laws and neglects to pay workers' benefits such as severance pay, accrued vacation, and year-end bonuses, the employees could feel justified in taking over the land as compensation. Chapter 12 covers this in detail.

However repugnant the idea of squatting may be to you, it is important to operate within the law. After all, *precaistas* have rights, like it or not. One woman who had just purchased some property told me that she had been informed that "the only way to deal with squatters is to burn down their houses," and that's what she intended to do if she ever found any on her property. I was horrified to think of someone on a tourist visa, a guest in the country, taking the law into her own hands! This is the way the problems start, and problems of this nature have been known to escalate into gunfire. Sometimes squatters are well organized and have their own ways of striking back; the best advice is to leave this problem to the law. The law may work slowly, sometimes not at all, but this is better than killing or being killed for a piece of farmland. I have friends who had no problem kicking the rascals off their land, and watched while the police burned the squatters' shacks.

If you are an absentee owner of undeveloped land and have reason to believe that your property is a target of squatters or property-theft scams, you should do the following: Make sure you are the legally registered owner; if you live out of the country, ask your attorney to conduct a title search from time to time to make sure you are still on the title, or at least check the Registro Nacional Web site yourself. (See instructions for checking the Registro in chapter 18. Let the neighbors know who you are and that you own the property. Fence the property if possible, and post signs. Have a friend walk the property boundary lines every two or three months and file a complaint against any squatters encountered. If you hire a caretaker or agent to watch the property, make sure you have signed receipts showing that you've paid the caretaker for this purpose. Understand, these precautions are only for undeveloped property that is left untended by absentee owners for long periods.

BUILDING **YOUR OWN HOME**

Okay, you've made the big decision? You've done your on-location research? You've traveled Costa Rica to check out climates and expat communities? You know exactly where you and your spouse want to settle in?

Congratulations! Your next decision is: Do you rent, do you buy, or do you build?

Unless you have the capital to invest, the obvious decision is to rent. The downside is that you'll have to accept whatever lifestyle and home designs are available instead of what you'd really like. Another problem is that many homes are used as vacation homes for the owners, so you'll be limited as to when you can stay in the house. Being forced to move from one place to another is a frequent consequence of renting. Even with a long-term rental, there's no guarantee the house won't be sold out from under you.

Buying is the best and simplest solution for most people. You choose from among the best-designed homes on the market and simply move in. More often than not, the house will come completely furnished, including refrigerator, washer, and dryer. Often these are turnkey setups: including kitchen utensils, bedding, and garden tools, especially when the owners are returning to their homes back in the United States or Canada. It wouldn't make sense to drag furniture back home.

Building your home is the third option, the one my wife and I adopted, but only after looking over the homes-for-sale market. We found features we loved in each of the homes we considered buying. Yet every home had at least one flaw we didn't care to live with. We decided to build instead of buy—that way we could incorporate all the nice features we'd seen and eliminate the problems.

First we needed a building site. We narrowed this down to two choices. The first choice: a lovely lot, high on the mountain side, with a gorgeous view of the beach. But the location was a ten-minute drive to the beach. We wanted walking distance. The second option was a lot where we could hear but not see the surf. Priced at one-third the cost of a view lot.

Next came the wonderful and exhilarating process of designing our dream home. We converted our dining-room table into a work space, and both began making sketches of how each of us envisioned the layout should look. Which features would be included. How bedrooms should be positioned. Where stairs to the upstairs living quarters would go. At first, none of the drawings had any similarities. We debated and argued for our designs, making changes over and over. Finally, we arrived at a consensus. The design retained all of the good features, and eliminated the bad. Or so we thought.

Our next step was consulting with our contractor. We handed him our final drawings and eagerly awaited his enthusiastic approval. Enthusiastic was not exactly his reaction. He pointed out several flaws in the design. One important flaw was that the stairway to the upstairs deck would end up in space beyond the house rather than on the deck. Another error: We forgot to allow for a door into the downstairs bathroom. Back to the drawing board. The process continued with our altering designs and the contractor correcting them.

Finally we all agreed on the design. Next steps: finding an architect to approve the plans and getting building permits from the municipality and a construction engineer's report on the suitability of the building site and septic tank capability. Costa Rican architects have a strong lobby in the National Assembly; the law says you must use blueprints from a licensed architect and the fee shall be a hefty percentage of construction cost. Actually, an architect here does much more than design: He/she is supposed to supervise all phases of the construction.

However, it turns out that there are many more architects in the country than building projects to keep them all busy. Architects who work part-time at their profession are often willing to negotiate the fee. Especially when the contractor is a friend or relative. This architect will look over the plans and recycle a similar blueprint for a negotiated price, resulting in significant savings for the client. Not all architects will do this, and those who have plenty of work will *not* do it this way. Again, it helps if your contractor is a friend or relative. If you are building anything more than a basic, plain vanilla house, you probably don't want to take shortcuts. Hire a skilled, reputable architect, and have your lawyer help negotiate, to be absolutely sure you are aware of the contract.

When estimating how long it would take to build our house, our contractor wisely said, "I might finish in three months. *No hay problema.* But since this is Costa Rica, I will promise *five* months. That way you will be delighted if I finish in only *four* months." Actually, he finished in four months to the exact day. He asked one of the workers to stop us that day, before we could get to the building site. The man took us to lunch and stalled for an hour while the crew installed the last of the windows. The contractor met us with a proud smile and took us through our new house.

When the day came to begin construction, the work crew set about cutting just enough trees to lay out the house. I watched over them to make sure they didn't cut too many. They thought this amusing. (Little did I know that trees here grow so fast they have to be continually trimmed and finally removed before they damage the roof and windows.)

I made friends with the workers by bringing cold beer for lunch. They started calling me "*don John*" (a term of friendship and respect accorded to those older than you and who are well liked in the community). They still call me *don John*—long after the house was completed. As I drive to or from the village, someone is always waving at me and saying, "*Hola, don John!*" I've gotten into the habit of waving at everyone for fear I might hurt someone's feelings at not being recognized.

Watching over the crew is a good idea, by the way—not because they will loaf, but because when you go away for a few weeks, contractors have a tendency to take their men and go work elsewhere. You can't blame them, because there is a labor shortage from time to time. They figure they can always get back to your house before you return. It does not always work that way.

During the early construction phase, I stayed at a nearby bed-and-breakfast and arose at dawn to hang around the building site and observe the wildlife that is so bountiful at daybreak. Monkeys, coatimundis, parrots, and other animals put on an early-morning show. Hanging around my building site at dawn brought surprises other than wildlife. I discovered something about the Ticos who worked on my project: Not only did they arrive on time for work, but most were early—quite unlike the case in other Latin countries I can think of. Starting time was 6:00 A.M., and at exactly 6:00 work commenced in earnest. They worked hard, with regularly scheduled breaks, until 3:30 P.M. (a nine-hour day). The famous *mañana* mentality wasn't apparent on this job. I'm not saying *all* Tico workers are like this; I'm only relating my personal experience.

Don't misunderstand: Our building experience was not all peaches and cream—all expected problems raised their ugly heads, and a few creative problems joined in the fun. We quickly learned a Spanish lesson: The difference between *Hay un problemcito* ("There's a little problem") and *No hay problema* ("There's no problem"). Essentially, it's as follows: *Hay un problemcito* translates as "We have a problem here, amigo, and it's probably going to cost money." On the other hand, *No hay problema* usually translates as "We may or may not have a problem, but it's not my problem."

CHAPTER ELEVEN

BUSINESS **OPPORTUNITIES**

Just a few years ago, the vast majority of those coming to Costa Rica for long-term stays were traditional retirees. By "traditional" I mean affluent couples about 65 years old, retired after forty years of loyalty to a benevolent company. They enjoyed a nice pension and looked forward to enjoying their "golden years" and a lifestyle of leisure. Retiring much earlier than 65 would have been unusual. Their ideal was a Costa Rican beach house overlooking the surf at Flamingo, or perhaps a stately home perched above Escazú with a gorgeous view of the valley and volcanoes in the distance. Ideally with a lifestyle that allowed ample time for bridge, cocktail parties, and golf with other expatriates, plus an occasional charter fishing trip.

A few years can make a lot of difference. For one thing, the retirement age has dropped—quitting work at 50 is not unusual. For many, retirement isn't voluntarily: 50 is the age at which many employers like to trim the payroll, before pension benefits accumulate. Today there are no such things as company loyalty or loyalty to employees. People are hired for whatever skills needed at the moment—and dropped the minute they're not needed. Many of today's retirees are casualties of the "dot-com" meltdown; since that time, most good jobs have moved

to India or China. Other people are simply tired of working for someone else and recall thirty years ago when "dropping out" was idealized. In the new millennium, "dropping out" becomes a goal as much as an option.

This creates a restless population of not-yet-ready-for-retirement people who are itching to do something interesting with the rest of their lives. In fact, the word "retirement" isn't in their vocabulary. These are the youth-oriented activists who in the 1960s and 1970s used to say, "Don't trust anyone over 30!" Determined not to get "old" in the way they perceived their parents to be, these youngsters are eager to get on with life. They have energy, talent, and workplace skills that they don't care to waste by playing bridge or swinging in a hammock. If they can't find a good-paying job in Costa Rica, the next option that comes to mind is going into business. And many of them do. Some popular tourist locales have more businesses owned by foreigners than by native Ticos.

A FRIENDLY **BUSINESS CLIMATE**

Many countries severely restrict foreign business investment as a way of protecting their national businesses and industry. Special tax breaks are given to local commerce, and roadblocks are thrown in the way of foreign investors. There's some justification for this, because many foreign businesses only want to take advantage of cheap wages, then ship the products—and the profits—out of the country. But Costa Rica takes a positive attitude toward foreign investment. Outside money is encouraged as a way to spur development, yet labor laws and wage minimums are enforced, giving the average Tico worker enough income that local stores, shops, and businesses flourish.

The end result is that Costa Rica is probably the most business-friendly country in Latin America. Foreign investment and foreign entrepreneurs are welcome. One obvious result has been the relocation of several high-tech corporations to take advantage of Costa Rica's educated and computer-literate workforce. This business-friendly climate has earned Costa Rica the reputation as Central America's "Silicon Valley." Companies such as Acer Computers, Microsoft, Abbot Laboratories, and General Electric have established sizable production facilities here. Intel Corporation's three production facilities here produce one-third of Intel's computer processor chips, creating thousands of good jobs for Ticos.

Any investment that promotes tourism, creates jobs, and doesn't harm the environment is considered welcome here. Another plus: Many foreign investors in Costa Rica actually live in Costa Rica. For them, the whole point of going into business is to be able to enjoy living in Costa Rica. They spend and reinvest profits in the country, further bolstering the economy.

To attract desirable businesses, Costa Rica offers generous incentives and tax breaks. Depending on the enterprise, there can be a twelve-year exemption from income taxes as well as waivers on import duties. When ecology is concerned—particularly projects involving reforestation—tax exemptions can be forever. Be aware, however, that continuing changes in tax laws may affect some of the tax breaks for tourist-oriented businesses.

Investments of $50,000 or more in specially approved projects can qualify the investor for immediate residency. With $150,000, the investment can be in any enterprise. Of course, to qualify for any of these special investment provisions, you need to proceed with government approval. Your lawyer can help you with this.

Remember that reforestation projects aren't just a matter of deciding to start sticking trees in the ground. You need to present detailed plans prepared by an approved forestry technical expert. If your reforestation project is a good one, you can also be eligible for government subsidies. (A friend is receiving about $5,000 a year under one of these programs.) Once planted, the property can be resold, as long as the purchaser agrees to continue with the reforestation project.

GOING INTO **BUSINESS**

Before we delve into the subject of going into business in Costa Rica, you should ask yourself some important questions. Do you really want to move to a beautiful country and spend your time working at a business? Ask yourself whether you'd be better off bird-watching, swimming, or tanning on the beach instead of doing bookkeeping, tending bar, or changing linens in your bed-and-breakfast. Do you feel up to the challenge of dealing with a quixotic, entangled bureaucracy, in a language you don't entirely understand? And finally, if it's so easy to start the business you have in mind—and make large sums of money from your idea—why hasn't somebody else already filled that niche?

Too often, dreamers feel confident that all that's necessary to become a successful business person in Costa Rica is to show up and dazzle the country with entrepreneurship. Well yes, this *can* happen but mostly to those who know what they are doing, who employ skills and special knowledge gained from business experience in their home countries.

Most North Americans who go into business in Costa Rica don't bother qualifying under the $50,000 or $150,000 investment laws, since tax advantages accrue to most qualifying businesses and because a Costa Rican passport isn't an enticement to those already holding U.S. or Canadian passports.

Since most businesses are registered in the name of a corporation or *sociadad anónima,* even a foreigner on a tourist visa can effectively control and manage the enterprise. While it is against the law for noncitizens to work at an ordinary job without permission, it's perfectly okay to oversee your own business. Discretion is required here, however, since part of the scheme is to create jobs, and if a business owner is doing work that could be performed by a Costa Rican, complaints could arise. This seldom happens, but it can happen.

Some North Americans have done exceptionally well in Costa Rican business ventures. They bring enthusiasm, expertise, and imagination, often re-creating successful enterprises they operated in their home country. One businessman from Illinois, who started a successful beach resort in Manuel Antonio about twenty years ago, said, "It's interesting to see who makes money here and who goes belly-up. Those who succeed are those who come here because of the attractive Costa Rican lifestyle and who go into business as a means of staying in Costa Rica. They usually make money despite themselves. Those who face one problem after another, and finally disaster, are those whose main interest is making a pile of money."

Foreigners often feel confident that they can be successful in tourist-oriented businesses because they understand the wants and needs of other foreigners who visit Costa Rica. That's often the case. Some restaurants and bars are popular with tourists because the owners know what tourists like. However, as in any business endeavor, you should know what you are doing, particularly in the restaurant or bar business, where the failure rate is unusually high.

Real estate development projects have created fabulous success stories as well as woeful tales of spectacular flops. Too many optimistic types start creating developments and resorts that look great on paper but never get past the fantasy stage. Be cautious about floating your investments on blue-sky dreams.

You needn't start your own business; numerous in-place enterprises are always available through ads in local newspapers. Of course, just as is the case back home, you need to investigate *why* the business is for sale. Maybe the reason is too much work, not enough profit, illness, or perhaps the owner feels it's time to cash in the equity and stash the profit. Don't consider buying a business unless you're competent to handle it and understand exactly why the enterprise is up for sale. What makes you think you can make money at this if someone else failed?

Among the many businesses advertised in the *Tico Times* are bed-and-breakfasts, car-rental agencies, pharmacies, travel agencies, and tons of bar-restaurants and discos. Apartment buildings, hotels, and beach resorts are always on the market.

A business consultant I once interviewed said: "Remember, it's just as easy to lose money in Costa Rica as it is back home. For a stranger in a foreign land, it's even easier. You must know what you are doing. My best advice is to come here for six months and look around. Study the existing businesses and find out why some are successful and why others fail. Above all, don't jump into a business just for the sake of being in business—particularly a business that you don't know much about."

BEWARE OF **SCAMS**

Because of Costa Rica's liberal attitude toward foreign business ventures and sometimes lax regulation, a surprising number of foreigners feel as though they have complete freedom to operate as they wish and that ordinary laws and ethics don't apply to them. This is probably why Costa Rica draws more than its share of swindlers, crooks, and con artists.

The Costa Rican government does what it can to keep on top of offenders, but it's impossible to do much more than prosecute crooks after the damage has been done. And this rarely happens, because the swindler simply skips the country before the trial date. For this reason, look very carefully at any business deal presented to you. Make sure you have a good, English-speaking lawyer check with all the proper government agencies and verify the integrity of your deal before risking your hard-earned money.

Popular scams include phony mutual funds, nonexistent banks, so-called tax-shelter investments, gold mines, hotels and resorts that never leave the drawing board, real estate that is sold to several people or property that didn't belong to the seller in the first place, and phantom teak, macadamia, and jojoba plantations—all the get-rich-quick schemes you can imagine.

After pointing out all the pitfalls of going into business, I have to admit that many people are having fun doing so. You can feel a dynamic sense of progress and excitement in Costa Rica. This is the country of the entrepreneur, of wide-open opportunity, inexpensive land, dependable labor, and a relatively honest government. Modern-day Costa Rica is reminiscent of the old frontier days of the United States and Canada, full of success stories about North Americans who've opted to "start all over again." Just be aware that there are stories of failure as well.

EXAMPLES OF **BUSINESS VENTURES**

The other day a successful expat businessman discussed the high rate of business failure by Costa Rica newbies. He said, "If you take restaurants out of the equation, business success rates are probably not much different than in the United States. The problem is, most start-up restaurants are by those who have absolutely no experience. Yet a restaurant is usually their first choice."

What happens is people fall in love with Costa Rica and decide to chuck everything back home and move to paradise. Too young to retire, they want either a job or a business. They've always loved to cook, and friends always praise their culinary skills. "Everybody always said I should open a restaurant when I retire." Good luck. One expat said to me, "It amazes me to see a new restaurant open up on a street where there are already eight other restaurants. I remember when one restaurant started to serve pizza in our village. Immediately, each of the other restaurants bought pizza ovens and put pizza on their menus. Unless you have something extra-special to offer, how can you possibly succeed?"

Sometimes this works. A very successful Italian restaurant in our community was started by an Italian insurance executive from Naples and his wife, who was an accountant for a chain of hardware stores. They knew nothing of the restaurant business, but their location was wonderful, and there were no other Italian restaurants in the region at that time. To succeed, food didn't have to be more than just okay.

But all too often, beginning restaurateurs have no clue as to what to do after making up a menu. Imaginative menus and good cooking are only part of the restaurant business. Without knowledge of buying, food spoilage, theft, and dealing with Spanish-speaking employees and suppliers, the new entrepreneurs are lost at sea.

GOURMET RESTAURANT The following business profile is an exception to a rule. Instead of accidentally going into a business she knew nothing about, Debbie Crawford studied and prepared. She opened the Vista de Paraíso restaurant in Nosara forewarned and forearmed.

Debbie says, "All my life I dreamed of becoming a chef. I was pre-med in college and got my degree in chemistry. I worked in restaurants while going to college and loved the life. I am a very social person and love to talk. Chemistry, though, fit the financial backing." After receiving her chemistry degree, she worked in environmental chemistry and plant processing for fifteen years before making a career change.

She explained, "I was earning a six-figure salary, but I wasn't satisfied. Then, I found an opportunity to go to chef school full time. I quit my job and went to the prestigious Alain & Marie LeNotre Culinary Institute for an intensive, full-time program. Most classes were taught in French and we needed a translator. A couple of the chefs spoke English, but all were master chefs, either in pastry or cuisine. After my time in culinary school, I applied and was accepted to the prestigious Accellis Culinary Arts Challenge. There were over 5,000 applicants across the United States and Canada, but only twenty were to be accepted. I came in third but felt like winner before I ever got there!"

Later Debbie was accepted to work in a three-star hotel/restaurant in Perigeux in the south of France. (Three stars is the highest rank a restaurant can receive in Europe.) "I worked there for three months and then another hotel/restaurant for three months. This was hard but a great experience."

When Debbie returned to the States, she decided to move to the tropics to open her own restaurant. Since she already knew Nosara and liked the people and the climate, her decision was easy. She found a gorgeous ocean-view property in an unbelievable tropical setting.

She says, "I named it Vista del Paraíso or 'Paradise View.' I built the house, the restaurant, and a new life here in the tropics. I have nothing physical left in the States except some of my best friends. My children are now both bilingual, and we are able to spend 100 percent of our time together in our home-restaurant. They play in the swimming pool while I prepare the evening's menu. I also have a wonderful Costa Rican boyfriend without whom I could not have gotten this far as fast as I did."

The restaurant features an international "fare with a flare," with imported tequilas, cognacs, and fun martinis; a beautiful pool for guests' enjoyment; seating inside or out (weather permitting); a baby pool; but most of all, really incredible food and view. Debbie says, "All food is always fresh and hand-picked by me."

BED-AND-BREAKFAST One of the more popular ideas of going into business in Costa Rica has always been bed-and-breakfasts. Seems like a natural for someone with little or no experience in business. What's so complicated? You just make beds and cook breakfast, right? There's a little more involved than that. For one thing, it is a hands-on, year-round business, just as any hospitality enterprise such as restaurants, bars, hotels is, when dealing with the public. As in any other business, it pays off to have relevant business experience. And it doesn't hurt to have an outgoing personality!

Starting a new business, or in the case of Angel Valley Farm B&B, near San Ramón, transforming an old business, can be challenging in any environment, particularly in a foreign country. However, compared to the United States and other Western countries, Costa Rica generally provides freedom for individuals with new ideas to bring them to the country and help support its strong tourism industry. A service or product of high quality can be very successful here, and Andrew and Beth are striving to provide accommodations, which, while modest, offer a friendly, family environment and some "extras" not found in many B&Bs.

From the time they met, Andrew Mastrandonas and friend/business partner, Beth Frischberg, both from Washington, D.C., talked about someday living overseas. Not just living overseas, but being in some kind of business there. Andrew, who has traveled extensively throughout the world, wanted to really "live the travel industry" by running a small travel business, and Beth wanted to try her hand at Latin cooking and bring new culinary methods to the business. It sounded reasonable to try a bed-and-breakfast.

They decided to give up their fast-paced lives in Washington and start anew in Costa Rica. In June 2005 they purchased Angel Valley Farm Bed & Breakfast (506) 456–4084; www.AngelValleyFarmBandB.com; in the small village of Los Angeles, just north of San Ramón. They remodeled inside and out, featuring custom-made furniture and other amenities. Although this was their first experience with a B&B, Andrew has experience as a head of Internet sales and distribution with US Airways and an international management consultant for two major nongovernmental organizations. Beth was an executive chef to a well-known corporate CEO and several Washington insiders.

Angel Valley Farm B&B caters to families and singles alike wanting an outdoor adventure experience. In addition to lodging and gourmet breakfast, the facility offers horseback riding, hiking, biking, outdoor sports, and tours. They also host retirement tours each month, bringing retirees to the area to learn about living in Costa Rica, searching for appropriate properties, and taking in the experience of being here, prior to moving here.

When asked what advice he might have for newcomers considering doing business in Costa Rica, Andrew says, "For many expatriates, the toughest thing about doing business in Costa Rica is the pace of business itself. Things don't often get done—by contractors, suppliers, and others—with the rapidity one often expects in the United States. If you adjust accordingly, pace yourself, and keep moving forward, things will get done, and you will fit in here well and be successful. Trying to do things as you do them in your home country won't often work, and we've learned that many times. Rather, understanding how Costa Ricans get things done and adapting to their practices is often the best route to take. Just because an idea, product, or service worked well in the United States or another country, doesn't necessarily mean it will work here, though when adapted for local circumstances, many good ideas can work here."

In addition to running Angel Valley Farm B&B, Andrew maintains a widely read blog on his move to Costa Rica and his life here. It can be found at www.travelblog.org/bloggers/andrewncostarica. Andrew also writes for the *Tico Times* and other publications on travel and social/cultural issues.

HOME RENTAL FOR TOURISTS A number of years ago, Tony Waddell purchased land in Puerto Viejo, on the Caribbean, and built a small house. Not with the intention of using it for business purposes; not even with the intention of using it for anything other than a place to use when he felt like getting away from San José.

Tony says, "Eventually, I had to question why I was living in San José and paying rent on a big house in the hills, when I owned a home at one of the more popular beaches in Costa Rica. I decided to try living there for a year and see how I liked it.

"Soon after moving all my furniture and possessions and settling in, I started renting out the second bedroom to tourists and other overnight guests. They received a comfortable place to sleep, and a secure environment with all the comforts of home, at a very low price. I enjoyed the extra income as well as the company. Guests ranged from groups of surfers who wouldn't pay more than $5.00 a night per person, to families traveling together from Italy or Israel or Brazil. I've had visitors from more than fifteen different countries around the world."

After staying for two years in Puerto Viejo, Tony realized he missed the conveniences and services of the big city (such as they are). He decided to move back to San José and "convert my little business of renting rooms to renting the entire house to tourists." He calls his rental Casa del Zorro with a Web site at www.caribecostarica.com.

He says, "I'm not interested in long-term rental of the property, even though that would be a lot less work on my part. After all, I want to use the house for myself from time to time. As a business, it's been successful and I am now getting reservation requests almost daily. This American-style home features two bedrooms, two baths, a fully equipped kitchen with all utensils, dishes, pots, pans, and appliances. My house has very large, open, and airy rooms, and the veranda runs the entire width of the house. Being only 100 meters [328 feet] from the beach and just 3 blocks from the main part of town makes it a convenient but peaceful and quiet place to stay."

Tony says that he now regrets that he didn't buy a larger lot in order to build another home. "Puerto Viejo has plenty of hotels and cabinas for rent, but the private-home market is largely untapped. Tourists, especially those traveling as a family, appreciate the comforts of a fully furnished home.

"The biggest challenge is attracting new guests. While word of mouth is the best adverting one can get, it takes a lot more than that at the beginning. Advertising in *AM Costa Rica* or the *Tico Times* is expensive, short-term, and not especially effective. The *Choose Costa Rica* bulletin board has been quite helpful in attracting new customers. For this type of businesses, various Web sites advertise vacation rentals, and some Web sites offer to list your property at no charge for a few months. I used these sites until I found which ones were providing the most referrals."

DOING BUSINESS **VIA THE INTERNET**

The Internet as we know it today didn't even exist when I wrote the first edition of *Choose Costa Rica for Retirement* back in 1992. Even three editions ago, few people had even heard of the Internet, much less knew how to use it. Today we routinely check our e-mail several times a day; we read the *New York Times, the Wall Street Journal,* and the *Tico Times* online, no matter where in the world we happen to be. In Costa Rica we can pay our bills online, check our bank account, connect with the Costa Rica Chamber of Commerce, and research just about any topic imaginable.

But Web technology goes far beyond convenience for consumers and communication with friends and family. Today's technology permits certain types of jobs and businesses to be located anywhere. Many employees no longer commute to their workplaces. Today they work from home and connect to the office by modem. It doesn't matter that their home computer and the office aren't in the same city, state, or even in the same country.

TRAVEL AGENCY   About four years ago, we profiled Casey Halloran's Internet business as an example of someone making a living on the Internet in Costa Rica. His experience is a classic example of turning a small business into a highly successful enterprise. We're happy to report on his progress.

Casey explains, "Originally I wanted to move to Spain. I lived there during my university days and loved it. But high prices and the ridiculous rules for non-E.U. residents to work changed my mind about Spain. After researching Spanish-speaking destinations from Mexico to Chile, I was impressed by the volume of online information coming from Costa Rica. This was in 1998, the early days of Internet, so I though it'd be wise to go someplace where the Internet wouldn't be starting from ground zero. It turned out to be a good choice."

At first Casey offered consulting and technical help to anybody that wanted to do business online. Then he decided to start an online marketing firm. Costa Rica had many tourism operators who needed to reach foreign markets, so Casey knew there was a need for services he could provide. His first two clients were a real estate firm and a travel agency. (In the end, those were the two industries he chose to enter as a business owner, not just a consultant.) After three years, his original Web directory grew into a five-person company with numerous Web sites and more than a hundred advertisers.

Casey said, "At that point, I found a great business partner and we started an online travel agency. Our focus was high-end vacations. Today the travel agency has expanded from a two-man shop to a thirty-three person organization with $5 million in sales, with offices in Costa Rica and Panama. We just recently expanded into real estate sales because so many of our vacationers were asking us for real estate advice. It's been a great time so far, and through all the difficulties and frustrations, I cannot imagine ever having had more fun trying the same anywhere else."

Asked what is the best part of living and doing business in Costa Rica, Casey replied, "Meeting so many great expats and locals who remind you that life is about what you leave behind, not just the money you make. You can find this anywhere, but being outside the very powerful influence of Madison Avenue and social norms of anyone's backyard can be very limiting intellectually. Being able to see the bigger picture has been the greatest gift Costa Rica has given me."

Casey's advice to others who are thinking of doing business in Costa Rica is: "Be patient. Last man standing usually wins in Costa Rica. If you're easily frustrated, this is not the place to do business."

AGRICULTURE **AS INVESTMENT**

Because of incredibly rich soil and year-round growing seasons, Costa Rica is an agricultural paradise. The country is checker-boarded with crops of all descriptions. Just about anything grows here, with bumper crops the rule rather than the exception. Therefore, agriculture would seem to be one of Costa Rica's best bets for investment. Actually, agriculture can also be one of the biggest investment disasters. Just because crops grow well doesn't guarantee you are going to make money. Furthermore, many native Costa Ricans are abandoning agriculture as a way to earn a living and going into less arduous occupations.

As an example: I have a Tica friend from a large Costa Rican family—twelve children. Her father was a farmer and so were all of his nine brothers. (Families of two generations ago were much larger than today.) Yet, my friend points out that not a single one of the male descendants went into agriculture as a living." They sold the land and went into some other occupation or business. Too much hard work for so little money," she explains.

One longtime agriculturist who has struggled to make a living in Costa Rica said, "Farming is a great way to go broke even if you are an experienced agriculturist. There are too many unknowns and too many marketing problems." He added wryly, "If I had invested the same amount in real estate as I spent trying to get an orange grove started, I would be a rich man by now."

Unusual or nontraditional crops that target overseas markets is sometimes a good idea, only if you personally are going to run the operation and you know marketing. You really have to know what you are doing and find a unique market niche. Expatriate farmers who farm successfully here specialize in crops destined for foreign markets or they develop a demand overseas for their specialty.

COFFEE FARM Ten years ago, Janet Blakeley, her husband, and her daughter Courtney (age 6 at the time) decided to make the move to Costa

Rica. They found a gorgeous home in the hills above Grecia, with a sweeping view of the city and high mountains on the other side of the Valle Central. (I've visited their home and can attest to the breathtaking layout.)

They discovered that in addition to the house and landscaped grounds, the property included several hectares of coffee trees—the type that produce the highest-quality Arabica beans. Janet's curiosity led her to learn more about coffee, how it should be grown and processed, and how it could be gourmet-roasted on a small scale. She made friends with neighboring coffee growers and soon became fascinated with organic methods of coffee production. She bought processing equipment and began packaging her own brand of gourmet coffee: Tesoros Del Sol.

When her husband left the picture via a divorce, Janet needed to do something with the coffee to supplement her income. She had already been helping neighbors convert to organic coffee growing and looking for ways to help farmers get fair prices, stop losing their land, and to help the environment. Together the group organized a collective of coffee growers.

Janet says, "We are licensed as an organic project, which means my company of Tesoros Del Sol gets them all certified. We make no-interest or low-interest loans for approved fertilizers and such. We train and monitor farms monthly. We pay higher rates to help them during the three years of transition to organic, and much higher rates for their organic beans. We've cut out the middle-man."

Farmers who participate in the program are also required to plant tree shade cover, which produces higher-quality coffee beans. They are urged to plant native trees, but planting alternate crop trees such as papaya, bananas, or citrus is also encouraged. Janet grows pineapples between the rows. Being certified organic enables her farmer associates to command a price commensurate with the cost of production.

Janet's marketing strategy: Package only top quality, hand-processed, pure Costa Rican beans (no blends), and market the product directly to consumers in the United States by way of the Internet. Coffee lovers there are delighted to pay a little more for 100 percent Costa Rican coffee that cannot be found elsewhere. It would have to be a low-volume business, Janet decided, but it could be done via the Internet. And it works!

Courtney thoroughly enjoyed her experience of growing up in Costa Rica and loves the *naturaleza* of their Grecia home. She is thoroughly bilingual and finds it easy to make friends with the neighbors. She says she finds them loyal and caring, and she feels as if they are extended family. Janet says, "I appreciate that I don't have to worry about drugs or violence, and that Courtney has grown up with 'people' values."

Janet maintains an exceptionally informative Web site (www.tesoros delsol.com) that gives complete information about coffee production in Costa Rica, how it is grown and processed, and the differences between varieties of coffee. The site also provides ordering information for North American consumers who would like to try certified organic coffee.

TEAK PLANTATIONS These have been promoted in Costa Rica for years. According to promoters, raising teak trees is a surefire venture that will pay huge dividends. Forestry experts I've interviewed dismiss this as mostly hype. It is true that after an eight-year growth (trees will be from 6 to 10 inches in diameter), they are typically cut into tongue-and-groove boards or into chips to make parquet floors. From what I understand, the profit from this first cutting sometimes just about covers the cost of planting and maintenance. Trees are thinned again every several years, with the last harvest at about twenty-five years when they finally become high-value lumber. The *Tico Times* once ran an interesting series of investigative feature articles on teak as an investment. The controversy is ongoing, so before you invest, do some investigation on your own. You're likely to find investors who feel they've made a mistake and others who are pleased.

Years ago, when the teak craze started, Tico farmers throughout the country planted stands of teak on steep hills where ordinary crops wouldn't do well. It didn't cost much, and over the years, they ignored the trees. But since teak should be planted on flat areas and loses most of its value without early pruning, this teak is not bringing high prices. Today, when you buy tracts of forested land, chances are you'll find teak trees, some possibly ready for harvesting on a small scale.

I have an expatriate friend who discovered that by using a relatively inexpensive and easily portable sawmill, his workers can turn out stacks of teak tongue-and-groove boards—very much in demand for home building today. Instead of the traditional method of cutting trees, dragging them to a point where they can be loaded on trucks, and selling trees to lumber mills, these entrepreneurs bring the sawmill to the trees. Workers process them on the spot, turning low-value tree trunks into valuable lumber.

This system is much better for ecology, since it doesn't involve cutting roads through the forest or clear-cutting to get at the teak trees. My friend turns a nice profit and feels good about the sensible way the profits are generated.

REFORESTATION The traditional way of marketing tree farms is to buy inexpensive, abandoned farms, then plant several thousand teak or pochote trees, then sell the land to investors. There are other ways of doing this: either sell shares in the project, or sell trees to investors rather than land.

Fred Morgan, from western New York, found another approach. Instead of planting hectare after hectare of a single tree crop, his idea is to re-create the original rain forest by interspersing cash-crop trees with varied native and rare species of trees that were originally present before the rain forest or primary forest was destroyed to create pasture for cattle. Later, when tree crops are harvested, the rain-forest trees are left standing, with a good start for the future. The land will then be withdrawn from further planting, restoring the land to nature. Information about this project can be found at www.fincaleola.com.

When asked his advice for those thinking about going into the reforestation business in Costa Rica, Fred Morgan wrote the following:

"We from the first world perceive that successful businesspeople are usually hard drivers. If you're that way in Costa Rica, you will find that, like walking chest deep in water, you will exhaust yourself by trying to run and not get anywhere much quicker. However, if you move at a reasonable pace (which is a little slower than you're used to), you will find that the water flows around you and even tends to support you when you stumble.

"Work with the characteristics of the culture: Here, community is considered more important than any particular business or enterprise. The labor laws reflect this way of life. You can fight against that for a while, but if your neighbors think it's against the good of the people, you can expect the current to start opposing you and to eventually wear you out. Our goals of re-creating rain forest and creating jobs are considered beneficial to the society, so not only do we rarely find ourselves fighting the culture, we also have been supported and carried by it at times.

"People buy trees from us with the understanding that after their trees are removed, the land will be maintained as perpetual rain forest. For people who want to help without owning trees, we have a program we call the Tree Avalanche that works by using donated trees to create a pioneer forest of valuable wood. Among these trees are also planted the 'succession trees' that will eventually make up the mature rain forest. When the pioneer cash-crop trees are removed, allowing the succession trees to form a forest, the money realized will be used to purchase more land and to plant more pioneer and succession trees.

"Since the money gained from the pioneer trees is more than it costs to plant, care for, and harvest them, the amount going into reforestation keeps multiplying. In the wake of this process, instead of leaving a path of destruction, the Tree Avalanche leaves a swath of new forest." (See the Web site for further details.)

REAL ESTATE **DEVELOPMENT**

The term "property development" usually stirs negative images in the minds of longtime Costa Rica residents. They picture a group of profit-hungry investors who have one goal: maximizing profits. If primary forest, mangrove wetlands, or wild animals get in their way, no problem. These kinds of developers show no conscience as their projects destroy the environment. The only thing of vital importance to them is getting the highest return for the lowest cost.

Those who live in Costa Rica for any length of time will understand what I'm saying. We've seen foreign companies—Spanish, German, North American—come in with bulldozers and chain saws to clear building sites and construct homes for wealthy foreigners. Lay waste to the countryside and invade the beaches. The biggest offenders are those who have the most money and thus have *pata* (connections) with local authorities. Big developers can afford to hire plenty of workers to speed up the process of transferring pristine beaches into gated golf courses and luxury homes. Local authorities are sometimes intimidated by wealthy and powerful corporations, and often are backed down when they try to control development.

LARGE-SCALE DEVELOPMENT It doesn't have to be that way, and not all developers *are* that way. A notable exception is the Bosque Verde development on a low mountain near the Pacific Coast village of Nosara. The developers, Julio and Barbara Batista, are originally from Phoenix, Arizona. Neither Julio nor Barbara had previous experience in land development or anything connected with real estate. Julio was an engineer working for Honeywell on the International Space Station, and Barbara was an educational consultant working with schools in Arizona.

This all changed when the Batistas first visited Costa Rica twelve years ago (after reading an early edition of *Choose Costa Rica*). They fell in love with the Beaches of Nosara region. They bought a lovely house with an ocean view and plenty of trees, where bands of howler monkeys, iguanas, and flocks of tropical birds compete for human attention.

By accident, they discovered a Tico family interested in selling their family farm. It was perched on a low mountaintop with fantastic views of the Pacific Ocean and coastline. Julio and Barbara couldn't resist. Heavily forested and not farmed for many years, the 285-acre property had become a veritable wildlife refuge.

They planned to build a new home on the very summit of the property. When they began looking into the expense of installing electric power lines, digging wells, and building three pumping stations to bring water up to the building site, they realized that they were looking at several times more money than they paid for the land. A natural solution was to subdivide the property into building lots and amortize the cost of the infrastructure among those who bought building sites. Each lot had ocean views yet were out of sight of neighboring lots.

Most developers would, at this point, begin selling lots to buyers, giving flowery promises of future water and electricity—a fast way to raise money to begin development. Julio and Barbara didn't care to do this. They decided not to sell even one building lot until water and electricity was in place, ready to start construction. They didn't want to disappoint buyers in the event that they couldn't come through with the promised utilities. When laying out the building sites, they made sure that each home would have maximum privacy from other homes. Even though it's a gated community, they wanted residents to get the feeling they are the only inhabitants overlooking the Pacific.

They hired a Costa Rican forestry and tropical-plant expert and proceeded to plant thousands of trees, shrubs, and vines. Sixty percent of the land is dedicated as an ecological easement for residents to enjoy, thus protecting the natural ecosystems from further development.

Being an engineer, Julio used his expertise to oversee the construction of the roads, culverts, electrical distribution, and water systems. Finally, after drilling wells, designing and building water-pumping stations, and bringing water to every home site, Bosque Verde was ready to begin selling building sites. All of the above took eight years of intensive (and expensive) work. But it was finally completed in 2005. Julio says, "We feel very good about what we have achieved. We

used our retirement money to create an ecologically friendly community where we can live with like-minded adventurers. It has been a creative journey."

Almost the moment the building sites were put on the market, one couple bought two of them—one for their home and one for future investment. An entry with lagoons and gardens for beauty and a gate-house for security are under construction.

Contact information and Web site: Greg Smith or Susan Loudenslager, 682–0616 or 876–0919 within Costa Rica; 011–506–682–0616 from the U.S.; www.bosqueverdereserve.com.

SMALL-SCALE DEVELOPMENT Property development doesn't have to be done with unlimited funds and investment. A few years ago, José Pelleya, a Cuban American from Florida and owner of a bed-and-breakfast in Alajuela, started looking around for another B&B to complement his business.

José says, "Unexpectedly I ran across a beautiful farm property, rolling hills and good views, on the outskirts of San Ramón. It had a large seven-bedroom, two-bath home (in need of remodeling), sitting on an eight-acre parcel. I loved it and could immediately see possibilities for a unique country bed-and-breakfast."

Formerly an attorney specializing in Florida real estate, José used his skills to negotiate a lease with the option to buy, with seller financing for one year once he exercised the option. José points out that both lease-option and seller financing are practically unheard of in Costa Rica.

So he set about remodeling and modernizing the building. This in itself was no minor project. Tico farmhouses are basic to say the least. Being a gregarious person, José realized it could be boring to live on all that property alone. "Why not invite others to share," he thought. So he asked for permission to do a subdivision into building lots (on paper only) and started planning.

"Six months later, I found my first buyer, so I exercised the option," he said. "Then I sold the lot, and away I went!" Divided into seven lots, four sold the first year. Only one lot remains, which José is keeping for himself. Incidentally, one of his clients, a lovely lady named Joanna, bought a lot, built a house, and then married José. He says, "At least she got a good deal on the lot!"

Things were looking good, so José purchased forty-seven acres adjoining his development and created twenty-eight more lots. Twelve of them sold in the last two years. So far eight homes have been finished, with three more being built, and three more planned for 2006. This is creating an interesting community of expatriates, pooling their energy, resources, and creativity. On a roll, José recently bought a nearby 112-acre tract with incredible mountain, gulf, and ocean views. Development is scheduled to come on line early in 2007.

As if that weren't enough, José's latest project is a business in downtown San Ramón called *Solo Bueno*, "only the best." This is a combination Internet cafe, public mailboxes, used-English-book store, as well as a real estate exchange for rentals and sales in the San Ramón area. Whenever local expats go into town, they naturally drop by for a cup of coffee, check e-mail, pick up a paperback, and catch up on what is happening in the community.

CHAPTER TWELVE

HIRING **EMPLOYEES**

During World War II the Costa Rican government passed a series of progressive labor laws that remain on the books and are strictly enforced. These laws seek to avoid conflicts between workers and employers by setting out concrete employment rules and a system of wages and benefits. In effect, these laws take the place of union contracts between worker and employer, guaranteeing individual workers benefits they probably couldn't negotiate on their own. If you look at the rules from the viewpoint of the worker, they are basically fair—and certainly not unreasonable from the standpoint of a considerate employer.

However, hiring a maid, a gardener, or an employee in your business involves more than an informal agreement about wages and hours of employment, as is the custom back home. Because we North Americans aren't used to such formal relations with employees, and because we are likely to be hiring workers, even if it's just domestic help around the house and garden, the rules need to be spelled out in some detail. Following the laws to the letter prevents unexpected and serious problems.

Briefly, here are some ground rules: Employers are responsible for making Social Security payments for an employee as well as deducting

contributions from the employee's wages. All workers are entitled to paid vacations. After a thirty-day trial period of employment, an employee is entitled to severance pay as well as notice before being laid off. A Christmas bonus is neither a gift nor a nice gesture; it's an obligation mandated by law. The employer is required to give three months of maternity leave at half-pay. All these rules are detailed below and should be studied carefully before hiring any help. One other piece of advice: Purchase an accident insurance policy for your employees, even if they are only part-time. Premiums are minimal, but your employees will appreciate the extra coverage. You'll also protect yourself should something horrendous happen to one of your workers.

GOOD **LABOR RELATIONS**

I once spoke with a woman who was visiting Costa Rica with the intention of starting some kind of business. "When hiring workers," she said, "I understand that the secret is to just hire them for eighty-nine days and then lay them off. That way you aren't responsible for benefits such as severance pay and vacations. Once they work ninety days, you are obligated; so you simply hire new workers every eighty-nine days!"

This upset me, and I told her so. Although her information was incorrect, that wasn't the point. Costa Ricans work very hard for a fraction of the wages employees receive in the United States or Canada, and the law guarantees them certain benefits. It's unfair to try to chisel them out of their rightful benefits. Attitudes like this can do nothing but tarnish the reputations of other North Americans. Those who have lived here for a long time generally realize the wisdom of paying their help more than the law requires. "I try to make it so my maid can't afford to quit," said one woman. "She is wonderful, and I couldn't stand to lose her."

Word quickly gets around the neighborhood if you are a good person to work for (or a difficult one). If you earn a poor reputation as an employer, your job applicants will be those who can't hold a job elsewhere. Then you'll wonder why your employees are lazy, don't show up half the time, or have a tendency to steal!

After I gave the newcomer a piece of my mind about her attitude, she explained that she had heard that if you lay workers off after they've worked more than ninety days, you must pay eight years' salary as severance pay. She heard wrong again. The facts are: For each year worked, an employee is entitled to severance pay of one month's salary—up to a maximum of eight months' pay. That is eight *months'* salary, not eight *years*.

From a worker's point of view, this is only fair. Let's suppose that after eight years of faithful service, it becomes necessary to let your housekeeper go. For eight years the severance pay amounts to about $1,500. Does that sound outrageous for eight years of loyalty and hard work? If it does, then maybe you deserve workers who are lazy, don't show up half the time, or have a tendency to steal.

The owner of a hotel and restaurant in Manuel Antonio told of his experience hiring Costa Rican workers. "It's important to gain their trust," he said. "They don't know anything about you or how you are going to treat them. At first I had trouble attracting the best workers. But I treated people fairly and tried to keep them busy during slack seasons so that I wouldn't have to lay them off. Before long I earned a good reputation. Now I have a waiting list of people who want to join my staff."

CONDITIONS OF **EMPLOYMENT**

1. **Length of employment.** The first thirty days of employment are a trial period, and either employer or worker can terminate without notice. However, vacation pay and *aguinaldo* (Christmas bonus; described later) must be paid in addition to wages if the employee has worked more than twenty days in that month's time period. Thereafter, for each month worked one day's vacation pay is due, up to two weeks of vacation for a full year's work. Many employees, either by custom or through union contracts, receive three weeks' vacation. My understanding is that an employee may work through his or her

vacation, provided that the employee receives an additional day's pay for each day worked. (I'm not a labor lawyer, however, so you will want to confirm this point if it arises for you.)

2. **Wages.** Just about every employment imaginable in Costa Rica has an official job description with a corresponding minimum wage. From taxi drivers to physicians, from clerk-typists to college professors, all are listed in a biannual list of minimum wages that requires several pages. Laborers who work with machetes are listed separately from those who mend fences or work with shovels. In addition, various regions of the country have different minimum-wage rates. My favorite wage scale is for journalists: They have the highest in the country, even above airline pilots! I assume this is because the legislators are afraid of journalists' clout. Their minimum is about $700 a month, compared with an unskilled worker's $225 (approximate), or $260 for a salesperson. (These wages are probably higher now due to regular cost-of-living raises.)

An interesting facet of the wage structure is that a maid, gardener, or chauffeur who lives in your home is considered to be receiving an additional 50 percent of his or her salary as "payment-in-kind." If, for example, you pay a live-in maid a salary of $150 a month, the actual salary is considered to be $225, or 50 percent more when figuring benefits. This is important, because the gross salary (salary plus payment-in-kind) is used to figure the *aguinaldo*, Social Security payments, and severance pay. A catch here is that an hourly employee who regularly receives a lunch at your home is also considered to be receiving a 50 percent payment-in-kind, so your Christmas bonus, severance pay, and vacation pay have to be based on this. If you feel that you are already paying the hourly employee enough, you can save money by sending them out to lunch! (To be fair, this is a rather extreme example; few employees would ever put in a claim such as this.)

3. **Working hours.** The maximum for domestics is twelve hours a day, although almost nobody expects more than eight. The standard is usually an eight-hour day and a five-day week. For regular employees other than domestics, work on Saturday and Sunday is at double-time rates. Often construction work-

ers work a half day Saturday for a full day's pay. For those working in businesses or industries that traditionally operate seven days a week, the rules are a bit different; check with your local Social Security office. Although the laws are quite specific, Tico employers often do not follow the laws to the letter, knowing that employees seldom complain. However, I earnestly advise expatriates to follow the rules; you have a high profile in the community, and cutting corners is really a penny-pinching tactic.

4. **Social Security.** An important obligation for employers, one taken quite seriously by the government, is Social Security. This critical institution pays for health care, sick leave, and disability pensions. You, as an employer, must pay 20 percent of a worker's gross salary and must deduct 9 percent of the worker's wages and pay both portions of the tax to the Caja Costarricanse del Seguro Social. Make sure your workers understand that you are withholding the taxes from their pay. Otherwise their share of taxes could come out of your pocket. Some people pay both sides of the Social Security payments as a bonus for a good employee.

   Within eight days of hiring a regular employee, you must notify the local Social Security office. Doing so is vital, because should a worker become ill or injured on the job, you could theoretically be liable for medical bills and 50 percent of the employee's salary for the duration of the sickness. When your employee is covered by Social Security, your liability is limited to the first four days' salary; Social Security takes over from there. To prevent abuse of this law, you, as the employer, are entitled to demand a health certificate from the worker (*carnet de salud*) when the employee is hired and every six months thereafter. This is provided at no cost to the employee by the Seguro Social Hospitals.

   Pregnancy is a different situation. Your employee's blessed event will obligate you to some additional employee benefits. Employees are entitled to a month's rest before the baby is born and three additional months afterward—half the salary to be paid by the employer and the other half by the government. By the way, firing a worker for being pregnant is frowned upon, and you might need to validate your reasons for firing other than pregnancy.

5. **Christmas bonus (*aguinaldo*).** Sometime between December 1 and 20, employees are due an *aguinaldo*. For those who have worked a full year prior to December 1, the bonus is a month's pay. For those who have worked more than the thirty-day trial period but less than a full year, the payment is prorated over the time they have worked. Thus, a person who has worked three months gets three-twelfths of one month's pay. Remember that employees who live in or who regularly receive at least one meal a day get a Christmas bonus based on the payment-in-kind, in addition to their salary, or an additional 50 percent.

6. **Notice and severance pay.** Workers employed more than ninety days and less than a year are entitled to two weeks' notice before being laid off. After a year, one month's notice is required. If you don't or can't give notice, you must pay the employee full wages for the notification period.

   Unless an employee quits, you are obligated to pay severance pay dependent on length of employment: up to three months, none; from four to six months, two weeks' pay; between seven months and one year, one month's pay. Then you must pay an additional month's pay for each year or fraction over six months worked. In no case can this payment be more than the equivalent of eight months' salary.

   Again, remember that this is based on gross pay (including 50 percent payment-in-kind, if applicable). It doesn't matter if the worker immediately finds a new job; you still have to pay.

   A worker can be fired at any time during the first thirty days for any reason, with no obligation other than the *aguinaldo* and wages due. Furthermore, a worker who fails to give notice (*preaviso*) before quitting forfeits the *aguinaldo*.

EMPLOYEE **OBLIGATIONS**

According to government regulations, workers can be held responsible for damages they have caused, whether intentionally or due to imprudence or "inexcusable neglect." A domestic worker can be discharged without receiving severance if "notorious lack of respect or civil treatment is shown," which should be backed up by witnesses. You had better have good proof, though, because in doubtful cases the Ministry of Labor tends to side with the worker.

When an employee quits or is laid off, it is a good practice to make things crystal-clear by having him or her sign a statement (in Spanish) to the effect that all benefits have been paid. Include the severance pay, vacation pay, Christmas bonus, and any salary due up to the time of separation. Have the employee sign the document in front of a witness. Should the employee be quitting voluntarily, be sure to note that in the document.

ACTUAL VS. **MINIMUM WAGES**

As long as Costa Rica's economy is booming, with little or no unemployment, you'll find competition for good employees. Consequently, actual wages are usually higher than minimum wages. Many workers earn commissions and bonuses on top of minimum wages, so in reality minimum wages are simply basic starting points. For a realistic figure of what to pay your household or outside labor, consult your neighbors and see what kind of rates they pay. Talk with local businesspeople and see what they consider appropriate.

We always pay a little more than our neighbors for two reasons. First of all, we want to feel like we aren't being cheapskates. Secondly, wages are so low in the first place we feel somewhat embarrassed on payday, as though we're exploiting our employees. Yes, we risk the ire of those who accuse us of "ruining it for everyone," but I can easily dismiss that. I reject the idea that paying our gardener an extra 40 cents an hour will "ruin it" for anyone. Neither can I believe that all this extra money will go to our workers' heads and cause labor unrest among our neighbors' domestic help. We try to be friends with our employees, not bosses. Our maid always gives us both a hug and kiss on the cheek when we see each other on the village street, just as we do with our good expat friends when we meet.

SALARIES AND **WAGE RATES**

Tico employers tend to be reluctant to pay higher wages than the law requires, but they are often forced to if they want good help. At times construction workers are in very short supply, so they can demand more

than minimum rates. In some parts of the country, workers could earn double what they could make in more depressed areas. Nicaraguan workers (most of them illegal) will usually accept the minimum or less, and are resented by Ticos who have to compete with them for jobs. North Americans who successfully operate their own businesses usually agree that paying decent salaries means happy employees who are loyal and hardworking.

Unlike the United States, the minimum wage in Costa Rica is set for every profession and job classification, not simply a base salary for all types of work. For example, a field hand or domestic servant presently earns $1.57 an hour. Every six months the government adjusts wages to compensate for inflationary trends through recommendations from the Consejo Nacional de Salarios.

Since wage rates change every six months in response to inflation, the wages quoted here can only be approximate. However, because inflation in Costa Rica is fairly predictable, with a slight increase every few months, figures quoted below are accurate only to early 2006.

Not only does just about every job classification have a specified minimum wage, but the level of education is considered, having its own minimum wage. For example, minimum wages range from 124,000 colones a month ($268) for gardeners, janitors, and unskilled workers, but for someone holding a master's degree from a university, the minimum is about

282,000 colones a month ($611). Our local librarian went to night school at the university for several years. Once she received her degree in library science, she was entitled to almost double her salary.

The highest-paid job title on the list is graduate journalist, which pays 327,856 colons a month or $710. My impression is that the legislators are sensitive to press criticism, so by awarding them the top pay rates, they might receive special consideration. Since this is my profession, I feel top pay is perfectly fair. (My publishers might quarrel with that belief.) However, most journalists in the United States earn more money than that per *week*.

Minimum Wage*

Workers	(colones)	(dollars)	(per hour)
Unskilled	125,500	$252	$1.57
Semi-skilled	136,200	$273	$1.70
Skilled	146,400	$293	$1.84
Technicians	157,700	$315	$1.97
University graduates	238,000	$475	$2.97
With graduate degree	287,000	$572	$3.58

* figures as of 2006

Foreigners considering finding jobs in Costa Rica can easily see a problem here. Jobs such as truck drivers, construction workers, and bartenders pay about $10 a day. So the problem is convincing an employer that you have some skills to offer that Tico workers do not have. And in order to get a work permit, you have to convince Immigration that you won't be doing work that a Tico could do.

WORKING IN **COSTA RICA**

A question often asked is "How can I get a job in Costa Rica?" The answer is, "It can be done but it's not easy." The Costa Rican government discourages foreigners from competing with citizens for work. In order to work legally, you'll need a special permit, which involves proving that you are uniquely qualified for a job that can't be done by a Tico. Foreign companies are entitled to a limited percentage of noncitizen employees, but in practice they seldom fill this quota. The reason is simple: They can hire all the qualified Tico employees they need, and most foreigners don't want to work for Tico wages. Twenty dollars a day is considered a generous wage.

To give you an idea of how difficult it is to obtain a work permit, only 410 Canadian, English, and U.S. citizens have been granted work permits in the past five years.

Since the collapse of high-tech employment and the dot-com meltdown, many highly qualified and skilled software engineers, technicians, and Web specialists are "at liberty," and many are eager to begin life anew in an interesting setting such as Costa Rica. They are aware that the country's computer technology is riding a wave of expansion as business, industry, and government become computerized and enter the Web universe. It's only natural that those recently unemployed and soon-to-be-downsized high-tech people who love Costa Rica will be looking in this direction.

Are there jobs for these highly qualified people? Probably not. You have to realize that Costa Ricans also see the future opportunities in the world of digital employment. Seems as if every other high school student you meet plans to major in computer science. At every one of the many satellite campuses of the universities, the most popular classes involve computers. Students come from miles around to take night classes in *computación*. The good news is that many high-tech jobs have been created through foreign investment. The bad news is that Intel and other corporations are limited to 10 percent of their workforce being foreigners on work permits, and they are committed to hiring as many Ticos as they can.

Other jobs that gringos try for are those that require some English, for example, bartenders, desk clerks, and office receptionists. But almost all of these jobs also require fluency in Spanish, and the pay will be at minimum-wage level. For example, the government-mandated minimum wage for jobs like these are less than $2.00 an hour! And, for many employers, minimum wage and maximum wage are one and the same. Finding a legal job normally requires some extraordinary skills. One exception is in the field of teaching. Qualified teachers can often find employment, although, again, for minimal salaries. More on this subject can be found in chapter 15, "Costa Rican Schools."

POSSIBLE **WORK-IMMIGRATION CHANGES**

This is not to say that a large number of foreigners aren't working illegally in the country. A large number are. Most work in real estate sales, property management, and tourism. You'll find them employed as waitresses, bartenders, tour guides, and hotel employees. Many are young and willing to take whatever pay they can get, just to live in Costa Rica. A number of them work as English teachers, usually tolerated by the government, ostensibly because they aren't taking work from Ticos. A few with special skills find work in construction. Often, foreigners working as building contractors don't get hassled by local officials, probably because they hire workers and provide jobs. Unless foreigners are obviously taking work from Ticos, their activities are often overlooked.

Let me emphasize: Over the years of updating this book, I've never recommended that people work illegally; I am simply reporting what is the case. The fact is, the Costa Rican government hasn't been enforcing existing laws.

However, in late 2005, the National Assembly passed a law that could radically change past practice. The intent of the law was to crack down on those working illegally in Costa Rica. Principally it was aimed at the flood of illegal immigrants from Nicaraguan, Panama, and other Central American countries, but the law could logically be applied to North Americans as well. Those working without work permits could face fines and possible deportation. The law also specifies fines for employers who hire illegal aliens and provides deportation for those who cannot prove they are in the country legally.

The new immigration rules also give the *Policía de Migración* (immigration police) broader powers to inspect documents and to detain and deport any person who cannot demonstrate his or her legal right to be in the country, including visitors who overstay their tourist visas. If this law is upheld, many "permanent tourists" who have been living in Costa Rica for years, going out of the country every ninety days to renew their visas, could be affected.

The law was to go into effect August 13, 2006. But when Oscar Arias—the new Costa Rican president—took office, he declared the new *ley de migración y extranjería* (immigration laws) "draconian." He requested that the laws be held in abeyance for eighteen months while the new government studies the laws and makes reasonable changes in the rules and regulations.

At this point, the situation gets somewhat complicated. The courts ruled that since the laws were on the books they couldn't be postponed for eighteen months. But the official in charge of administering the law, the *Ministero de Seguridad* (Security Minister) pointed out that no funds or immigration agents were provided to enforce the new regulations. He confirmed that it is an impossibility for the immigration service to apply the new regulations, saying that "no one is obligated to do the impossible."

Meanwhile, the Arias government seems determined to push ahead for a deferral of the law for at least six to nine months, saying they need time to make changes to the existing legislation for a more "practical" law. Needless to say, strict enforcement of these laws could affect many people living and working in Costa Rica more or less illegally. People who could be technically in violation of immigration laws should be aware of what is happening.

This is the state of affairs at the time of writing, when this book is about to go to press. My personal opinion (and it's only an opinion) is that the government is not going to do anything drastic that might affect the status quo for those who are technically in violation of immigration rules. Nevertheless, it would be prudent to keep abreast of events, should there be any question in your mind. You can do this by watching the online newspapers, reading the *Tico Times* and local Costa Rican daily papers. You can also follow my Internet bulletin board at http://discoverypress.com and my Costa Rica Update Web site at: www.discovery press.com/update.

CHAPTER THIRTEEN

GETTING TO **COSTA RICA**

The quickest and easiest way to get to Costa Rica is by air, but this, of course, restricts the amount of belongings you can take—things you may need for a long-term stay. Those who live here full- or part-time always enter with as much luggage as we can get away with, packed with personal things we need from home and items difficult to find in Costa Rica. We send "wish lists" to our friends to carry in their luggage when they visit. They brought us everything from paperbacks and videotapes to bedding and automobile parts.

A number of airlines schedule regular service to Costa Rica—American Airlines, United, and Continental, among others—and inexpensive Canadian charter flights fly from Vancouver and Montreal. Mexico's Mexicana Airlines flies to Costa Rica, as do several other Central American airlines, such as TACA, Aviateca, COPA, and SAM, which fly from Miami, New Orleans, Houston, San Francisco, and Los Angeles.

Costa Rica used to have its own airline, LACSA, which is now part of TACA, an El Salvador line. Occasionally LACSA beats the price of other airlines, but generally all carriers keep their prices within a dollar or so of one another.

Getting the best fare may involve shopping around a bit. My experience with travel agents is that not all of them can find the least expensive way to travel. You can often save money by going online and shopping for the best rates. Check directory assistance for airlines' toll-free telephone listings. You'll spend time on the phone, listening to boring music while waiting for a clerk, but you could save dollars. Be sure to ask about special promotions, which can save you plenty of money. Sometimes the clerk won't know until a month in advance just how much, if any, of a discount will be available.

COSTA RICA'S **MAIN AIRPORT**

Totally renovated and ultramodern, the Juan Santamaría Airport, near San José, has streamlined its arrival and departure procedures and is almost a pleasure to use. Customs inspections are relaxed yet professional. Airport taxis to downtown San José are plentiful and prices are controlled. The standard price to downtown San José is around $15. Drivers readily accept dollars. By the way, some airport taxis aren't supposed to go to more than one hotel or address per trip, so if you share a cab with someone, make a deal with the driver, if necessary, perhaps a tip for the extra stop. Also, a bus stops on the main road in front of the terminal; there are inexpensive buses for downtown stopping every few minutes.

When returning from Costa Rica, paying the departure tax used to be paid by buying stamps for your passport from hawkers on the sidewalk. Today you stand in one of two lines in the terminal and pay the tax ($26) at special desks. You can use colones, dollars, or even a credit card (which I don't recommend, since they have to add about $4.00 or so to the bill). You'll hear travelers complaining about this tax, but consider that U.S. airports also have hefty charges, which customers often aren't aware of— they simply add it to the price of your ticket.

A new international airport near the northwestern city of Liberia opened a few years ago. It had been completed and ready to open for some time, with the first official inauguration held twenty years ago and several other grand openings since, each time with service predicted to begin shortly. At each inauguration ceremony officials from the tourism ministry, travel agencies, and businesspeople all celebrate the impending opening of this new facility. This time they are finally open for business.

LACSA flies several times a week from Miami, and charter flights from Canada are now landing. Continental, Delta, and American have added flights to Liberia's Daniel Oduber International Airport, and other airlines are said to be planning on initiating service.

With the Liberia airport in service, Guanacaste's Pacific Coast towns and resorts will boom. The economy of this region is already healthy, but increased airline traffic will boost it even higher. A friend flew in from Miami the other day, with about two and a half hours' flight time and two and a quarter hours' drive time from Liberia to a Pacific beach resort—a total travel time of less than it used to take to drive from the San José airport to his destination!

DRIVING TO **COSTA RICA**

For a while civil war in Guatemala, El Salvador, and Nicaragua brought tourist automobile travel through these countries to a virtual standstill. But even then some intrepid tourists insisted on driving, merely changing the route somewhat. They traveled the Pacific coastal route through Guatemala, avoided El Salvador by detouring through Honduras, and then carefully skirted trouble spots in Nicaragua. We tried to get through in 1984 but returned to Mexico after tiring of gun barrels being pointed at our foreheads at every military stop. Today, with the return of peace to the region, automobile travel is once again routine.

Our last adventure took place in 1999. The actual driving time from the Arizona border at Nogales was around nine days of no more than eight to ten hours of relaxed driving per day. But not being in a hurry, we spread the trip over a full month. We stopped to visit friends in Lake Chapala and Guatemala City. We also detoured to spend some time at the marvelous Mayan ruins in Copán, Honduras.

Not everyone would have enjoyed the trip as much as we did, but we had done it before, and for us it was a pleasant adventure. From the time we entered Mexico until we reached our home in Costa Rica, we encountered not one military stop, saw no military presence, and were halted only a few times for routine checks of the car—presumably to make sure it wasn't stolen. At none of the borders did they inspect our luggage or do anything other than glance in the back of our station wagon. Also, we were careful not to do anything stupid, like driving after dark.

Please don't think I'm suggesting that everybody will have a breeze. It's a long trip, with bad roads as well as good ones. Sometimes the accommodations are awful; sometimes they're delightful. If you can speak some Spanish, it would be helpful, but we met many travelers who spoke very little Spanish yet were making out just fine. Some people will enjoy traveling through Mexico and Central America, others will not. Those who won't enjoy this kind of journey are those who probably wouldn't think about going in the first place. You'll know into which category you fall.

I've interviewed more than a dozen travelers who made the trip between 1995 and 2005; all shrugged off these inconveniences. Most described their trip as an adventure they wouldn't have missed for anything. The secret to stress-free traveling in Central America is to "hang loose" at the customs stops—try to laugh at the process. A smile will do a lot to smooth your path across borders. A smile and a $5.00 bill will do even more. Those who can't handle a trip like this are those who probably wouldn't try it in the first place. With the exception of the excellent and efficient toll roads through Mexico, the Central American portion of the Inter-American Highway today consists of low-speed pavement—sometimes pockmarked, occasionally smooth with dual lanes.

Every day on the road was a new adventure, a new challenge, full of photo opportunities and stimulating encounters with other travelers and local people. The most annoying part of the journey was the delay and inconvenience while crossing borders. Sour-faced officials examine your papers with suspicious eyes, then hand out a sheaf of forms to be filled out in triplicate. Then they rubber-stamp everything in sight. (Oh, how they love rubber stamps!) You go from one official to another for what seems an eternity. Finally, you are allowed to leave the country, only to drive 50 feet into the next country and start the process all over again at the next customs office.

Even if you speak Spanish well, I highly recommend that you hire a *tramitador,* someone to help you through customs, at the busy crossings. (You can generally tell when you need one: when the lines are long and not moving.) You'll usually find kids hanging around who, for a fee, will run your passport and car papers around to the places where they will be rubber-stamped, have stamps affixed, and signatures scrawled upon them. Which of the kids to hire? I always pick one who appears to be the most aggressive. He will not be shy about elbowing other tourists aside to shove his way to the front of the line so that the officials can look at your papers first. The cost is usually $10, but it's worth it. Get the price fixed before you start. If things appear to be moving smoothly, you may not need to hire a helper.

We didn't drive through El Salvador this last trip, though not because we wanted to avoid it; our visit to Copán, Honduras, just happened to route us around El Salvador. The border crossing from Guatemala to Honduras at that point is exceptionally easy and painless. So few cars cross there that the border guards seemed delighted to have someone to chat with.

ON THE ROAD From the U.S. border at Brownsville, Texas, to Costa Rica, the drive is 2,300 miles (3,701 kilometers). From Mexicali the distance is 3,700 miles (5,955 kilometers). Your car should be in good condition, with new tires, a spare, an emergency tool kit, road flares, and flashlights with extra batteries.

Always get out of the car and supervise the gas station attendant while he services the car. Attendants have been known to accidentally put diesel fuel or leaded gas into a car requiring no-lead fuel. And make sure they turn the pump back to zero before they start so that you don't end up paying for gas you don't get. (I've never had this happen in Costa Rica.) You might carry a hand calculator to make sure you are paying the correct amount and getting the right change. Even if you don't know what you are doing, the attendant will think you do, and he won't cheat. A trick that station attendants in Mexico might try to pull on you: When you hand them a 100-peso bill, they quickly switch it for a 50-peso note, to make you think you made a mistake. The cure for this is to carefully hand them the note and say, "*Billete de cien pesos*" ("hundred-peso bill").

Don't forget car insurance. Your U.S. or Canadian policy isn't recognized south of the border, but carry it with you anyway as proof that you have a valid policy, just in case. You can buy a special insurance policy for Central America. Before you cross into Mexico, contact Sanborn's Insurance at (210) 686–0711 (fax 210–686–0732), or write to P. O. Box 310, McAllen, TX 78505-0310. The Web site is at www.sanbornsinsurance.com. This company can write Central American policies by telephone and will take credit cards. Most people purchase a fifteen-day policy, which should be more than ample time to drive all the way to Costa Rica. For fifteen days of liability-only coverage, the cost is probably around $100. Ask for a *Travelog* with detailed directions, maps, and hotel/restaurant listings for Central America (free with insurance).

The first country to cross is Mexico. You will be issued a tourist card at the border without hassle, or you can obtain one in advance at your nearest consulate by showing your passport. If your vehicle is financed, you'll need a notarized statement from the bank or finance company with permission to take the vehicle out of the country. It's best to have it notarized at a Mexican consulate if possible. Mexico has been closely checking cars coming into the country to combat a rash of stolen automobiles. Rules are in a state of flux at the moment; you may have to pay a small fee and post a bond to ensure that you don't sell the car in Mexico. (You must use a credit card for this bond; no cash changes hands.) When you exit the country, they'll cancel this bond. The Mexican crossing is easy; you won't need anyone to help you, and you won't have to tip anyone. Be sure to do the paperwork as soon as you cross the border, because it's easy to drive across and then be stopped 20 miles (32 kilometers) down the road at the Immigration checkpoint and have to turn back to get your papers in order. If you are carrying household goods or items you will need in Costa Rica, make sure you let customs officials know you are "in transit," and they'll so note on your car papers.

Unless you want to visit places like Puerto Vallarta, Acapulco, or other spots on the west coast, the best route is one of Mexico's new high-speed toll roads. Driving through Mexico on the nontoll highways will add a day or so to your travel time, but you'll see more of Mexico. Figure four or five days to make the trip to the Guatemalan border. You ought to take at least an extra week and enjoy a minivacation, visiting some of Mexico's recreational and historical sites.

Keep an eye out for speed-limit signs and slow down to the posted limit; that way you won't be bothered by cops. They won't stop you unless you're breaking some traffic law. This is pretty much true anywhere in Central America, so obey the signs and avoid problems. Important: Never drive at night in Mexico or anywhere in Central America. Highways are generally in fair condition, but they are built as cheaply as possible. This means the road often ends at the edge of the pavement; when there are shoulders, it's purely by chance. In the dark you have no idea what lies alongside the pavement—a stretch of gravel, mud, or a 10-foot drop-off. You might even find a bull sleeping on the pavement. Repeat after me: Don't drive at night! (I have to admit that I violate this rule when using Mexico's toll roads; they are wide and safe, and they have almost no traffic, even in daylight.)

The recommended place to cross into Guatemala is near Tapachula, Mexico, at the Guatemalan town of Tecún Umanán. Good overnight accommodations can be found in Tapachula, so you'll be ready for the Guatemala run in the morning. Start early, since the border sometimes closes for siesta from 1:00 to 3:00 P.M., sometimes earlier if personnel feel in need of a nap.

From Guatemala City to Costa Rica, you have two choices: through Honduras or through El Salvador (which includes a few miles through Honduras). The shortest, quickest route is through El Salvador, yet until the cessation of the civil war here, most drivers preferred the slow, safe route through Honduras. Nowadays travelers describe driving the El Salvador leg as uneventful. The advantage of the Honduras route is a side trip to the fabulous Mayan Ruins at Copán.

By the way, Honduras must have found a lot of extra money somewhere, because the highways are new, wide, and marked with a line in the center—and they actually have shoulders! The same for Nicaragua. My understanding is that several European countries as well as Japan and Taiwan put up a lot of foreign aid money to help these developing countries improve their highway infrastructure. Because they consider Costa Rica wealthy in comparison, they ignore the potholes in our roads.

The drive from Guatemala City to the city of San Salvador takes about six hours, depending upon the delay at customs at the border. From El Salvador another early start will get you across a short stretch of Honduras and into Nicaragua. It's only a 190-mile trip from the Honduras border to the Costa Rican border. For an overnight stay in Nicaragua, you might consider the interesting city of Granada.

By the time you've reached the Nicaraguan border, you'll probably be eager to get to Costa Rica. Driving the length of Nicaragua can be done in a few hours, so there's no real need to stop over there, although you might be tempted to linger in one of the colonial cities or stay at a beach hotel not far from the Costa Rican border. Nicaragua is sometimes plagued with strikes and protests, which can slow traffic down, so try to make the earliest border crossing possible.

Once in Costa Rica, be sure to make copies of your papers and your passport—and keep them in a separate place, just in case you lose the originals. Be sure to copy the passport page with the entry stamp for the date you entered the country.

Remember that the car permit and your insurance are good for ninety days. Unless you choose to pay the import tax and apply for a Tico title and license plates, you'll have to take the vehicle out of the country at the end of ninety days. Depending on the way the rules are being applied, there is a possibility of renewing your papers for another ninety days, but eventually you'll have to decide whether to bite the bullet and pay the duty, take the car out of Costa Rica for ninety days, or return home with it. Be sure to check with customs when crossing the border and find out the current policy regarding car importation. You can sell the car in Costa Rica, but you'll have to drop the price to compensate the buyer for having to go to the trouble of legalizing the vehicle.

CENTRAL AMERICA **BY BUS**

For those with lots of time, patience, and a sense of adventure, it's entirely possible to travel from the Mexican border to Costa Rica by bus. As a matter of fact, my wife and I did exactly that during our first visit to Costa Rica, thirty-three years ago. We didn't do it to save money (although it's a cheap way to travel), we used to enjoy bus travel in foreign countries and happened to have unlimited time for our vacation. With somebody else driving, you get to see the countryside and enjoy visiting the cities in a much different way from flying over at 33,000 feet. Like driving to Costa Rica, however, a bus trip is something you need to think over carefully. It takes a stalwart traveler with a highly developed sense of adventure and plenty of free time to enjoy this trip. (Today my wife and I prefer to fly anywhere we can't drive.)

Friends related the following itinerary for the trip they took a couple of years ago. They caught the *Ticabus* at its San José bus terminal and headed toward Guatemala City; tickets cost around $50 each. The bus stopped at the Nicaragua–Costa Rica border for customs inspection. The total border cost for both Costa Rica and Nicaragua was $8.75.

They spent the first night at the Ticabus terminal in Managua. They stayed in the small hotel at the bus station, humorously called the "Ticabus Hilton." Rooms cost $6.00 per person and were modest but clean. The bus left early the next morning and stopped at the Honduras border for passport stamping and $4.00 for exit and entry fees. (An alternate route stops over in Tegucigalpa, Honduras, instead of San Salvador.)

Going through Honduras was fairly fast. The bus's next stop was at the El Salvador border, and exit stamps again cost $4.00. Entering El Salvador requires a visa that you can get from an embassy by mail at no charge. If you don't have a visa, you'll have to pay $10 for a tourist card.

The bus stopped for the night in the city of San Salvador. At the nearby San Carlos Hotel, the room rate was $10. The bus left at 6:00 A.M.

At the Guatemala border another stop was made for exit from El Salvador and entry into Guatemala. The costs were $2.00 each. The bus finally arrived in Guatemala City at about noon.

In Guatemala they caught a bus that went to Tapachula, Mexico, for a fare of $21. This was the Galgos Bus line, comfortable and providing very good service. From Tapachula to Mexico City, they traveled on the Cristobal Colon line—the best bus on their entire trip. The bus had hostesses and plenty of room to stretch out and enjoy the sixteen-hour trip to Mexico City. The tickets were $40. From Mexico City a twenty-four-hour trip to Juárez (on the border across from El Paso) cost $80.

Even though Mexican first-class buses are okay—often having a bathroom, stereo music, and sometimes even an attendant serving coffee and soft drinks—this was the longest, most difficult leg of the trip. Because of the long distance between the United States and the Guatemala border, the numerous bus changes and long hours made for an uncomfortable trip. (An alternative might be to fly from Tapachula or to break up the trip with stopovers for sightseeing in Mexico.)

The total cost per person for bus fare and fees came to about $222. This is not a trip for the fussy or overly fastidious because hotel accommodations are basic to rustic, and you'll feel constrained to staying near your hotel and/or the bus station. I don't advise exploring the cities of San Salvador or Managua during the overnight stops, except in the company of other bus passengers—preferably Central Americans who know what they are doing.

The fun part of this bus trip is making friends with other travelers. Those passengers who live here are eager for you to enjoy their country, and they'll point out landmarks and highlights as you cruise along. While having lunch at the rest stops, passengers make plans for having dinner together at the next overnight stop. By the time my wife and I reached San José, we had made many friends and received several invitations to visit Costa Rican families.

CHAPTER FOURTEEN

TOURING **COSTA RICA**

Every nook and cranny of Costa Rica has something special to offer, something to dazzle the eyes or gratify the other senses. Newcomers are never satisfied until they have seen it all; longtime residents tend to repeat their travels, to see everything again and again. Fortunately, getting around the country is easy. Within a few hours you can visit just about any section of Costa Rica you choose, and you usually have several modes of transportation available to you.

The quickest way to travel about the country is by SANSA, Nature Air, or charter flights. Planes fly regularly, serving San José, Quepos, Golfito, Palmar Sur, Barra del Colorado, Nosara, Tamarindo, and Sámara. Ticket prices used to be inexpensive, but in the past few years, they have become costly, and service often leaves much to be desired. Charter flights cost only a few dollars more than scheduled flights. SANSA offers a 50 percent discount for residents with *cédulas* (permanent residents), but it's still five to ten times as expensive as bus travel. Flights to anywhere in the country take far less than an hour, including stopovers. Check with travel agents or Web sites for schedules. They can change overnight or be canceled entirely.

Because flights are popular and the planes are small, they are frequently booked solid. Make reservations well in advance. And since regular service can be crowded, "air taxi" or charter flights are popular. Small five-passenger planes will take you anyplace in the country with an airstrip. What's nice is that you can have a driver awaiting your arrival, who rushes directly to your charter flight, and you don't need to overnight in San José. (Pause for cheers and whistles.) Sample fares: to Carrillo or Nosara, about $80 one-way (minimum of two passengers), or $280 for five passengers to Tortuguero.

What if you are a pilot and would like to rent a plane and fly yourself? Not so easy. Even if you are a certified pilot with a license from another country, you can't rent a Costa Rican plane until you've earned a Costa Rican license. You need to show proof of your total air hours logged in your country as well as log a certain amount of time in Costa Rica. To import an airplane, see chapter 16.

TRAINS AND **BUSES**

Guidebooks sometimes rave about the scenic wonders of the country's train system. Especially tempting are descriptions of a spectacular railroad trip from San José to the Caribbean city of Limón. However, when you read about train trips in Costa Rica, you know the book is a bit out-of-date. Since the earthquake of 1991, passenger trains no longer journey to Limón, or anywhere else for that matter. Sad, but true. Some roadbeds and a few ancient bridges slipped downhill—common occurrences during Costa Rica earthquakes—but this time the government decided not to rebuild. The lines were losing money anyway.

It's possible that service to the Pacific port of Puntarenas could be resumed sometime in the future, with a private company taking over the operations. In early 2000 a test run to Puntarenas had people sleeping in line overnight to get tickets. Two hundred disappointed would-be passengers watched the train roll away without them. The train to the Caribbean Coast, however, definitely appears to be history. The cost of repairing the bridges and tracks would be prohibitive.

Buses are another story. In addition to excellent city bus service, eight intercity bus companies provide frequent service to just about anyplace you'd care to go. Unlike the situation in the United States, where monopolistic intercity bus fares sometimes border on extortion, tickets between Costa Rican cities are downright cheap. A four-hour ride from San José to Limón, for example, costs little more than $4.00.

San José has no central bus station; bus lines depart from separate terminals, ranging from a new, full-service terminal to a curbside parking place in front of a small ticket office. For example, to go to Quepos and Manuel Antonio, you take the buses that leave from the "Coca Cola" terminal. (The Coca Cola terminal gains its name in a typical Tico fashion: There used to be a Coca-Cola bottling plant in the neighborhood.) Buses for Limón, Cahuita, Puerto Viejo, and other Caribbean destinations have their own terminal on Calle Central, 6 blocks north of the Metropolitan Cathedral. Often reservations need to be made a day or two in advance. The better tourist guidebooks list the bus terminals, destinations, and travel times.

A number of smaller bus companies (often with only one or two buses in the fleet) carry passengers to all imaginable sectors of the country. Few towns or villages in the republic lack bus transportation of some sort. Often while I was negotiating impossible backcountry roads, bouncing through deep potholes, skirting boulders in the trail, and wondering whether my rental car could ever make it back in one piece, a passenger-laden bus would appear from out of nowhere, sound its horn impatiently to move me aside, and then rumble past as it hurried on its way.

These country buses tend to be of an older, rattletrap variety, usually secondhand school buses bought at surplus in the United States. Sometimes the owner-drivers don't bother to change the paint, and the bus finishes its transportation career bouncing along dusty trails in Costa Rica with the legend Maplewood unified school district still painted on its side. Sometimes you'll be pleasantly surprised by an air-conditioned vehicle of late manufacture, which makes the backcountry surprisingly luxurious. Of course, there's nothing to guarantee the driver will actually turn on the air-conditioning, which draws power from the engine. And since Ticos open the windows from force of habit, the air-conditioning is redundant.

Since the distance between San José and any destination in the country is not very far, bus trips don't take too long. From San José to Quepos, a popular tourist destination, bus travel time is less than four hours. By air it is only twenty minutes or so, but by the time you get out to the airport an hour early, wait for the plane to leave (often a half hour to an hour late), and then wait for a bus to take you from the airstrip to town, you haven't saved all that much time. Plus you've missed a lot of interesting scenery. However, be aware that different bus lines have varying schedules. For example, travel from San José to Puntarenas takes two hours on one bus line but four hours on another line.

I knew Costa Rica had a lot of competing bus companies, but for a while I was astounded at how many different bus lines there appeared to be in and around San José. It seemed that the bus lines' names were very creative. Then I discovered that the name painted on a bus's side or on the back wasn't the name of a bus company at all but, rather, an imaginative name given to the bus by its driver as an expression of his individuality.

The *Tico Times* ran a feature article on these names, at which point I realized that the Papa Lolo bus that passed by my house every morning as I waited for my ride was not owned by Papa Lolo Bus Lines but driven by a driver with the nickname Papa Lolo. Some buses are named after family members; other names are exercises in imagination. Additional names the article noted were Desert Storm, *Krakatoa*, *El Principe Azul* (the Blue Prince), *Mil Amores* (Thousand Loves), the Dancing Queen, and *El Guerrero del Camino* (the Road Warrior).

A MULTITUDE OF **TAXICABS**

Costa Rica enjoys an excellent system of taxis, with about 7,000 drivers zipping along the streets of San José and the suburbs—double what there were a decade ago. Almost all cabs are late-model Japanese imports, usually Toyota or Nissan. Occasionally you'll see a Volkswagen or a Volvo. By law taxicabs are painted bright red. You can't miss them.

Not only is taxi equipment usually in good shape, but fares are inexpensive. In San José you can go practically anywhere in the city from downtown for between $1.00 and $3.00. Between 10:00 P.M. and 5:00 A.M., drivers are permitted to charge an additional 20 percent. Drivers don't expect tips, but I always round the bill up to the next 100 colones, and they drive away happy.

All San José taxis are supposed to have meters, and except for the "pirate" cabs, most do. Ticos refer to a taxi meter as a *maría*. Why *maría*? Some years ago Costa Rica's president decided that taxis should have meters rather than have drivers and clients haggling over the price of each ride. So he ordered a batch of taximeters from a company in Argentina for a trial run. The company's name contained the word María-something-or-other. But with typical Costa Rican bureaucracy, customs officials in Limón refused to allow the contraptions into the country until all the proper papers and forms were filled out in triplicate and stamped. By the time all the red tape and tax stamps had been glued to quadruplicate copies and signatures affixed, the meters—which were mechanical, as opposed to the electronic ones they use today—had rusted in Limón's damp climate and had to be trashed. Ticos thought this so funny that they adopted the word *maría* for a taximeter.

Avoid cabs parked in front of hotels or discos. The drivers will tell you that they don't have to use meters because they pay more insurance or some other baloney. The truth is, they charge from two to four times the normal rate. When in doubt, ask, "*Hay una maría?*" If the driver claims the meter isn't working, don't enter the cab until you've established a price (provided, of course, that you know about what the price should be). If the driver quotes a ridiculous price or if you haven't any idea of the correct fare, take another cab with a meter. At certain times of the day, drivers are reluctant to turn on the meters because they know they can get all the customers they want and don't want the cab's owner to know exactly how much was taken in.

Often you'll find cabs without meters, known as *piratas,* or "pirates," private autos illegally operating as taxis. Usually the fares quoted by these nonmetered cabs are about what you'd pay in a legally operated vehicle. The problem with *piratas* is that some of them aren't in safe operating condition. And unless you know what the fare should be and you know enough Spanish to negotiate, I'd recommend waiting for a cab with a meter. All in all, I think Costa Rican taxi drivers are fairly honest. Rarely have I been overcharged, and that was during times of heavy rains or rush hours, when the extra cost was worth it to me.

Although the law says that taxicabs must use meters, bear in mind that any trip over 12 kilometers (7.5 miles) is exempt. A trip from the airport to San José, for example, should cost between $12 and $16, depending on what part of the city you are going to.

Why are most cabs new? Because one side benefit of owning a taxi is that it can be purchased free of import duties, as long as it is used for three years before selling it as a used car. This means that after three

years of generating income, the vehicle can be sold for almost as much as it cost in the first place.

Up to this point we've been discussing taxicabs around the Central Valley. Taxis aren't only for city folk: You'll find them all over the country, sometimes in places so isolated that they would seem implausible. Not all villages will have a taxi, but most have access to one from a neighboring village. Away from the city's paved roads, four-wheel-drive taxis are the norm—and in the rainy season, a must. Four-wheel-drive trucks commonly serve as taxis, with the truck bed used to transport furniture, appliances, or more passengers. In rural areas, where buses and taxis are rare or non-existent, private autos and trucks often provide free rides to local people walking from one village to another. I do the same and find that locals appreciate rides—the hospitality enhances their opinion of foreigners.

TAXI CHAUFFEURS Driving a car around San José or through the narrow roads in the immediate countryside isn't exactly a relaxing pastime. I sometimes find myself so involved with traffic and confusion that I see very little. My passengers see even less, since they spend a great deal of their time praying, cursing, or shouting at me: "Watch where you're going, you dummy!" For that reason I rarely drive in downtown San José, even though I have my own car. It used to take me ten minutes of sweating and cursing to get from our condo to the center of town, whereas it takes only five minutes of sweating and praying in the average taxi. (My idea of hell would be driving a taxi in San José through eternity!)

There is a better way to explore the Valle Central: Rent a cab! Taxi drivers much prefer the idea of one fare for the entire day, instead of wandering all over town waiting for someone to flag them down. One fare isn't nearly as hard on the cab, since passengers always want to stop, get out, and spend time looking around, giving the taxi and driver a deserved rest.

Not only is it convenient to let someone else drive (someone who knows what he's doing), but renting a cab costs about the same as renting a car for the day. A competent, English-speaking cabdriver will chauffeur you around the Valle Central for five or six hours for about $50. A rental car for one day, with insurance and gasoline, would cost almost $60—and $1 million worth of tension. In other words, after you buy the driver's lunch and give a small tip, you're about even. Most any cabdriver will rent for about $10 per hour, but you're better off making prior arrangements with an English-speaking driver.

Taxicab rental will also save you hours of time and frustration when checking out neighborhoods for real estate. The driver can whisk you to a half-dozen suburbs in less time than you can stumble onto one. This is also a great idea for sightseeing trips around the Valle Central. Instead of four people paying $25 to $45 per person for a five-hour commercial tour, a cabdriver can show you the same sights, with individual attention, for much less. Some drivers will even take you on longer trips, anyplace in the country you care to go—Monteverde or Manuel Antonio, for example—as long as you also take care of their hotel and meal expenses.

Not all drivers are willing to rent by the hour, and not all can speak English well enough to explain what you are seeing. To find one who does, check with your hotel clerk or a travel agency. Many English-speaking drivers are available and eager to show you around the Valle Central.

COSTA RICA **RENTAL CARS**

Renting a car is by far the most convenient way of touring the country. When you get serious about looking for a place to live for a few months or for the rest of your life, renting a car for a week or two allows you to travel about freely in search of your dream location. You don't have to bother with bus schedules; you can check out side streets or country lanes, and you can stop whenever you find a particularly interesting view. With a car, you needn't worry about hotel reservations; chances are, if one hotel is full, another will have room. You can drive around, checking out FOR SALE or FOR RENT signs. You can investigate for yourself instead of being under the control of a salesperson, a rental agent, or others with a vested interest in showing you only their own properties.

At present, automobile insurance is a government monopoly, and it's mandatory that your rental-car insurance be purchased through the government agency. This could change soon, bringing much-needed competition to the field. The way it is now, there's usually a hefty $750 deductible in case of an accident with a rental car. Should the car be totaled or stolen, the deductible is $1,500. Since auto theft of rental cars is common, this calls for keeping your rental car in a safe place at night. Nowadays you can pay extra and have full collision insurance, and pay a little more and insure against theft. The insurance isn't cheap, but if you have a gold or platinum credit card (such as Visa or American Express), it should cover the deductible in case of an accident. Check with your credit-card provider to be certain. Be sure to report a mishap to the credit-card company within twenty days, even if the rental agent assures you that the other driver's insurance covers the repairs.

Accessories such as antennas, radios, tires, and mirrors aren't covered by rental insurance; if they are stolen, you are liable. The answer to the insurance problem is to keep your car in a guarded parking lot overnight when in the vicinity of San José. Auto-accessory theft is not common in smaller towns, but in San José and other large cities, be aware.

Important: Unless you purchase full-coverage insurance, before you accept a rental car, check the car for dents, scratches, and blemishes! Make sure the rental-car employee notes each of them on your contract. Unscrupulous employees in some car-rental agencies have been known to work a scam by charging for the same damage over and over. If the damage is there but not duly noted, you could be blamed and may have to pay. Generally, this only happens with smaller rental companies. Discuss the issue before you sign a contract.

Finally, insist on good tires. A sharp rock can penetrate a tire if the tread is thin and the sidewalls weak. If the tire is destroyed, you're liable for that, too. Insist on another car if the tires are not in good shape. If the car-rental agency gives you trouble about this, consider finding another agency.

DRIVING **COSTA RICA ROADS**

Your regular driver's license is perfectly legal in Costa Rica for ninety days from the time you enter the country. After that you need a Costa Rican license. For residents or for those awaiting *residente* status, a license is relatively easy to get: Simply apply at the local office of the Ministry of Public Works ("MOPT" for us gringos; ask a friend to help you find one locally) and present a certificate of health from one of the doctors' offices nearby. The license is issued while you wait.

As a tourist, you are permitted to drive with your home country's license as long as your passport indicates you are in the country legally— that is, if your passport shows you haven't been here more than ninety days. If you leave the country long enough to get a fresh stamp on your passport, you'll be okay for another ninety days. Take this warning seriously. Some MOPT offices issue driver's licenses to nonresidents; some will not. However, the advantages of having a driver's license are nebulous unless you are a resident or have made application for residency.

Some people believe that with a Costa Rica driver's license, you needn't have to carry a passport. Not so. If you can't show either a passport or a resident's *cédula* to prove you are in the country legally, you could have a problem. A photocopy of the passport is acceptable, provided you have a copy of the page showing the date you entered. The original passport is much preferred. Photocopies of your driver's license are *not* acceptable. In fact, without your original driver's license, car-rental agencies won't even rent you a car.

The first rule of driving in Costa Rica is one that should be followed in any country: Do not leave anything valuable in the car, even out of sight. They say that a favorite trick of thieves is to monitor the car-rental desks at the airport and watch who rents a car and fills the trunk with interesting luggage. They then follow the car to the hotel, and while the passengers are inside at the registration desk, the thieves open the trunk and help themselves to the luggage, extra money, cameras, and so on. Frankly, I've never known anyone to whom this happened, and I think this is a bit far-fetched, but why take chances? If possible, leave someone in the car during that crucial first stop. Once you are outside of San José, the chance of something like this happening is almost nil.

Driving through the Costa Rican countryside isn't difficult, it's just slower. With all that gorgeous scenery, who wants to travel fast? Be especially careful when passing. Make sure you have time to get around safely, and be cautious near hills and curves. Always drive as though you expect trouble. That's just common sense in any country, but particularly in Costa Rica. Too many drivers have a daring attitude that urges them to pass on hills and curves. For this reason accident rates in Costa Rica are unusually high. Drive defensively, and keep an eye on the speedometer.

Americans, used to high-speed, paved highways, sometimes have difficulty keeping their speed under 65 miles per hour; it doesn't seem normal to drive slower. But you must realize that 65 miles per hour is about 110 kilometers per hour, an illegal speed anywhere in the country. Most Costa Rican highways have a 80-kilometer-per-hour speed limit. That's only 48 miles an hour—not a normal speed for North American drivers, those used to 65 mile limits with most everyone driving 10 miles an hour faster than the limit. Depending on the quality of a Costa Rica highway, an 80-, 90-, or an occasional 100-kilometer-per-hour speed might be permissible.

Watch for oncoming drivers who flash their headlights off and on. That means trouble ahead, usually a radar speed trap or occasionally an accident. Another sign of danger is a tree branch or piece of shrubbery lying across one lane of the pavement. That signifies that an accident, a washout, or some other nasty surprise could await you ahead.

Driving in city traffic anywhere around San José can be frustrating. As you get the knack of it and learn the system, it gets easier, but never easy. Theoretically, finding your way around San José should be simply, because downtown city streets are logically organized on a north-south, east-west grid. *Calles* (streets) run north to south, and *avenidas* (avenues) run east to west.

However, nothing in Costa Rica is as simple as it sounds. For one thing, street signs are usually missing. Sometimes they'll be posted on the corner of a building or sometimes on a signpost, but just when you need to know exactly where you are, you'll not find a clue. Furthermore, most downtown streets are one-way, sometimes without arrows to indicate which way! You are expected to know. Okay, so you know that Avenida 9 is a one-way street going west, but how do you know the street you are looking at is Avenida 9 when there are neither street signs nor one-way signs? All you can do is watch to see which way traffic is flowing. If no cars are coming either way, you don't dare take a chance.

In the surrounding towns of the Central Valley, traffic is lighter than in San José, but the problem of missing street signs becomes even worse. Some streets are one-way and others two-way, but often there aren't any signs to clue you in as to which is which. An arrow painted on the pavement should indicate which direction is permissible, but often the arrow has faded into history. It's especially disconcerting to be driving along what you believe to be a two-way street and suddenly notice that all the cars parked on both sides of the street are pointing in your direction. Since parking on either side of the street is okay in Costa Rica, you have no way of knowing if they just *happen* to be facing your direction or if you are traveling the wrong way again.

Away from the cities and major highways, you find bumpy roads that demand slow driving. Going too fast over rocks can cut tires, marooning you several kilometers from a repair shop. You may have to change a tire yourself! When this last happened to me, I stood around looking perplexed until two young men stopped to change the spare for me. They refused to accept money. Next I drove to a sort of auto-repair place where two kids fixed my tire in a jiffy using strips of an old inner tube, some kind of glue, and what appeared to be a steel crochet needle. They didn't even have to take the tire off the rim, as I expected. They charged the equivalent of $1.50; that included putting the repaired wheel on the car and stashing the spare in the trunk.

MAPS AND **DIRECTIONS**

Maps of Costa Rica are notoriously inaccurate. I've only seen a couple that are up-to-date, many of them showing roads that haven't been traveled in years, having been abandoned long ago. New roads take forever to show up on most maps. The one map I am familiar with and in which I have faith is published by a company called Berndtson & Berndtson. It's rather expensive, but it's printed on a plastic-coated fiber that ought to last forever.

One of my favorite Costa Rica map incidents occurred while I was trying to find my way from Zancudo back to the highway. I had been there several times before, but I was forever getting lost. This time it seemed hopeless; I knew I was about two hours away from the pavement up north. I saw a truck approaching and flagged it down. With my three maps, I approached the driver and asked him to give me a clue as to how to find the sandy trail that headed north.

He puzzled over the maps, shaking his head in despair. "This map is wrong, Señor," he said. "This town is not here, it is way over here, and this road has not been used for years." He took a pencil and began tracing what he thought might be the road I wanted. Finally, with a flourish, he marked the last portion of the horrible road that connected with the pavement near Golfito. He explained once again how to find the correct turning points and, as an afterthought, said, "But Señor, I don't under- stand why you don't return to San José on the paved road instead of such a bad road."

"Paved road?" I interjected. "These maps don't show a paved road!"

"Of course not. This is a new road and not yet on the maps. Just go 2 kilometers in the opposite direction and you'll reach the pavement!" (Actually, the road had been there for several years, but mapmakers are notoriously slow updating Costa Rica maps.) A few minutes later we were cruising along the road that follows the Panamanian border, with Panama on one side and Costa Rica on the other, headed for the Pan-American Highway!

TRAFFIC COPS **AND SPEED TRAPS**

I often hear reports of tourists being harassed by Costa Rican traffic cops. No doubt these things happen, as is the case anywhere else in the world. A few bad guys can get on the force. Yet after driving many thousands of miles and receiving numerous traffic tickets (all deserved), I have found the overwhelming majority of Costa Rican traffic police to be courteous and rarely stop someone without due cause. With all the crazy drivers in this country, cops have little reason to stop somebody for "nothing at all." Let's face it: Issuing a ticket for speeding, illegal passing, or no safety belt, is *not* police harassment! In the United States it's known as law enforcement. Tourists aren't exempt from traffic laws, even if they don't thoroughly understand them. Why should they be?

Yet you'll continually hear gringos complain that "the cops only stop rental cars. Why not Tico cars?" This is partly true, because Ticos know a little secret: When they see a speed-limit sign of 60 kilometers per hour

(38 miles per hour), they slow down because they know there's a good chance that there's a radar gun ahead. Tourists, used to 65-mile-per-hour highways back home, however, blissfully pass the slowpoke Ticos in front of them. And guess what happens.

Paved Costa Rican highways usually are posted at 80 kilometers per hour. This may seem ridiculously slow (49 miles per hour), but you can avoid being stopped and will be money ahead if you simply relax and drive the speed limit. Ticos know that those occasional long, straight stretches of good pavement are also favorite places for radar guns. Maybe it seems sneaky, but when 80 kilometers per hour is the maximum, you're asking for trouble by going any faster. I've come to love those speed traps; if it weren't for them, all Ticos would be traveling 80 miles an hour! The fine for speeding is about $40 for ordinary violations, or $100 for *velocidad temerario*, that means: "frightful and reckless" driving, defined as 120 kilometers per hour (75 miles an hour) and above.

As is the custom in Mexico and all Central American countries, motorists cooperate with each other by giving a flashing headlight warning of a speed trap ahead. So when you see an oncoming vehicle flicking headlights on and off, bring your speedometer down to the proper range, and you'll avoid being "stopped for no reason."

Allow me to offer some advice for when you're stopped by traffic police (I've had lots of experience in this department):

1. **Be calm, cool, and courteous.** After all, a ticket is no big deal. Until you're officially a resident, a traffic ticket doesn't affect your driving record or insurance. I've escaped several well-earned tickets simply by joking with the officers.
2. **Do not get belligerent or raise your voice.** Shouting won't help; it only makes things worse. When a cop feels he's being harassed for doing his job, don't be surprised if he retaliates in kind. I suspect this is where many cases of true police harassment originate: A tourist isn't aware that he's done anything wrong and becomes angry and abusive. The cop loses his temper, too.
3. **Don't offer a bribe.** Even the best cops will accept money if you force it on them. This encourages a bad practice. The department is continually trying to enforce standards of profes-

sionalism. Wages have been doubled, crooked cops are being dismissed, and intensive training programs are under way.

If the cop suggests that it would be easier to pay him than have to go to some distant place to pay your ticket, just politely decline and calmly wait for the ticket. Don't even discuss it with him. Sometimes, when the cop realizes you aren't going to give him a bribe, he figures it isn't worth his while, so he might let you off with a warning. Example: One day while driving up the Inter-American Highway toward Liberia, I happened to pass another car on a bridge. On the other side of the bridge, I was flagged down by a waiting traffic cop. He asked in Spanish if I knew why I was being stopped.

When I replied, "Of course" [*claro*], the cop asked: "Why did I stop you?"

My reply: "Because I passed on a bridge."

"But, don't you know that's against the law?"

I shrugged and said, "Of course."

The policeman looked puzzled as he said, "Then *why* did you pass on the bridge?"

"Because I didn't know you were here."

Knowing he stood no chance of collecting, the cop laughed and motioned for me to get out of his life. It doesn't always work that way, but it's better than apologizing and pleading and then getting a ticket anyway.

Again, traffic tickets are no big deal, and you can pay at any national bank or simply give them to the auto-rental company when you return your rental car. The agency will pay them for you and add the fine to your credit card. Ticos and expat residents routinely save their tickets and pay them once a year, just before it's time to renew their auto license plates. If a cop tries to insist on a bribe, make a good mental image of him, including his badge number, and report the incident to the Ministry of Public Works (MOPT) at (506) 227–2188 or at the MOPT office on Calle 9 between Avenidas 22 and 23.

I might add that since I've grown accustomed to watching the speedometer, I haven't received a speeding ticket in more than six years, even though I make frequent round-trips to the Nicoya Peninsula—past a dozen speed traps—sometimes with California plates, sometimes in a rental car, usually with my Tico plates. Having no speeding tickets in six years is a Central America record for me.

Traffic tickets used to be so ridiculously cheap that drivers routinely ignored traffic laws, preferring to pay the occasional ticket rather than drive safely. This contributed to an appalling accident rate. Speeding tickets were less than $6.00, so why worry? Even with today's $40 fines, people still keep traffic cops busy.

FINDING HOTELS
AND LODGING

The tourist bonanza over the past few years made the hotel situation somewhat tight at times. To compensate, new hotels were constructed and private families converted homes into bed-and-breakfasts as quickly as they could. Many North Americans joined this bed-and-breakfast boom, partly financing their retirement by renting out spare bedrooms. In smaller communities, hotels and ecotourism facilities raced to accommodate demand. Today you can often find a room for rent in isolated places where camping was the only choice before. This trend has caught up with demand, at least temporarily, because now there seems to be a slight oversupply of rooms.

The tightest hotel-room market in Costa Rica is during the Christmas–New Year's weeks. Not impossible, just tight. Easter week and spring break are other busy times. During the rush seasons, making reservations before you leave for Costa Rica, even if only for the first couple of nights, is a good insurance policy. After you arrive, you can check around and locate something to suit your taste and/or the size of your pocketbook.

Around San José, hotels come in all sizes and flavors, with expensive rooms costing $100 a night and up and cheap rooms under $15. For medium-priced hotel rooms, expect to pay from $45 to $65 a night during the tourist season. I looked at one room for under $10 recently, but shivers ran down my spine when I peered into the gloomy-looking room, with dirty linens on the bed, housed in a ramshackle wooden building that looked like a firetrap. For my personal tastes a $30 room would be my bottom choice, yet many of the younger set and the backpacker brigades believe that anything over $8.00 is far too expensive. My wife's preferences fall into the $60 range or above.

If you're on a budget—as long-term travelers usually are—don't expect too much in the way of luxury. You may find an affordable rate for a room with a private bath, only to discover that the shower is plumbed for cold water only. When a hotel advertises hot water, you'll often find one of those rinky-dink electric heaters attached to the showerhead. This contraption, known as a "suicide shower," has a lever that can be set to one of three positions: HOT, WARM, and OFF. The position that says OFF is the only one that works all the time. This encourages short but exhilarating showers. Ideal for anyone considering celibacy. The secret is to let the water flow at its lowest possible volume, in the hope of coaxing warmth from the heating element. You'll usually get a satisfactory WARM stream of water.

Truly inexpensive hotels sometimes use low-wattage light bulbs to save on electricity, so weak that you have trouble reading in bed. The solution is to carry a seventy-five-watt bulb in your luggage and substitute it whenever you feel like reading. (Make sure you aren't on a twelve-volt system!) Other items you might keep in your bag are a drinking cup, a roll of toilet paper, and some nylon string and clothespins so that you can wash out undies. Important: Pack a set of earplugs. I've suffered several nights made impossible for sleep by inconsiderate people partying all night or standing outside my door making plans for the next day's trip— at 2:00 A.M. One additional item is insect repellent: One buzzing mosquito can make sleep difficult, a dozen of them can make sleep impossible. Understand that most of the foregoing advice is geared toward the low end of the hotel range. Ordinary places are much better.

Should you be stranded out in the country, unable to find a place to stay, your ace in the hole is the local *pulpería*. This is the Costa Rican equivalent of a country "general store"; it also serves as the social center of the community. Drinks and snacks are sold, as neighbors congregate to exchange news and tidbits of gossip as well as purchase necessary items ranging from matches to machetes. The proprietor of the *pulpería* can sometimes find you a room with a local family. This is a unique opportunity to see how country folk live in Costa Rica, but don't expect luxury. A *pulpería* is also an excellent place to inquire about real estate. If anything is for sale or rent in the neighborhood, the proprietor will know, and she might even know the bottom-line price as well as the asking price.

CHAPTER FIFTEEN

COSTA RICAN **SCHOOLS**

Because of Costa Rica's high literacy rate and extensive education system, a higher percentage of people speak English here than in any other Latin American country. English is a required course in grade school and high school. But don't expect every Tico you meet to understand English: They forget high school English just as quickly as you forgot your high school Spanish. The fact that most Costa Ricans have at least a smattering of English makes it easier for those who are struggling with Spanish conversation. When a certain word eludes you, you simply toss in the English word and forge ahead with your discourse, knowing there's a good chance the listener will understand either the word or its context. Fluency and learning are greatly enhanced when you don't have the tension of pausing and searching your memory for the proper word. Tension is an enemy of language acquisition.

Surprisingly enough, many North Americans live in Costa Rica for years without ever learning any more words than needed to deal with the gardener or the gas-station attendant. But those who do take the trouble to learn Spanish find they are highly respected by their Tico friends and neighbors. Knowing the language opens many doors that would otherwise be closed to you. Being able to communicate with

anybody, instead of only those who speak English, permits interaction with a whole new set of potential friends and acquaintances.

SPANISH **LANGUAGE SCHOOLS**

An excellent way to study Spanish and to learn about Costa Rica at the same time is to enroll in one of San José's many Spanish language schools. Language acquisition is big business here, with at least twenty schools in and around San José offering intensive Spanish classes. (Teaching Spanish is a popular cottage industry here.) Throughout the country you'll find individuals who are eager to give you private, one-on-one Spanish lessons. Some schools keep the class size to three or four students, ensuring each person maximum attention from the teacher.

Most schools offer programs that include living arrangements with a Costa Rican family. By interacting with a local household, you might learn how Costa Ricans cook, where and how they shop, and how to deal with servants, as well as other everyday routines of life that can be so different from back home. Combining classroom study and a homestay with a Costa Rican family puts you in a round-the-clock Spanish-speaking environment, speeding up the learning process. Some schools include tours of farms, factories, archaeological sites, museums, conservation projects, national parks, and other places of ecological and cultural importance as part of the curriculum. Some schools will pick you up at your door every morning and return you to your homestay in the afternoon.

An important observation about homestays comes from a former student, who says: "It's best to find a situation where you are the only guest in the home. When three or four students stay in the same house, you'll find yourselves talking to one another in English instead of to your hosts in Spanish."

No matter where you are in Costa Rica, there'll be a language school nearby. You can study Spanish in downtown San José, on the beach in Quepos, in the cloud forest at Monteverde, or even in a typical rural village. The sheer number of schools makes it impractical to list them here. Also, the varying quality of instruction makes it impossible for this book to make recommendations; we just don't know enough about them to vouch for their quality. The *Tico Times*, various tourist publications, and the Internet are full of information about Tico language schools. Your best source for recommendations are from those who have attended a language school in Costa Rica.

YOUR CHILDREN **IN COSTA RICAN SCHOOLS**

A remarkable difference between Latin American children and their North American counterparts is their behavior toward one another and toward authority. Gringo kids are typically boisterous, full of energy, and extremely competitive. On the other hand, Latin American children, especially Ticos, tend to be polite, calm, and well behaved. Bullying other students is all but unknown. Both in the family and school, cooperation is approved and competition discouraged. Classroom discipline is no problem for the teachers, which makes Tico kids a delight to work with. (I can say this from experience, as one who has taught language classes both in the United States and in Costa Rica.)

Your children can select from three types of Costa Rican schools: 1) private English-only schools, 2) private bilingual schools, or 3) free public schools. The farther you live from Valle Central, the more limited your choices. When you live in an area where private schools are too far away to commute, your choices could be a public school or home schooling.

Most foreign residents I've interviewed about their children's progress in private schools heartily endorse the educational and cultural experience their kids were enjoying. Tuition costs vary from the most expensive private school, with tuition and fees of about $7,500 per year (plus bus transportation), to some of the more inexpensive bilingual schools that offer tuition as low as $60 a month. Again, it's way beyond my scope of expertise to even try to make recommendations. You'll need to interview your neighbors and interview the school personnel.

PRIVATE **SCHOOLS**

Most North American parents prefer an American-credited school with a curriculum equal to that offered stateside. Around the San José area, you'll find a choice of twenty or thirty English-only or bilingual private schools. Some present classes half in Spanish, half in English; others are basically English-language schools. Some offer classes from pre-kindergarten through high school, others just the first three to seven grades. English-only schools are popular with Costa Rican families who can afford the tuition. They want their children to learn English, and these schools are essential for those preparing for U.S. universities.

At the end of this chapter, you'll find a partial list of well-known private schools that cater to North American students. Tuition varies from moderate to expensive, and selections will depend on the location of the school facility and the distance from your new home.

PUBLIC **SCHOOLS**

For the most part, Costa Rica's public schools are patronized by expatriate children living too far from the larger population centers to attend a conventional private school. Despite the fact that Costa Rica spends an inordinate amount of money on education, schoolrooms and facilities can be crude and rustic when compared with the average U.S. or Canadian classroom. Often library books are scarce or nonexistent, and the quality of the teachers varies widely.

The daily hours of a public schoolday are usually shorter than those at private schools. Also, when a teacher is absent, classes are canceled and children are sent home early. This is partly due to an irrational government policy of assigning teachers to schools based on need, without considering where a teacher's home is located. Schools provide housing for teachers during the week, and they go home every weekend. Of course, teachers look for any possible excuse to cancel Friday-afternoon classes so that they can get an early start on the trip to their hometowns.

Depending on where you live, your only alternatives could be home-schooling or a Spanish-only public school (sometimes both). Parents of kids enrolled in public schools give mixed reviews. Some children are immediately befriended and accepted by the other children and love their teachers. Others feel lonely and ignored. None reported their kids being mistreated, bullied, or teased because they are different—these things are often a problem in U.S. schools. Much depends on a combination of the individual child's ability to adjust and the particular situation in the school (the attitude of the teachers, the friendliness of the other students, etc.).

I know a couple from Holland whose three children attend an all-Spanish classroom located in a small village on the Guanacaste coast. The youngest (in second grade) absolutely adores the school, the teacher, and her classmates. The next oldest (fourth grade) hates school as much as her sister loves it. The older brother, who has Down syndrome, enjoys school so much that his parents have trouble making him come home after classes. The students his size encourage him to play soccer (which he loves), and they treat him with extraordinary kindness and respect.

The bottom line is that not all children can adapt to a public-school setting in Costa Rica, and some could do poorly. It seems to be an either/or situation that becomes apparent rather quickly. They either love it or they hate it. Whatever you do, don't force the issue if the child is not happy with public school.

COSTA RICA **HOMESCHOOLING**

Some families choose home schooling as an alternative to expensive private schools, or to supplement the public school curriculum. To be honest, while children benefit immeasurably from immersion in Spanish language and Costa Rican culture, a public school can't provide the background needed to be accepted at a North American university. Homeschooling can be crucial here. Also some children will not like public schools; homeschooling could be their only alternative. A recent poll among parents with school-age children indicated that 30 percent of the parents responding described themselves as homeschoolers. Those attending conventional schools were divided between 25 percent in public schools and 75 percent attending private schools.

Sharon Wallace, who has homeschooled three children over the years and sent them away to be accepted in universities in the United States and France, has this to say about homeschooling in Costa Rica: "The nitty gritty is that homeschooling isn't recognized as a legal entity, yet the government takes a typical laissez-faire attitude. The official word is that kids must be in an educational program until age sixteen, but this is not enforced. In fact, local schools are delighted to not have the burden of more students in an already crowded environment. So, like almost everything here, it's considered tacky to butt into someone else's business.

"We've been homeschoolers in Costa Rica for more than thirty-five years. Parents all use a wide range of techniques. Among them are: online classes, standard curriculum, various mixed media courses, supplementary classes, mentor situations, and none of the above (a k a: 'unschoolers.') My husband and I are *unschoolers*, meaning no prescribed course of study; instead we facilitate the kids' interests. And it's worked out beautifully for us. It's interesting that many of us who are totally sold on homeschooling also work as volunteers in local public schools, teaching English, helping set up computer access, teaching CPR (I did that), and whatever is needed."

One common objection to homeschooling is that children miss the social interaction of being in a traditional classroom. However, homeschooling parents in Costa Rica typically get together on a regular basis, bringing the children into social groups, doing ad hoc classes in creative writing, book reviews, science, drama, art, and other subjects. Since the Costa Rican school day is a half-day, at any given time half the school kids are available for an out-of-the-classroom social life. A homeschooling in Costa Rica mailing list can be obtained by E-mail from hscr@codina.org, or from sharon.wallace@gmail.com.

CHILDREN **LEARNING SPANISH**

Whether your children go to public or private schools, you will be astounded at how quickly they become fluent in Spanish (while you struggle and can't seem to get anywhere). It's nothing short of miraculous how kids can absorb a language simply by sitting in a classroom and listening to strange words and mixing with children using these same words. With most adults, it's too late to simply "pick up" the language; you're going to have to work at it.

My favorite example of this instant-learning process comes from Hilary Aeschliman, originally from Kansas City. Her daughter Stephanie had been placed in a very rustic village school on Costa Rica's Guanacaste coast. She started class not knowing a word of Spanish.

After a few weeks, they wanted to purchase Stephanie another school uniform. Hilary says, "We went to this little village store, but despite my Spanish lessons, I couldn't understand a thing the owner was saying. We were just talking in circles—my husband and I in English, the lady who was running the shop spoke only Spanish. We exchanged plenty of smiles and *lo siento's*, but neither had a clue to what the other was saying. After about fifteen minutes we gave up.

"As we were leaving, I said, 'Well that wasn't very productive. I have no idea what she was trying to tell us.'

"At that point, Stef piped up and explained, 'She said that the lady who makes the uniforms is in Nicoya today and for us to come back next week. She'll be here Monday and Tuesday.'

"I could have strangled her!"

ATTENDING THE **UNIVERSITY**

Students from abroad are welcome at Costa Rica's many universities. There are four public universities and nine listings for private institutions. The largest school is the University of Costa Rica (UCR), with about 35,000 students, located in San Pedro, on San José's northeastern edge. Tuition for Tico students is about $70 a semester; foreign students are charged considerably more, with rates available on request. The other large school is Universidad Nacional. It has about 13,000 students and has several campuses scattered about the country, as does UCR.

Most satellite campuses are rather basic, with instruction geared to Ticos who can't afford to take time off from work to study in the San José area. Most classes are held in the evening and offer studies in computers or bookkeeping or preparatory classes for entering a full university setting. I doubt that many gringos could benefit from attending one of these schools.

Private universities offer programs ranging from MBAs to degrees in theology, tropical agriculture, and conservation. Most accept and welcome foreign students, charging tuition of about $100 per class and $5,600 for an MBA degree.

EXCHANGE-STUDENT OPTION If you're convinced that you'd like to relocate to Costa Rica but just aren't ready for it right now, an interesting idea is to send your offspring here for a school term as an exchange student—or maybe just for a class during summer vacation. This gives the youth a head start in learning the language as well as a great cultural experience. And you will have an interpreter when you do decide to make the move. You can contact the Iberoamerican Cultural Exchange Program and inquire about their various exchange-student programs in Costa Rica. The address is 13920 93rd Avenue NE, Kirkland, WA 98034; (206) 821–1463, fax (206) 821–1849.

Christen Kemp, a Spanish and international business major at the University of Tennessee at Knoxville, tells of her experience as an exchange student in a Costa Rican university where she studied Spanish under ISEP (International Student Exchange Program) for a year. The Universidad Nacional is one of few schools offering an optional fee-paid ISEP Spanish program outside the United States and is designed to provide study opportunities beyond those offered typically only through reciprocal exchange.

Christen says, "I studied at the university's campus in Heredia and, though it's not the nicest school in Costa Rica, it was better than I had expected. Some foreign students who studied at other universities claim their schools are better. Apparently Universidad Nacional enrolls many Ticos who can't afford the tuition to attend the better schools. I spoke to one who told me the tuition for a Tico at the school was only about $30 a semester. (I can't help but wonder what happened to the thousands I paid.)

"Technology at this university is not up to U.S. standards. There are only a few computers in the library, and students line up to use them. I found it easier to go to one of the many Internet cafes around town. An hour's Internet connection costs only a dollar. And then there's McDonald's, where you can use the Internet if you buy a Value Meal.

"Registering for classes was quite confusing. They don't use a computer system, so you end up making several trips to classes and the registrar's office. Another big difference is that the teachers are on Tico time. In my first class the teacher was always about forty-five minutes late. The students told me that teachers can be up to an hour late and, unlike the United States, where a class meets for an hour three days a week, at this school a class was held once a week for three to four hours. It's hard to keep focused for that long, but the teachers were actually pretty good. I had an excellent literature teacher from Chile. You do not buy books for your classes. Instead your teacher places a packet of photocopies at a designated copy shop and you go there each week and make copies. They are really cheap, like ten colones each.

"Living with a Tico host family is awesome. This was probably the best part of my education in Costa Rica. Being introduced to and actually accepted into a traditional family and being part of their religious-holiday celebrations was an unexpected gift.

"There are many advertisements for families looking for students. The exchange program from the University of Tennessee paid my family $300 a month. For this I received a nice room, three full meals a day, and all my clothes and linens washed and ironed (sheets, pajamas—everything was ironed!). The family had a maid from Nicaragua whom they paid $100 a month to cook and clean five days a week."

TEACHING **ENGLISH**

I maintain a very popular Internet Costa Rica bulletin board as a public service to those who want to know more about traveling in or moving to Costa Rica. It's also used by those who have already moved to Costa Rica and want to keep in touch with one another. Nearly 200,000 visitors have visited the bulletin board over the past four years (http://discoverypress.com/CostaRica).

Hardly a day goes by without requests for job information from young people who want to live in Costa Rica so bad they'll work for any amount of money. The most frequent question is "How can I get a job teaching English in Costa Rica?" Many queries come from those who assume that just because they speak English, they are competent to teach English. This obviously can't be true or else people wouldn't waste time in universities earning teaching credentials and studying classroom techniques or the latest ESL (English as a Second Language) methods. Believe me, as a credentialed ESL teacher myself and one who passed courses in these techniques, I can vouch for the awesome magnitude of facing a class of eager faces and hoping they will learn more from today's lesson than I will. (Even though I have university training in ESL, have taken all the requisite classes, and have even coauthored textbooks in language acquisi-

tion, I am the first to admit that I am not a very good teacher. I have neither the temperament nor the patience.)

That's not to say that you can't find a teaching position without an ESL degree. Mike Curls, who teaches ESL at two schools in the San José area, points out that it's not essential to be an experienced English teacher. But you should have some teaching background, he says. "Myself, I have a degree in business administration (accounting major) and teaching experience from the Air Force. I was a classroom instructor in Resource Management School with extensive background training." By the way, many local colleges offer classes in teaching English to foreigners. It will go a long way toward your finding a job if you have some experience before you move to Costa Rica.

How to find one of these jobs? Something that ought to be obvious is that you won't find a teaching position while in the United States or Canada. You'll have to apply in person, in Costa Rica, ready to go to work. Every day schools receive job queries from people 6,000 miles away; the schools routinely ignore them. Why waste time corresponding with someone who may or may not ever come to Costa Rica—who is very likely just daydreaming about an adventure that will never happen? You'll have to be on the ground, ready to go to work.

Claudia Jenkins taught ESL in Costa Rica and points out an exception to the rule of applying in Costa Rica. "One way for an experienced ESL teacher—or one with a master's degree or at least an ESL certificate—to get a job with a Costa Rican language school might be to go to the annual springtime TESOL conference, which is held in different parts of the United States and sometimes other countries. While there, I showed copies of my résumé to two school administrators from the Centro Cultural Costarricense-Norteamericano. They wanted me to start teaching in ten days! I couldn't do it because I was a full-time teacher and only looking for something during my summer vacation. Later I did teach at that school for a ten-week bi-semester."

Claudia also points out an enormous drawback to teaching English in Costa Rica: the pay. She says, "At that time (in 1990) my net pay in Costa Rica was $2.00 per hour. My hourly pay in California at the same time was more than ten times that amount! Fifteen years later the school is paying $4.00 an hour. And it's mostly part-time work." Today Claudia is a volunteer ESL teacher for an expatriate-sponsored library in Nosara and does teacher training of volunteer college students who come to Nosara every winter to teach classes for university credit.

Mike Curliss reports on today's salaries, saying, "The pay is not adequate if someone needs to live on the salary. The Pro English school where I work pays $5.75 per hour, but most classes are two hours a day, two days a week ($23 a week). Where I teach in Cartago, they pay by class size. For example, a class of six to nine students pays $114 a month; twelve or more students pays $142 per month."

Why such low wages? Obviously because of the excess of applicants for the jobs. This is one of the few jobs foreigners can obtain without a work permit being absolutely necessary. Technically, one would think that schools would demand work papers, but they get around this by hiring their teachers as *servicios profesionales* (independent contractors). Technically, they aren't really working for the school. Mike Curliss says he is aware of only one school at the moment requiring working papers: Berlitz. Apparently they had a problem a few years back with people without work permits, so they are somewhat fussy about it.

Claudia Jenkins says, "Teaching adults at a private school in Costa Rica is simply a wonderful experience. The students pay a lot of money, by local standards, for the classes, so they are motivated to learn. Since Ticos like to *quedar bien,* even the most disinterested adult student would never be disruptive in class!"

Many Americans and Canadians earn extra money by tutoring in English in their homes. Sometimes a lack of formal training isn't that much of a handicap because the students merely want an opportunity to practice their fluency in one-on-one conversations.

LIST OF **PRIVATE SCHOOLS**

A full list of private schools is far too long for this book, and I have no way of evaluating them. Below are a few of the more popular and prestigious schools that have come to my attention. As in any educational situation, you'll need to ask other parents for recommendations and personally interview school personnel before making any decisions.

- Country Day School is a prestigious institution in Escazú, with classes from pre-kindergarten through the twelfth grade. It is Costa Rican accredited and has 650 students, with classes all in English. There is also a Country Day School in Flamingo. Tuition is moderately expensive. Phone (506) 289–8406; fax (506) 228–2076; e-mail codasch@racsa.co.cr; Web site www.cds.ed.cr.

- Costa Rica Academy is another popular school and charges similar tuition. It is accredited by Costa Rica and in the United States by the Southern Association of Colleges and Schools. It's located in Ciudad Carrari, west of San José, on the way to the airport. Phone (506) 253–1231; fax (506) 225–9762.

- Lincoln School in Moravia is the largest, on the northeast side of San José, with 1,600 students. Tuition is somewhat less than the above-mentioned schools. Phone (506) 247–0800; fax (506) 247–0900; e-mail director@ns.lincoln.ed.cr; Web site www.lincoln.ed.cr.

- Escuela Britanica teaches half in English and half in Spanish, kindergarten through eleventh grade. It's located in Santa Catalina on San José's west side and has 800 students. Tuition is very affordable. Phone (506) 220–0719.

- American International School is located in Cariari. This is a coeducational day school and college-preparatory school, with classes pre-kindergarten through twelfth grade. Phone (506) 239–0376.

- Marian Baker School in San Ramón de Tres Rios offers a United States- and Costa Rican-based curriculum to prepare students for colleges and universities in the United States and Costa Rica. Phone (506) 273–3426; fax (506) 273–4609; e-mail mbschool@racsa.co.cr; Web site www.marianbakerschool.com.

CHAPTER SIXTEEN

IMPORTING YOUR
BELONGINGS

Importing an automobile is one of the first things newcomers consider. Public transportation in Costa Rica is more than adequate, and many folks here do perfectly well without an automobile, yet having your own wheels is a luxury some refuse to forgo. Since car rentals cost between $800 and $1,200 a month, before long the savings involved in owning your own car will become quite evident. The equivalent of a year's car rental would purchase a nifty used, four-wheel-drive vehicle.

There are places in Costa Rica where it just isn't practical to visit without a vehicle. True, buses make it just about anywhere you can imagine—some places I'd hesitate to take a four-wheel-drive vehicle—but after you get there, then what do you do? If you have to walk 3 miles (5 kilometers) to the nearest store or restaurant, you are stuck. Without a set of wheels, your choice of hotel accommodations is governed by where the bus stops—if there is a bus. With your own transportation you can shop around for the best place to stay and then use your wheels to select the best restaurants or hunt out the nicest beaches (which are usually a long way from a bus stop).

BUY OR IMPORT **YOUR VEHICLE?**

Chapter 13 gives details on driving your vehicle down from the United States. That's an option for the hardy, one not to be undertaken lightly, but it can be fun, too. If you choose not to drive, you are left with the alternatives of buying a vehicle in Costa Rica or shipping one down from the north. There are advantages to both options. Which option is better depends on several conditions in effect at the time you need a vehicle.

There are two schools of thought about buying vehicles in Costa Rica. One claims that cars here are maintained in excellent shape because they are so expensive; folks protect their investments with loving care. The other school of thought is that Costa Rican roads are so full of bumps that cars age quickly beyond their years.

No matter which school of thought you favor, take my advice: Never buy a refurbished taxicab! Taxis in Costa Rica go through absolute hell, driving all day and all night, cruising over rough streets—stop and go, stop and go—the worst kind of wear. I know a mechanic in San José who restores taxicabs for a living. He has a great body-and-paint man and has a skilled upholsterer on his staff. I've seen vehicles limp in looking hopeless and strut out looking brand-new. I've studied these cars in minute detail, and I swear, each looks showroom fresh! How can you tell if a car is a rebuilt taxi? You need to find an expert mechanic you trust and have him inspect the vehicle.

This is sometimes easier said than done. I happen to have a good friend who is also a great Tico mechanic and has agreed to help put people in touch with a mechanic qualified to inspect a vehicle and give you a report and/or a recommendation to buy. Two years ago I asked him to find a trustworthy four-wheel-drive for me. He had a mechanic search Heredia and Alajuela for reliable vehicles and found five to recommend. I bought the first one I looked at, which was his first choice, too. He charged a reasonable fee for his time, and I've been very happy with the deal. Since most mechanics do not speak English, I made arrangements with a friend who can be contacted by e-mail and who will contact a mechanic for you, with no obligation. The e-mail address is reydenosara@ice.co.cr.

IMPORT TAXES ON AUTOS Customs duties are responsible for the sky-high prices of new and used cars in Costa Rica. At one time taxes were more than 100 percent of the vehicle's value. They are a bit lower now but still range from 60 to 85 percent of the appraised value, depending on age. Tax rates keep changing as the Congress and Ministry of Customs vacillate on how to apply customs duties. Decisions change every year or so.

I know, this sounds like highway robbery (excuse the metaphor), but the government presents two arguments for high customs duties. One, of course: They need the money. Ticos dodge as many taxes as they can, but they can't avoid customs on that new Mercedes because it's collected before they get their hands on the steering wheel. The other justification is that high prices discourage people from adding more vehicles to already overcrowded streets and highways. This strategy doesn't seem to be working, at least not the last time I tried to drive along Paseo Colón.

It doesn't do any good to argue about the value of your vehicle with the customs people, because they go by a printed list of market values. If your vehicle is in bad shape, they may deduct for that. But you wouldn't be bringing a junker here in the first place. My recommendation is to hire a customs agent or a *tramitador* who knows how to get things done and can tell you exactly what you'll need to pay in taxes.

SHIPPING **YOUR VEHICLE**

Cars can be shipped from either Atlantic or Pacific ports to Costa Rica. But the cheapest and fastest way is from Florida or New Orleans. Most people say they paid $400 to $800, depending on the shipping line and availability of space. From California, costs are higher: I paid $1,300 from San Francisco. From Florida, the destination port is Limón; from California it's Puerto Caldera (near Puntarenas). The shipping line will prepare the documents stateside and take care of details once you deliver the car. Don't fail to ask for full-coverage insurance; it's not terribly expensive. You will also need to obtain a smog certificate from the state of origin of the car before shipping it to Costa Rica.

Once the car arrives at the port, you have the option of picking it up at the port or waiting until it arrives at the main customs house in San José. In either event, you then have the decision of taking possession and going through customs yourself or hiring a Costa Rican customs agent to handle the paperwork for you. If you speak a bit of Spanish, you can do it yourself, but I'd advise asking a Tico friend to walk you through the hurdles of red tape and forms in triplicate. The friend needn't be an expert, just someone who speaks good Spanish and who can ask which line you must stand in—and which line after that.

MY PERSONAL EXPERIENCE I chose the option of shipping my first automobile to Costa Rica rather than buying one there. I realized that it was going to cost a small fortune, but I figured it was worth the trouble; the car was in exceptional shape and had exceptionally low mileage—a 1967 Volkswagen Bug that had spent sixteen years of its life in a garage.

We began the process by calling shipping companies in nearby San Francisco, shopping for the lowest cost. Estimates ranged from a high of more than $2,000 to the bid we accepted of $1,300. The difference was that for $2,000, you got a container for your vehicle alone and for $1,300 other merchandise was included in the container.

The shipping line (Maruka) handled most of the paperwork for us and gave us a date to deliver the car to the docks. We said good-bye to our little car, apprehensive of its voyage, despite the full insurance that was covered in the fee. We were told that the car would arrive twenty days later at Puerto Caldera, near Puntarenas. So we flew to Costa Rica to be ready to greet our Bug when it arrived.

After our anxiously calling Puerto Caldera every day, the ship finally arrived fifteen days late. We found out that three days one way or another is average for cargo ships on the West Coast. A Tico friend and I hurried to the port and began our first inquiry of a long day of asking questions, standing in line to fill out papers, getting signatures, and standing in line for more papers and signatures. We also had to drive into Puntarenas to purchase three months' worth of liability auto insurance. This cost only $20, one of the lesser amounts for the day.

The most expensive cost was $85 to open the container. Another gringo was trying to get his car at the same time, and when he complained about the $85, he was told, "You don't have to pay it. If you'd rather, you can wait until the container arrives in San José and wait until the customs officials get around to opening it. That could take a month or more." He paid the $85.

I highly recommend taking a pleasant-mannered Tico with you if you go through this process. My friend handled things very smoothly. He joked with the clerks, he patted them on the back, and we bought soft drinks for a couple of helpful workers. Not once did anyone suggest a bribe, nor did we offer one. The result was that by the end of the day, we had a bevy of friends in all corners of the huge customs office. (In fact, when the ordeal was over, one of the clerks came out and towed my car to get it started when I discovered the battery was dead.)

Finally, with fifteen minutes to go before the customs office was ready to close for the day, I was told, "All you need now are four copies of each of these documents, and you can pick up your car."

I eagerly rushed over to the copy machine and stood in line. Ten minutes to go, and my turn was next! But to my extreme dismay, the clerk shrugged and said, "Sorry, the machine is out of toner. You'll have to come back tomorrow."

This is where our friendships paid off. One of the clerks we had been joking with rushed over and took the documents from my hands. "Wait here," he commanded." I'll copy these in my boss's office." He came running back with the copies with four minutes to spare.

When I finally got my VW started, I drove to the exit gate and handed the guard a stack of documents that weighed almost as much as the car. He looked through them carefully, handed me the originals, tossed the rest into what looked like a wastebasket, and motioned me on. Now I believe I know what they do with all those duplicate and triplicate forms.

At this point the car was in the country legally, but only for ninety days. In order to make the car a naturalized "Tico," it had to go through the main customs warehouse in San José. Supposedly, this is a simple matter requiring two days in the warehouse while papers are filled out, the car gets inspected, and license plates are issued. Unfortunately, the government was in the middle of a campaign to cut the number of warehouse workers, so employees were protesting by working "by the book," as slowly as possible. In Costa Rica this can be very slow.

"When can I get my car?" I asked hopefully.

"Ordinarily, it would be two days, *Señor,* but with this slowdown, it will take two weeks. God willing."

I called my customs agent to complain. He calmed me down by saying, "I'll talk to the chief. We can get your car in a week. God willing." I returned to the customs warehouse in two days to see if I couldn't hurry things along, and I arrived just in time to hear the chief explain to another gringo that his car would be out of hock within a month. "God willing."

I was about to inquire how long God had been involved with Costa Rica customs when the chief saw me and smiled broadly. "A miracle! The papers came through on your car just an hour ago." To be fair about all this, I must point out that the strike was an untimely event, and that God probably only works part-time for customs. Most people tell me they've had to wait no more than the expected two days for their cars.

I drove away in ecstasy, thinking that my problems were over, that my car was a genuine Tico now, entitled to all the freedoms of the road of any other Tico automobile. Not so. Next I had to go through a safety inspection in order to get papers that could then be presented to another office for clearance to get a piece of paper that was pasted on the windshield until my license plates were ready.

At this point I gave up and turned the papers over to a *tramitidora,* who went to work. She knew exactly where to go, what line to stand in, and whose bread to butter. Three days later my VW Bug was a naturalized citizen of Costa Rica! After waiting a year and a half for my license plates, I found someone who earns a good living by making plates in his garage, so for an additional $25 I now had license plates. Eventually, I assumed, they would have the plates for me, God willing. However, I sold the car three years later, still without an official license plate. (By the way, it is illegal to have license plates made, but the police never hassled me.)

SHIPPING YOUR **HOUSEHOLD GOODS**

Although many will disagree, I wouldn't bother shipping household goods and belongings to Costa Rica, unless they were items that I couldn't replace or couldn't live without. Just about anything you can think of to import into Costa Rica can be purchased for less than what you would pay in the United States or Canada including the import duties and shipping.

Another idea is that you can make a trip to Golfito or to the Panamanian border and buy your appliances—duty-free in Golfito and $500 per person duty-free at the border (a couple gets $1,000, and they can do this every six months). A recent development: I've been told that the government decided that automatic washers and dryers are no longer luxury goods; they've reduced, if not eliminated, import taxes on them. This brings prices down to U.S. levels.

Many of you will go ahead and import everything but the proverbial kitchen sink. If so, you will need a shipper in the United States to make sure things are packed properly and stowed away on a ship. When your cargo arrives, you will need a customs broker to handle things on this end. You can get your personal items out of customs yourself, but I'm convinced that an experienced hand, someone who knows whom, when, and where to schmooze, will save you aggravation.

Some people I know have shipped by air, as long as it wasn't too much weight, because the cost is about a dollar a pound. The cost is much less by cargo ship, and unless you have an inordinate amount of stuff, your things will share a container with other merchandise. Shipping from Florida or New Orleans is much less expensive than from the West Coast.

A problem with cargo ships is they are seldom on schedule. This makes it difficult to arrange a definite date to meet the ship and usher your belongings through customs. You'll have to wait until the unpredictable day when the ship finally docks in Costa Rica. As noted previously, when we shipped our car from San Francisco, we were told it would arrive within a three-day spread. Would it surprise anyone that the ship was fifteen days late? We called every day, and they promised it would be there within two more days, God willing. (God was most unwilling during those two weeks.) By the way, shipping from San Francisco was three times more expensive than it would have been from Tampa.

Packing your goods correctly will save them from damage when tossed around in the loading process. Labeling them properly will help keep duty down. Marking boxes "used household goods" and "not for sale" will also help. Some people take grease pens and mark *usado* on the items themselves to make it clear that they aren't going to be sold.

Duty assessed can be rather erratic, depending on the mood of the customs official, so this is where your suave customs representative can earn his pay. I will say that I've always been treated with respect when dealing with customs, with one exception: I was bringing in a computer that the customs official wanted to mark on my passport as my exempted duty. After a shouting match (which I won), we both apologized.

You are entitled to import a certain amount of items for personal use tax-free (as well as $500 per person of normally taxable goods). The amount of duty you pay on additional items can be minimal or very high according to a highly involved and subjective combination of import duty, consumption tax, sales tax, and other miscellaneous charges. These are multiplied by the value of the item (a combination of estimated cost plus freight plus insurance). Depending on the article, there could be a 37 percent tax or, sometimes, no tax at all.

I've heard about different experiences from people who've brought a lot of belongings into the country by automobile, and they've been mostly favorable. My own experience is that when entering Costa Rica from Nicaragua with the back of our station wagon stuffed to the max with household goods, power tools, and who knows what, the only inspection we got was from a Costa Rican guard, who asked whether we had electronic items such as TVs or VCRs. When we said no, he waved us on without even looking. Maybe we were lucky. By the way, two things you don't want to get caught bringing in without proper papers are arms and munitions!

BRINGING AN **AIRCRAFT TO COSTA RICA**

(The following information was supplied by Peter Todd, manager of Helicorp S.A. Maintenance at Tobias Bolanos Airport in Pavas.)

There are two options the private owner has regarding bringing an aircraft to Costa Rica.

As a tourist: You have the same privileges as the local aircraft do for three months. No duties, no taxes, no local insurance required. At the end of three months, you will have to take the aircraft out of the country for *at least three months*. You may then bring it back again for another three months.

Import the aircraft into Costa Rica: To do this, you will need the following: Either here or in the United States you will need to get a DAR (Designated Airworthiness Representative) to issue an Export Airworthiness Certificate naming Costa Rica as the importing country. For the DAR to do this, the aircraft will need to have had an "Annual Type" inspection within the last thirty days and be airworthy.

When this is done you will have to de-register the aircraft from the United States This can be done from Costa Rica, and the FAA will issue a letter confirming this. The AOPA can assist with this function. Once this is done you may start the registration proceedings in Costa Rica. This is fairly simple and should only take about two weeks if you have your ducks lined up. The DGAC will inspect your aircraft, review the documents, and issue you a TI number and local certificates.

You will also have to pay the import taxes, which are about 20 percent based on market value. I have been told that the taxes are in reality pretty reasonable, but things can change! You will also have to purchase the local liability insurance from the government insurance agency, INS.

Some other items for aviators coming to Costa Rica: There is no night VFR here, and you have to file a flight plan no matter where you go. There are four international airports in Costa Rica: the main ones in Alajuela and Liberia, and two smaller ones in Pavas and Limón. Your FAA private license will get you a Tico private license just by showing it. For a commercial license you will have to take the test. I have heard conflicting stories about it being available in English and Spanish.

BRINGING PETS **TO COSTA RICA**

Those of you who refuse to relocate anywhere without your faithful furry companions will be pleased to know that there is no legal problem bringing them to Costa Rica. You will, of course, have a certain amount of paperwork.

You begin the process with a visit to your local veterinarian for a complete examination of your pet to make sure that your companion is free of all infectious and/or contagious diseases and that all vaccinations are up-to-date against rabies, distemper, hepatitis, parvovirus, and leptospirosis. The rabies shots should be at least thirty days but less than one year old at time of departure. The examination report will identify the pet's name, breed, sex, and color, as well as the owners' name and address. This health certificate must be signed by a licensed veterinarian. The papers are supposed to be good for ten days after issue by the consulate, but customs people say thirty days is okay. Many travelers report that they weren't even asked for papers when they arrived in Costa Rica, but it makes sense to shoot for the ten-day deadline if possible.

I have a friend who doesn't bother with papers going in either direction; she just tucks her toy poodle into her large handbag and marches aboard the airplane. That's taking a chance, but she claims that if there's a problem, she has a thirty-day grace period to straighten things out. (Presumably, little Fifi could be incarcerated in a doggy jail in the meantime.) I highly recommend getting all the proper documents, with precisely crossed *i*'s and correctly dotted *t*'s—or whatever.

Some unusual animals, especially endangered species, require special papers, from both the U.S. and Costa Rican governments. Another friend's son insisted on bringing his pet Tasmanian monitor lizard (or some such thing), and although she had the proper papers, the freaked-out customs inspectors at the San José airport refused to allow the large reptile to enter until a veterinarian certified that it wasn't venomous.

Yet another friend wanted to bring Oliver, her daughter's blue-and-gold macaw, into the country (akin to carrying coal to Newcastle). After three months of paperwork in both the United States and Costa Rica, paying fees and duty and such, Pam made a special trip back to the States, only to spend a lot more time cutting through red tape. "The only hassles I ran into were in the States!" she said. "When I arrived in Costa Rica, the customs guy peeked into the large carrier, glanced at my paperwork, and sent me on my merry way, never asking to see the health certificate or declaration papers that cost me so much time, effort, and worry!"

Once you have your pet's papers, you still have to figure out how to get the animal to Costa Rica. I find it difficult to give advice in this area because airlines keep changing their policies. Some airlines (and maybe all) are currently refusing to carry pets in the cargo holds in summer because of possible heat danger to the animals. Some airlines are refusing to accept animals, period; others are more pet-friendly. The last I heard, Delta was the most friendly, still allowing small animals to be carried into the passenger cabins (although they could balk at accepting a large Tasmanian reptile). With the current uncertainty about rules and regulations, you'll need to check individual airlines to find the right carrier. I'll try to post current info on my Web page for the book update (www.discoverypress.com/update).

To leave the country, your pet needs an exit permit, just like human *residentes*. For this you'll need a health certificate from a Costa Rican veterinarian (well actually *you* don't need it, your pet does). The vet usually accepts your original papers as valid and fills out the proper Costa Rican exit permit without having to personally inspect the animal. The vet can do all the paperwork, obtain the proper stamps, and pay fees. Some people arrange this by fax; the vet or an assistant then meets them at the airport with the necessary permits. Call your vet or contact the Departamento de Zoonosis, Ministerio de Salud, Apartado 10123, San José; (506) 223–0333, ext. 331.

Contrary to the situation in some Latin American countries, pet food is readily available at most Costa Rican supermarkets and sometimes in the local *pulpería*. Veterinarians are numerous, with at least a dozen practicing in the San José area. Some will even make house calls. Actually, a few villages are without a small-animal veterinarian because most vets specialize in treating large animals such as horses and cattle. They have little experience taking care of pets and some don't like to be bothered with them. Those vets with small-animal practices are often reluctant to travel 30 or 40 kilometers to your beach-village home just to give a distemper shot to Fido or to neuter Miss Pussycat. Expats sometimes bring their pets together and have a "veterinarian party." They'll have a dozen animals ready for the vet to work on when he arrives for his monthly visit. The party guests enjoy themselves, eating *bocas* and sipping cocktails, while the unfortunate *animalitos* are experiencing the business end of needles—and possibly losing some precious parts of their anatomy.

CHAPTER SEVENTEEN

BECOMING **A RESIDENT**

Because the rules for entering Costa Rica are so liberal, most people who live in the country for six months or less at a time do not feel it is worth the effort of applying for residency. My wife and I fall into this category. We seldom live in our Costa Rica home more than three months at a time, and when we do we leave the country for a seventy-two-hour stay in Nicaragua or Panama before returning and receiving another visa.

Although the laws seem clear—you are entitled to one visa extension—many people have spent years in Costa Rica, leaving every ninety days and "renewing" their visas at the border. For years, many haven't even bothered doing that, since the fine for having an expired visa used to be a ridiculous amount, about $6.00 a month. However, a few years ago the government did away with the fines and began cracking down on those overstaying their visas. Several persons have been picked up and deported for having expired visas.

As mentioned earlier in the book: For some time, little or no action has been taken against those "permanent tourists" who continue to go out of the country every ninety days. Generally tourists who do get deported are those who are somewhat undesirable in the first place.

But be aware that at some point, the Ministry of Immigration could become serious and begin enforcing regulations. Once your application is in, you don't have to worry about leaving while your residency is being processed. I must emphasize that I am in no way encouraging people to do this "ninety-day turnaround" to get around the rules. I am merely reporting the situation at the time of this writing. If you are going to stay in Costa Rica year-round, you would be well-advised to consider applying for residency. (This is discussed in detail in chapter 12.)

Even though Costa Rica's rules have tightened somewhat, they are still exceedingly liberal compared with those in most other countries. In the United States, for example, if you stay even one day over your visa, you might never be permitted to return!

It's embarrassing to contrast the openness of Costa Rica's immigration with the way the United States treats Costa Ricans when they want to vacation in Disneyland or Las Vegas, or visit friends and relatives who have immigrated to the States. To receive a temporary visa, a Costa Rican must visit the embassy, hat in hand, pay a nonrefundable application fee and prove beyond the shadow of a doubt that he or she has every intention of returning to Costa Rica and has no possible motive for staying in the United States. It must be a humiliating experience to be denied a visa because your job doesn't pay a salary high enough to convince an embassy employee that you're sufficiently trustworthy to visit Hollywood and return. A large percentage of those requests are turned down with no explanation. Supposedly, a daughter of a Costa Rican vice president was once rejected because a clerk doubted her character, thinking her to be a prostitute looking for employment abroad.

Compared with U.S. immigration rules, Costa Rica's are very liberal. To become a legal resident, all you need to do is prove you have either $600 or $1,000 a month income and do not have a serious criminal record. From time to time the Costa Rican congress considers raising income requirements, thinking that they may be unrealistically low. In my opinion, it is unlikely they will take any action. If they do, I will report it on my Choose Costa Rica Update website at www.discoverypress.com/update.

Also, from time to time, the government declares an amnesty; those who've been in the country illegally for a certain amount of time—say, two years or longer—can apply for permanent residence. (However, this has not happened recently.) And people who are operating successful businesses are sometimes permitted to apply for residence papers. Those who qualify under amnesty rules are particularly lucky because they don't have to certify that they won't work for a living and therefore aren't restricted from holding jobs.

Again, I'm not recommending that anyone overstay his or her visa or try to ignore Costa Rican laws. I'm simply reporting how the laws are being enforced at this time and how they are being applied toward foreigners who have the wherewithal to support themselves, who may invest much-needed capital in the country, and who won't be taking jobs from Costa Rican citizens. Those who are indigent or who get into trouble may not find the laws applied quite so gently. Having said this, I again bring your attention to chapter 12, under the heading "Possible Work-Immigration Changes." There you will find a discussion of recent legal changes that could make a big difference in the lives of those who repeatedly renew visas and more or less live here permanently without legal residency. For those who contemplate staying in Costa Rica more than six months at a stretch, it isn't very difficult to obtain legal residency, so why not bite the bullet and make it legal?

COSTA RICAN **RESIDENCY**

The government fully recognizes the economic value of foreign residents living in Costa Rica, bringing dollars to spend and deposit in banks. People from North America and Europe create jobs by building homes and hiring domestic help. To encourage foreigners to apply for residency, the government used to offer some enticing benefits to *pensionados*. Retirees received huge exemptions from import duties on household goods, appliances, and automobiles. With import taxes on automobiles in the 100 percent range, you could bring in a new car, drive it for five years, and sell it for as much as you paid for it!

For years these valuable duty-free imports were major attractions for wanting legal residency. As you might imagine, these tax-free imports became a point of contention between Costa Ricans and foreign residents, with the local people complaining that it was unfair for them to pay more taxes than foreigners. Because of complaints from citizens and pressure from the World Bank and the International Monetary Fund, the Costa Rican government canceled these benefits for newcomers in 1992. Those who entered the country before the laws were changed were granted "grandfather" status.

Today, with longer stays possible, the necessity of obtaining legal status is not as pressing as it once was. For people like my wife and I, who can be satisfied with living half the year in Costa Rica and the other half in my home country, there's no clear advantage to becoming a legal resident. We can own property or a business and can travel about the country with nothing more than a tourist visa. On the other hand, there are restrictions and obligations on *pensionados* and *rentistas*—not ponderous ones, but they involve a certain amount of red tape. For example, you must prove that a certain amount of monthly income has been deposited in a Costa Rican bank. On a regular basis, you must provide police certification of good conduct, and you must live in Costa Rica for at least four (nonconsecutive) months of the year in order to hold on to your *residente* status.

For those who will be staying pretty much full-time in Costa Rica or who plan on entering business and working as a manager in the business, the resident option is no doubt the best way to go. Once you have the papers and fulfill the residency obligations, you are completely legal and can enjoy all the rights of a Costa Rican, except voting. Becoming a legal resident of Costa Rica doesn't affect your U.S. or Canadian citizenship in any way.

CATEGORIES OF RESIDENTS   Immigration and applications for residency are handled by the Costa Rican Tourism Institute. Basically, it recognizes three classes of legal immigrant residents: Residente

Pensionado, Pensionado Rentista, and Rentista Inversionista. After two years of residency under one of these categories, you may apply for permanent residency, and then you have fewer restrictions, for example, you can work without permission from the government.

Residente Pensionado. This category pertains to retired people with pensions of $600 or more per month. Social Security is usually sufficient to qualify for this status. A total of $7,200 a year must be deposited to a colón account in a Costa Rican bank and proof of this shown to the government every year. No law says that you can't take the money out of the bank right away and change it to a dollar account or that you have to spend all of it; you have only to prove that you've brought that amount of dollars into the country. Some people deposit the full amount at the beginning of the year to get the requirement out of the way.

For a married couple the person without retirement income is considered a dependent, and no extra income is required (that is, only one pension per family). Children under the age of 18 (or under 25 if in school) are also considered dependents. Social Security is sufficient proof of income. This is the option most retired people go for.

Pensionado Rentista. This category is for those who are not old enough to retire or who do not have a pension, yet who want residency in Costa Rica. Applicants must prove $1,000 a month income ($12,000 a year), deposited in colones to a Costa Rican bank under the same rules as regular *pensionados*. The income must come from an investment such as a certificate of deposit, an annuity, or some other source that guarantees at least $1,000 per month. Younger people and those who want to go into business often choose this option.

For some people, qualifying for this status is difficult because of the large investment needed to return $12,000 a year income. Others would prefer to use the money to start a business or build a home. One way to immediately acquire residency status is to deposit $60,000 in an interest-bearing dollar account in a Costa Rican bank. The bank then pays you $1,000 a month, or $12,000 a year (plus interest), from this account for a period of five years. Deposits in state-owned banks are government guaranteed without limit, and most bank interest in Costa Rica is not taxed by the Costa Rica government.

Rentista Inversionista. People who are serious about going into business prefer this category. It requires a $50,000 investment with an approved tourism or export business, $100,000 in a reforestation project, or $150,000 to $200,000 in any other type of business. If the investment is in an existing company, you need to submit the firm's latest balance sheet and a statement indicating its profit-and-loss situation.

You understand, of course, that you needn't become a resident to own or operate a business in Costa Rica: You can do so on a tourist visa. Many foreigners invest far less and don't bother with residency. However, they are ostensibly restricted to management duties and not permitted to work at ordinary tasks in the business. This is not usually enforced, especially if the person working isn't displacing a Costa Rican worker.

When it comes to investment in a business or a reforestation project, please exercise extreme caution. As mentioned elsewhere in this book, Costa Rica is teeming with sharks just waiting for fish like you and me. Reforestation investments are highly promoted as lucrative investments. You should be cautious of overly optimistic claims; teak promoters have poor track records in fulfilling their promises. Consult a good lawyer first.

What Do You Get with Residency? As a resident with any of the aforementioned three statuses, you have the following benefits and requirements:

1. You have all the rights of citizenship except voting.
2. You can own and manage businesses, but you cannot earn a salary from a Costa Rican employer. You can pay yourself dividends, however. Once your residency is permanent, you can work for anyone.
3. You must reside in Costa Rica the equivalent of at least four months a year, not necessarily contiguous months. Once you have permanent residency, you are expected to visit Costa Rica once a year for at least one day.
4. You must renew proof of stable and permanent income annually until you have full residency.

RED TAPE The question of whether to become a legal resident or to visit using a tourist visa varies with the individual. Some feel that four or five months is all they want to stay, so why bother with the red tape of papers? Others plan on making Costa Rica their primary home and therefore see benefits in becoming residents. It all depends on your circumstances. One

benefit is that residents receive a 50 percent discount on in-country airline flights as well as certain other breaks, such as reduced entrance fees to parks.

To make an application, you can either do it yourself or hire someone to go through the red tape for you. The process requires a deposit of about $100 and about $30 for fees, stamps, and forms. It could take from a few months to a year before approval comes through, depending on the thoroughness of your preparation and who is assisting you. Meanwhile your residency status is legal and won't be challenged.

Ask around the North American community for recommendations of a good lawyer or an experienced *tramitador* (a person who knows which lines to stand in and knows whom to see to get your papers processed promptly). Some people I've talked to have had good experiences with *tramitadores* they located through classified ads in the *Tico Times*. But be careful: Hiring someone who doesn't know what he or she is doing not only takes a lot more time but could be a waste of money if the person does not or cannot follow through.

ASSOCIATION OF PENSIONADOS Yes, some individuals have done the paperwork on their own, but you'll hear sad tales of woe from those who have tried it without knowing what they were doing. Few people enjoy standing in line, facing the indifferent attitudes of some clerks or the hard-to-understand questions and information in Spanish. One way to avoid this is through the Association of Residents of Costa Rica. Among other things, this organization specializes in obtaining residencies, and it charges reasonable fees, considering the amount of time you save. A provisional membership is $100, entitling you to apply for residency through the group and to attend social events and meetings. Regular membership is $50 a year.

Further benefits are as follows: The association can make sure your annual papers are up-to-date, translate and notarize your documents, renew the required Costa Rican ID card, help you get a driver's license and other special permits, and assist you in many other ways before your move. The organization will also do English-to-Spanish translations and authenticate a photocopy of your resident's *carnét* so that you can leave your original at home.

Members with residency are eligible to receive doctor and hospital care in the National Health Services System, under terms of a special contract. This relieves you of the obligation of standing in line each month to make your payments. The organization pays it on a three-month basis and sends you proof of payment for the current month, which entitles you to medical service. The association also publishes a newsletter six times a year. For more information, write ARCR, Apdo. 1191–1007, Centro Colón, San José, or call (506) 233–8068 (fax 506–255–0061). The ARCR has a comprehensive Web site at www.casacanada.net.

PAPERWORK In any event, the process of getting your resident papers is best started by you, right in your home country. It's much easier to get these at home than by mail from Costa Rica. The four main items you need are listed below, and in all cases processing must be done through your local Costa Rican consulate. They charge about $40 per document.

1. **Income certification.** This is the first and most important step; it's often complicated and difficult. Rules and proof of income differ between *Residente Pensionados* and *Pensionado Rentistas*. Social Security or other government pension money is the easiest to prove. Ask for a statement from the pension source confirming that you have at least $600 a month pension, and have that notarized at a Costa Rican consulate in your country. If the pension is nongovernmental, you'll need notarized letters that the pension is for life and two letters from bank officials testifying to the soundness of the company's pension plan.

   The guarantee of income for *rentistas* is $1,000 in interest and dividends from banks or investment houses. The decision on whether your income qualifies is made on a case-by-case basis. You'll need statements establishing that this income is guaranteed for at least five years, and you'll need to renew these guarantees every succeeding five years. The Costa Rican consulate can help you with this. Again, it's important to have the notary certification and authentication of the documents done by a consulate in your home country.

2. **Birth certificate.** This is needed for you and each of your dependents.
3. **Marriage certificate.** Proof of previous divorce is not necessary.
4. **Police certificate of good conduct.** Obtain this at your last place of residence, and make it the last document you receive. Have the police certify a set of fingerprints as well; ask the Costa Rican consulate for the necessary forms. Make the good-conduct verification your last step because it's only valid for six months from the time of certification. If you get this document first and then spend a lot of time with the other papers, it could expire before your application gets under way. I know of people who've had to return to the United States to get another conduct certification because theirs was more than six months old. You'll also need certificates of good conduct for dependents over eighteen.

Note, too, that if you are traveling with children, some special rules apply. Apparently, these rules apply more for Costa Rican citizens than for tourists, and even though they don't seem to be strictly enforced, it's important that you be aware of them. When a child traveling without both parents stays beyond thirty days, the child falls under the jurisdiction of the Patronato Nacional de la Infancia, a children's welfare organization. In order for a child to leave the country without both parents, it might be necessary to have a permit notarized by the Patronato offices on Nineteenth Street and Sixth Avenue in San José. I've never heard of any tourist being hassled for this, but if just one parent is traveling with a child for long periods, it might be a good idea to have a notarized statement of permission from the other parent. And remember, just having your documents notarized is not enough.

The documents must be taken to the Costa Rican consulate in your country to verify the notary's validity and certification. The notary isn't merely verifying your signature but also that the documents are valid and that they belong to you. Not following each step correctly is responsible for the many delays and obstacles you often hear people complain about.

Other details can be taken care of in Costa Rica at the time you make a formal request for residency. Several certified copies of your passport are required, and you'll fill out a questionnaire of personal information. As a retiree, you'll have to sign a statement that you won't work for pay while in Costa Rica (without authorization) and that you'll spend at least four months a year in Costa Rica. (As stated earlier, the months needn't be consecutive.)

From here on, it's filling out forms, standing in line, waiting for stamps and signatures, standing in more lines to put a deposit in the bank, going hither and yon to stand in still more lines—most of which can be done by your surrogate, the *tramitador.*

CHAPTER EIGHTEEN

LEGAL **MATTERS**

In chapter 10 we discussed the pros and cons of buying real estate in Costa Rica. The nice thing is that property ownership is open to anyone, no matter what citizenship; it's fairly easy to gain a clear title, and you can feel absolutely confident about your ownership. The nasty part is that a lot of charlatans and swindlers are out there ready to take advantage of your trusting nature. Don't worry: They haven't a chance if you do things correctly and don't skip any steps in the process.

The following information comes to us courtesy of my friend Carlos Umaña of Tacsan & Umaña law offices in San José. For those of you with connections to the Internet, another source of Costa Rica legal information can be found at www.discoverypress.com/crinet. Another connection for understanding Costa Rica rules and regulations is the Association of Residents of Costa Rica (ARCR) Web site at www.casa canada.net/rulesandregulations.html.

Your first step is to cultivate a relationship with a lawyer who knows what the score is. In Costa Rica it's much easier to become an attorney than it is in the United States or Canada, so just because someone can legally assume the title *licenciado* doesn't guarantee he knows what

he's doing, or even that he's ever practiced law. You'll find many Ticos who are entitled to call themselves attorneys but actually practice law as an occasional sideline. A poor attorney isn't necessarily crooked; he could be lazy, inefficient, or incompetent, which is just as bad.

A second important point, mentioned earlier: Make certain the lawyer is working for *you*, and exclusively for you. If you use the other party's attorney to represent both interests, you're facing the probability that the lawyer is primarily working for his first client and isn't on your side at all. Unlike the situation in the United States, this is how it can work in Costa Rica. So insist on having *your* attorney handle your part of the sale, buying or selling.

PURCHASING **REAL ESTATE**

To make it easy to check on land ownership, all property, with a few exceptions, must be registered at the Property Department of the Public Record Office, known as the *Registro Nacional*. This office is located in Zapote and is open to the public. You can access the records on the Internet also. It's a rather easy system to research, however, it's best to have your attorney do the checking because he knows what to look for and where.

The first step, before you hand over any money, is to run a thorough title search of the public records to see whether the property really belongs to the seller, whether the seller is who he claims to be, and whether any mortgages, liens, encumbrances, or easements come attached to the property. Mortgages and liens must be properly registered to have any effect on the buyer. So if the title is clear, you needn't worry about outstanding debts. If a lender didn't register a second deed of trust, he's out of luck. A title search should cost less than $50, and it is well worth it. If the seller was untruthful, you won't waste any more time. Actually, to get started you can research a title or plot of land yourself in the Registro Nacional, simply by going to the Web site and filling in a form. If you find nothing wrong with the title, you can authorize your attorney to investigate further. (For details, see the end of this chapter.)

You'll remember that all property is registered, with some exceptions. These exceptions are important. Let's review the three basic categories of Costa Rican properties:

1. **Recorded land.** This includes all properties you'll find registered at the Public Record Office. The vast majority of properties for sale today fall into this category.
2. **Nonrecorded land.** This is property that could be registered at the Public Record Office but has not yet been recorded. This applies to farmland, *fincas* (ranches), and homesteads— places that haven't legally changed hands for many decades or perhaps have been changed through a private contract. Nonrecorded land requires an attorney familiar with the procedure. It takes a judicial procedure to register land for the first time into public records. This kind of sale lacks the security granted by the Public Record Office.
3. **Nonregisterable land.** This is property that cannot be legally recorded at the Public Registry. This is the case with most beachfront property. In some instances beach properties can be possessed legally by individuals or corporations through a concession granted by the government. The lease is always through the government, but you must acquire possession from the previous possessor, if there is one.

TRANSFERRING **RECORDED LAND**

Any individual or company, national or foreign, may legally own land sheltered by the Registro Nacional Public Record Office system. But for legal and economic reasons, you should consider placing your property in the name of a Costa Rican corporation, or *sociedad anónima* (more about this later in this chapter).

Recorded land transfers must be granted through a public deed. That is, buyer and seller must appear before a Costa Rican lawyer, or to be more precise, a notary public (to be chosen by the purchaser), who will insert the title transfer in his protocol. (A notary public is a licensed attorney who is endowed with "public trust" and the right to validate and legalize all contracts and deeds. Again, to protect your investment, you should insist on having your own attorney to perform as your notary public in the transaction.)

The purchase deed, as well as any liens or mortgages agreed to by the buyer, are then presented to the Public Record Office to be registered.

It's also the notary's duty to complete all recording procedures necessary to provide the title transfer with full efficacy. (This is another reason to have a good attorney working for you, someone who knows what the word *efficacy* means.)

Expenses and legal fees involved can range from 6 to 7 percent of the total amount of the transaction and on the assessed price of the property. These costs are customarily shared by buyer and seller on a fifty-fifty basis, unless agreed otherwise. My attorney recommends not to agree otherwise. Any deal you make should be on a fifty-fifty basis, with your lawyer involved to watch out for your interests.

BEACHFRONT **PROPERTY**

Because of special regulations, some areas are not subject to private ownership. This is the case with most beachfront property, which is leased through concessions granted by the government. This is where things become complicated. Public Law No. 6043 of March 1977 established a restricted coastal zone called the Zona Marítimo/Terrestre. This law covers a strip of land, 200 meters (656 feet) deep, along both the Pacific Coast and the Atlantic Coast. The restricted zone is divided into two sections:

1. The Public Zone (*Zona Publica*), that first 50-meter strip of land starting at the mean high-tide line. This is public property; the public has full access to the Public Zone.
2. The next 150-meter strip of land is called the Restricted Zone (*Zona Restringida*).

The law states that no private individual or corporation is allowed to build on or use for private purposes "any portion whatsoever" of the Public Zone. However, it's sometimes possible to obtain a lease/concession on Restricted Zone properties for private or business use. Understand that when this happens, it isn't a deed, it's a "lease concession." At first the lease is with the local municipality; later on, after a procedure, the lease is with the Costa Rica Tourism Institute. Beneficiaries of lease concessions can be granted the use, occupation, and possession of the land, including the right to build. But the municipality can withhold building permits under certain circumstances.

Now comes a sticky point. The law says, "No lease concessions are granted to non–Costa Ricans who have resided in the country less than five years, nor to foreign companies, nor to national companies of which 50 percent or more of its stock is owned by non–Costa Ricans."

While that may be the law, the fact is that many if not most of the desirable Zona Restringida properties are held by Costa Rican corporations that are owned entirely by foreigners. This is, of course, difficult to verify, because ownership of a Costa Rican corporation is impossible to substantiate. (Tips on how to start a corporation are found later in this chapter.)

These lease concessions can be transferred from one person or company to another, subject to the approval of the municipality and the Costa Rican Tourism Institute. Leases are generally granted for periods that range from five to twenty years. The local municipality is entitled to charge a small leasing fee. At the end of the leasing period, the lessee can apply for an extension of the lease concession, and extensions are normally granted with the previous approval of the Tourism Institute.

Beachfront land *not* regulated by this law can be found, but it's extremely unusual to find titled property in areas within the restricted 200-meter zone. True, some beachfront land isn't regulated because it was in use before the beach laws were passed. These exempt parcels are so-called "grandfathered" properties. However, be cautious: Many people think that their property is grandfathered when it really is not. Some sellers claim that their property is grandfathered when they know it is not.

The danger is that somewhere down the road, the government can decide that your lovely beach house is illegally constructed on property you do not own. All the more reason to have a good attorney, to protect your investment.

OFFSHORE **CORPORATIONS**

For a variety of reasons, banking-secrecy laws such as those in Switzerland attract a great deal of interest among certain folks who have motives for hiding assets. As far as I know, there is no law against this as long as these accounts aren't used to defraud creditors or to evade paying taxes. Like Switzerland, Costa Rica has strict rules on nondisclosure of bank accounts.

An interesting angle of financial secrecy is the use of Costa Rican "offshore" corporations. Like bank accounts, these corporations can be started by anyone—citizen, resident, or tourist—and are supposed to be totally secret. Since there's no way of knowing precisely whose names are on the corporation books, it's almost impossible to discover who actually controls these corporations. In fact, the legal term *sociedad anónima* means "anonymous society." That's why Costa Rican corporation names are appended with "S.A." instead of "Inc." or "Ltd."

One common example of a legitimate use of a corporation is when buying or selling real estate. If the property belongs to a corporation, transfer of ownership is simple. You merely transfer the corporation's stock; the property belongs to whoever holds this stock. The ownership of the property hasn't changed hands, only the corporation shares, and the owners of the shares are now in control of the property.

Having stressed all of this about secrecy, I have to say that I feel uneasy about the extent of the anonymous nature of a corporation. Some feel that the U.S. government, using the pretext of "containing terrorism," has been pressuring the countries that allow offshore corporations to relax their rules on anonymous corporate officers. It stands to reason that Washington has pressured Costa Rica. A few years ago, the Costa Rican government insisted that all *sociadad anonimos* (corporations) file a special one-time, year-end tax form that requested details about the officers of the corporation and how much income, if any, the corporation made. Whether any of this information will be surrendered to outsiders is questionable. For those who use their corporations for the usual legal purposes, such as property ownership, there is no problem. For those who have something to worry about, I would suggest a talk with your attorney and possibly changing to a new corporation.

Before we go any further, you need to understand a few crucial points. First, I am not an attorney, and even if I were, you would be foolish to accept legal advice from a book, particularly when it comes to activities as complicated as offshore corporations or foreign banking practices. Second, while most corporations and bank accounts in Costa Rica are legal, used for perfectly legitimate purposes, the ones used for illegal schemes are frequently toppled, sending overly creative schemers to jail. I suspect that what happens is that the corporation originally starts off with legal goals in mind and then branches out into a small tax fraud, which grows until it gets out of hand. Some schemes are so obvious that the IRS has little trouble spotting the smoke and flames. My final point is a reiteration of the first: I am not a lawyer, nor am I in any way urging readers to get involved in offshore corporations or secret bank accounts. I am merely reporting what Costa Rican residents and attorneys have passed along to me: Controlling real estate through a Costa Rican corporation is perfectly legal.

YOUR COSTA RICAN **CORPORATION**

Costa Rica's corporate structure allows any person or persons (Costa Rican or not) to control a company without his or her name appearing in the public records. A Costa Rican lawyer (who must be a specialist in this) sets up a corporation without the real owner's name ever appearing in the record. It is termed a *sociedad anónima con acciones al portador,* or "anonymous society with all stock owned by the bearer." This means that although there is a legal president, secretary, and treasurer (often simply employees of the attorney), the actual ownership of the corporation is invested in whoever physically has the stock certificates in his or her pocket or safe-deposit box. Even the attorney has no way of knowing whether the original clients still own the shares. This arrangement is prohibited in the United States but is perfectly legal in Costa Rica.

This corporation is free to engage in many types of business activities, both in Costa Rica and in other countries. Theoretically, because it is considered a "foreign corporation" as far as the IRS is concerned, it pays no taxes in the United States. (There's talk about changing this.) Because it's a Costa Rican corporation, it pays nothing on what it earns outside Costa Rica. This doesn't relieve the individual of the responsibility of reporting income and paying income taxes in his or her home country. New laws require that a yearly report of a corporation must be filed; should there be no income to report, there are no tax consequences, but not filing the report makes the corporation liable for a fine. So if you already have a corporation in Costa Rica and haven't been filing reports, see your lawyer.

Be aware that from time to time there can be arbitrary changes in tax rules for corporations. No matter that your corporation does not make money. For example, if the corporation's only asset is a house or an automobile, there could be an extra form to fill out to state that there is no income. This happened in 2003, and many people were caught unaware. The process was simple, but if you happen to be living in the United States or Canada, you might not hear about this. To avoid any fines for not filing, you should have someone in Costa Rica monitoring the situation and notify you when something new comes up. I have my lawyer take care of things like this for me—it's done automatically. If you prefer to do it yourself, you should watch the *Tico Times* or one of the online newspapers, such as *Costa Rica A.M.* or *La Nación,* or at least have a friend in Costa Rica give you a "heads-up" on the rare occasion some special law change happens.

ADVANTAGES OF A CORPORATION Again, it's always advisable for both foreigners and Costa Ricans to own land through a corporation. Among the advantages is a reduction of personal liabilities and taxes. The ownership of assets, such as real estate, boats, and automobiles, is the main purpose of most registered corporations in Costa Rica.

A corporation can be owned by a group of shareholders or fully owned by one shareholder. This way a single individual or a small group of people can operate the company in a relatively simple and inexpensive manner. The asset (your house or your car) can be sold or transferred simply by handing over the shares of the corporation, because it is owned by the corporation, not the individual, even though he or she may own all the shares. Your attorney will show you the best ways to ensure control of the company and the overall handling of corporate power.

An important point about corporations is to make sure you are getting a full-fledged corporation; there are shortened versions that have some serious drawbacks. Don't go for a cut-rate, partial incorporation, because you'll not get all the required services, and it could expire at the end of a brief period. Later you'll find you have to go back and spend more money to put the company on a par with other corporations. Most attorneys will charge from $350 to $900 to form a complete corporation.

LEGAL DETAILS There are four main stages in the process of forming a Costa Rican corporation. (The details herewith were supplied by my attorney, who knows what he is doing, so I merely present them here, without any attempt to explain or even understand them!)

1. A document called the Articles of Incorporation or Constitutive Charter of the company will need to be prepared. This document will be drawn up by your attorney. The Constitutive Charter determines the organization, administration, and bylaws of the company. This is signed by all the shareholders, the appointed members of the board of directors, the controller, and the *agente residente*.
2. Before registration in the Public Record Office, your attorney will announce the company's constitution in Costa Rica's official newspaper, *La Gaceta*. This takes about two weeks. Also, you must make a deposit of the amount of the capital stock indicated in the Constitutive Charter—usually 1,000 colones—in a national bank. The amount of shares in the corporation and their denomination are determined by the founders. All shares must have equal value and must be worth at least 1 colón, but there's no top limit to a share's value. The money deposited

can be withdrawn once the company has been duly recorded.

3. The company must be registered in the Public Record Office. This registration is essential to legally constitute a corporation in Costa Rica. The registration process is performed by the notary public (your lawyer). The whole process takes from one to three months, depending on the time it takes for the Public Registry to approve the company's bylaws, including the books.

4. You'll receive a set of three accounting books (*Diario, Mayor,* and *Inventario y Balances*) and three "legal" books (Shareholders' Record, Shareholders' Assemblies, and Board of Directors' Meetings). Your attorney will present the books to the Ministerio de Hacienda for their initial authorization. Once duly legalized, these books should register all internal affairs of the company (as well as stock transfers) and are kept privately by the shareholders. You can leave them with your attorney or place them in a secure place, such as a safe-deposit box. Remember, whoever has the books in hand also has control of the assets.

To form a Costa Rican corporation, you need a minimum of two initial shareholders. Once the company is formed and properly inscribed in the Public Record Office, the shares can be transferred to a single person, who becomes the sole shareholder of the company.

The name of the company must be in Spanish, Latin, or any native dialect. Of course, a name can't be identical or equivalent to that of an existing corporation. And names with a meaning in a foreign language (such as English or German) are not allowed without special exceptions. Your attorney in charge of preparing the Articles of Incorporation will ask you for a list of names (in Spanish), and he'll research them and determine whether they will be accepted by the Public Record Office.

There must be a board of directors with at least the following officers: president, secretary, and treasurer. The president must be the principal representative of the company. Other members of the board can also be made representatives of the corporation, depending on how the founders of the company decide to do the Articles of Incorporation. (The attorney who sets up the corporation takes care of this.) The members of the board may or may not be shareholders. The directors must be present when the company is legally formed, to personally accept their designation and sign the Corporation Charter along with the shareholders or power of attorney.

The controller cannot be a shareholder or a member of the board of directors. The person appointed as controller has to sign the Articles of Incorporation. Usually this will be someone on your lawyer's office staff.

Every Costa Rican company must designate an *agente residente*. The *agente residente* will probably be your Costa Rican attorney, who will be a formal representative for official matters. He has no powers to act on the company's behalf. The fee for this service is usually $100 a year.

BANKING **SECRECY**

Traditional tax havens such as the Cayman Islands, Switzerland, Luxembourg, the Channel Islands, and the Netherlands Antilles have always tempted those looking for ways to hide assets. Secret bank accounts are often used for this purpose. I've been told that medical doctors routinely hide as much of their holdings as possible in these places to avoid disaster should a multimillion-dollar malpractice suit top their insurance limits. Like the aforementioned countries, Costa Rica maintains a strict policy of banking and commercial secrecy. The amount of money you have in a bank account is supposedly sacrosanct and unavailable to curious outsiders.

One banker said, "If I disclosed information about someone's account—even to a policeman or a government official—I could go to prison." The *Tico Times* illustrated this point with a story about a suspect accused of stealing and forging checks. The crime could easily be solved if authorities could access bank records and see whether the stolen checks had been deposited to the suspect's account. But bank officials refused to help the police solve the crime because, in the process, they would become criminals themselves!

Having said the foregoing, I have to qualify it by expressing my personal belief that the U.S. government, through its Homeland Security Act, has pressured the Costa Rican government and financial institutions to modify their policies. I doubt that this secrecy deters the IRS from snooping about, and I suspect not without some success. (Realize that failing to report a foreign bank account on your income tax return is a law violation.) Sometimes fraud is so transparent that all the secret bank accounts or anonymous corporations in the world wouldn't help. The bottom line is that there is nothing illegal about U.S. or Canadian citizens owning a bank account or majority stock in an offshore corporation, as long as profits are reported and taxes properly paid.

CHECKING PROPERTY **ON THE INTERNET**

Costa Rica may be somewhat backward in some aspects, as are most developing countries, but we must admire the way the government has utilized the Internet to open the Registro Nacional to the public. What used to be a time-consuming and bewildering process of investigating the legal status of a piece of real estate or ownership of an automobile has now become a simple matter of calling up a Web page and entering a few numbers. Within a few seconds, you can find out if that beautiful house with a view of the valley actually belongs to the person who is trying to sell it to you. Does he have a mortgage on the property that he neglected to mention? Are there any liens against the house because of an automobile accident or a liable judgment? You can discover who the previous owners were, in case you would like to talk with them to see if they have any information for you. In some instances you can find out who the neighbors are. Before you decide to buy that bargain four-wheel-drive Toyota, you might be interested to know that it hasn't been reported stolen, or that the title is not held encumbered by a bank loan. The previous owners are also listed.

The Registro Web site can be found at http://196.40.22.10. Navigating the site is fairly straightforward. You'll probably need a dictionary or, better yet, an online Spanish-to-English virtual dictionary to understand some of the terms. (Go to www.wordreference.com and install the Spanish-to-English module.) To look up real estate, click on "Bienes Inmuebles" and then "Catastro." You'll find several search choices; first click on "Consultas," then on "Bienes inmuebles," then the type of search. In the case of real estate, searching by "Consulta por Cédula" works best for me, since my property is in a corporation, and I enter the corporation's *cédula* number. If your property is registered in your name, click on "Consulta por Nombre."

UNITED STATES **INCOME TAX**

U.S. citizens living abroad must file income taxes. You can file through the U.S. Embassy, and you have until June 15 (instead of April 15). The general rule is: U.S. citizens are taxed on their worldwide income and must file and pay U.S. income taxes regardless of where they live. In 2006 more than four million Americans living outside the country filed income tax returns. However, most taxes assessed by a foreign country are deductible from U.S. taxes.

With the general rule comes an exception that could be valuable for some workers. For 2006, qualified taxpayers can exclude from gross income as much as $80,000 in income earned while living abroad. To qualify, this income has to be earned at a job with wages received in the foreign country. Money earned from rentals, investments, bonuses, or pensions in the United States do not fall under this provision.

The tax-free foreign earned income includes foreign-source wages, salaries, bonuses, commissions, cost-of-living differential, home leave, tips, professional fees, and any other form of compensation for personal services rendered. It even includes noncash income, such as the use of a car. To be eligible, you must have a job that's expected to last for not less than one year, and you are expected to spend at least 330 full days out of any twelve consecutive months outside of the United States. This is generous of the IRS, however, I can't imagine many expatriates earning enough wages in Costa Rica to make it worth their while to file an exemption.

You are required to file with the Costa Rican government on all income earned within the country. Your attorney can file these tax forms. You're also required to file a tax statement for any corporation that owns property, even if there's no income. If you own a house or land, chances are it is held in the name of your personal corporation. If the house has earned no income, you won't pay taxes, but there is a fine for not filing.

Until 2006, income earned in the United States and Canada was exempt from Costa Rican income taxes. However, in 2005 the National Assembly passed a law to the effect that certain foreign income will be taxable. The problem is, at this point in time, nobody knows what this means, just what income will be taxable, at what rate, and what deductions will be allowed. Furthermore, it is unclear how the government will know how much taxable income an expatriate receives in his home country. These details could take some time to figure out, and in the meantime, most foreign taxes are deductible from your U.S. taxes. I'll try to keep folks informed via my Web site: www.discoverypress.com/update.

A caveat here: I am *not* a tax expert. Please check with a tax professional before making any major tax decisions.

APPENDIX

EMBASSY OF **COSTA RICA IN THE UNITED STATES**

2112 S Street NW, Washington, DC, 20008; (202) 234–2945; fax (202) 265–4795. Tomas Dueñas, ambassador

COSTA RICAN CONSULATES **IN THE UNITED STATES**

ARIZONA

Phoenix (area of coverage: Arizona): Andrew P. Burke, Honorary Consul, 7373 E Doubletree Ranch Road, Suite 200, Scottsdale, AZ, 85258; (480) 951–2264; fax (480) 991–6606

CALIFORNIA

Los Angeles (areas of coverage: Arizona, Hawaii, Nevada, Southern California, and Utah): Percy Calvo Cartín, Consul, 1605 West Olympic Boulevard, Suite 400, Los Angeles, CA 90015; (213) 380–7915; fax (213) 380–5639

San Francisco (areas of coverage: Alaska, Idaho, Montana, Northern California, Oregon, and Washington): Manuel Escoto, Honorary Consul, P. O. Box 7643, Fremont, CA 94537; (510) 790–0785; fax (510) 792–5249

COLORADO

Denver (area of coverage: Colorado): Tito Chaverri, Honorary Consul, 3356 South Xenia Street, Denver, CO 80231-4542; (303) 696–8211; fax (303) 696–1110

DISTRICT OF COLUMBIA

(Areas of coverage: all U.S. territory): Alejandro Cendeño, Consul General, 2112 S Street NW, Washington, DC 20008; (202) 328–6628; fax (202) 265–4795

FLORIDA

Miami (area of coverage: Florida): Oscar Camacho, Consul General, 1600 NW 42nd Avenue, Miami, FL 33126; (305) 871–7485

Tampa (area of coverage: Florida): Erica Salgado, Consul Genera, 14502 North Dale Mabry Highway, Suite 200, Tampa, FL, 33618; (813) 969–3837; fax (813) 969–3357

GEORGIA
Atlanta (area of coverage: Georgia): Emilia Trejos, Consul General, 1870 The Exchange, Suite 100, Atlanta, GA 30339; (770) 951–7025; fax (770) 951–7073

ILLINOIS
Chicago (areas of coverage: Illinois, Indiana, Iowa, Kentucky, Michigan, Minnesota, Missouri, North Dakota, Ohio, South Dakota, and Wisconsin): Juan Salas Araya, Consul, 185 North Wabash Avenue, Suite 1123, Chicago, IL 60601; (312) 263–2772; fax (312) 263–5807

LOUISIANA
New Orleans Temporary (areas of coverage: Alabama, Arkansas, Louisiana, Mississippi, New Mexico, Oklahoma, and Tennessee): 1514 Martens Drive, Suite 210, Hammond, LA, 70401; (504) 581–6400 and (985) 549–5454

MASSACHUSETTS
Boston (area of coverage: Massachusetts): 175 McClellan Highway, East Boston, MA 02134; (617) 561–2444; fax (617) 561–2461

MINNESOTA
St. Paul (area of coverage: Minnesota): Anthony L. Andersen, Honorary Consul, 2424 Territorial Road, St. Paul, MN 55114; (651) 481–3616; fax (651) 645–4684

NEW YORK
New York City (areas of coverage: Connecticut, Maine, Massachusetts, New York, New Jersey, Pennsylvania, and Rhode Island): 80 Wall Street, Suite 718, New York, NY 10005; (212) 509–3066; fax (212) 509–3068

PUERTO RICO
San Juan (area of coverage: Puerto Rico): Avenida Ponce de Leon, Edificio 1510, Oficina P1, Esquina Calle Pelaval, San Juan, Puerto Rico 00909; (787) 723–6227; fax (787) 723–6226

TEXAS
Houston (area of coverage: Texas): Sergio Valverde, Consul General, 3000 Wilcrest, Suite 112, Houston, TX 77042; (713) 266–0484; fax (713) 266–1527

San Antonio (area of coverage: Texas): Marta Rojas, Consul, 6836 San Pedro, Suite 116, San Antonio, TX 78216; (210) 824–8474; fax (210) 824–8489

COSTA RICAN CONSULATES **IN CANADA**
BRITISH COLUMBIA
Vancouver: Antonio Arreaga, Honorary Consul, Suite 430–789 West Pender Street, Vancouver, BC V6C 1H2 Canada; (604) 681–2152; fax (604) 688–2152

ONTARIO
Ottawa (areas of coverage: all Canadian territory): 325 Dalhouise Street, Suite 407, Ottawa, ON, K1N 7G2 Canada; (613) 562–2855; fax: (613) 562–2582

Embassy of Costa Rica, 135 York Street, Suite 208, Ottawa, Ontario K1N 5TA Canada; (613) 562–2855; fax (613) 562–2582

Toronto: Peter Alexander Kircher, Honorary Consul, 164 Avenue Road, Toronto, ON M5R 2H9 Canada; (416) 961–6773; fax (416) 961–6771

QUEBEC
Montreal: Roy Thompson, Consul General, 1425 René Levexque-West, Suite 602, Montreal, Quebec H3G 1T7 Canada; (514) 393–1057; fax (514) 393–1624

INDEX

ABOUT THE **AUTHOR**

John Howells and his wife, Sherry, know Latin America well. John lived with his family in Mexico as a youth and has traveled extensively throughout Central and South America, Spain, and Portugal, publishing several guidebooks about living, retiring, and investing in these foreign locations. His thirty-three-year love affair with Costa Rica and Central America uniquely qualifies him as an expert on what it is like to be an expatriate in this charming little country known as "the Switzerland of the Americas." John and Sherry divide their time between Costa Rica and California.